My Final Ride

The Thrilling Canada-to-Mexico Journey
of Charles Morris Christensen

A story of hope, perseverance, and triumph

LeAnn Bednar

Published by:

GOWITH
Books

Cover photo, Chuck and Teancum, taken by Fritz Kaufman while riding to Canada.
Cover design and layout by Jeremy Bailey.
Author photo by Lyndsey Kunz.

Library of Congress Control Number: 2013935370
ISBN: 978-0-9891574-0-7

Published in the United States of America by:
Gowith Books
P.O. Box 1421
Driggs, Idaho 83422

LeAnn Bednar is available for speaking engagements. Please contact her at LeAnn@LeAnnBednar.com or call 703-409-9999.
Visit LeAnnBednar.com

Dedicated to my Father, Charles Morris Christensen, who, through his example, helped me believe I could do anything—even write a book. Thank you, Dad. You're in my heart always.

"Great things are done when men and mountains meet."
- William Blake

DISCLAIMER

This book is not, and does not claim to be, an accurate representation of the Great Western Trail. The ideas, thoughts and observations are Chuck Christensen's alone.

This book is not, and does not claim to be, a thorough treatise on cancer or how it is approached by the medical field. The experiences and musings expressed are Chuck Christensen's alone.

The location where Chuck Christensen crossed over into Mexico is left intentionally vague. The border is not secure and can be very dangerous. Hence, this book is not meant to serve as a road map from Canada to Mexico.

SPECIAL THANKS

Endless appreciation to Stephanie DeMartin, Natalie Christensen and Jolene Houston, my writer club buddies, who offered wonderful suggestions and always were encouraging and supportive, even when I was beyond the brink of discouragement; to Marlene Berry, for her hours of expert editing; to Stevens Anderson, for his final polishing efforts; to Kate Hull, for another pair of editing eyes; to Luther Komonaseak, who sent me my father's whale-hunting notes; to Sharon Skenandore, for sharing her personal journal, which was crucial in finding the northern route; to Rich Bednar, for his technical support; and to Morrissa Rich, who copied photos and spent much time writing as my father dictated his personal history. Thanks also to Rudy Puzey, ElDean Holliday and Elwood Clark for sharing their stories and experiences, to Bryce Berry for his knowledge and expertise maneuvering in the publishing world, to the readers who gave of their time and thoughts: Leland Christensen, Jim Wilson, Janelle Mattson, and to those many un-named others who were willing to open up their lives and experiences to me. Ongoing thanks to my mother, Sarah Christensen, for her unfailing support of this project and her countless draft readings.

Most of all, much thanks to my father for his personal history and journals–but mostly for his inspirational legacy.

APOLOGIES

I apologize to those many family members, friends and acquaintances who rode with my father on his journey, but are not named in this book. Please understand that this in no way reflects my or my father's lack of love for, or appreciation of, you for your sacrifice. Due to length considerations, I had to condense and streamline the story.

ACKNOWLEDGMENTS

I wasn't with my father on his ride, so the errors and omissions are mine, not his. I have taken poetic license to recreate scenes, conversations, interactions and events in more detail. And for those individuals I didn't have the pleasure to meet personally, I used my imagination. I've tried to maintain the best I could the integrity of the events as written in my father's journals, his life history, newspaper and magazine articles, interviews with those who rode with him, and the videotapes he made.

The periodic "philosophies" randomly portrayed in the text are quotes from my father's trail journal, as are the infrequent italicized quotations at the close of some entries. This book is my creation, however at times, throughout the work, I've chosen to use my father's exact words and phrases, because he so often said it best.

Names have been changed in the telling of certain events to protect the privacy of those individuals. This story is based on factual events. Any slights to people, places or organizations are unintentional.

PREFACE

Partly out of my fear that my father would die alone in the mountains, and partly out of my intense love for him, I was one of the vehement naysayers of my father's mule ride from Alta, Wyoming to Mexico and then Alta, Wyoming to Canada. I wanted to hold him tight and keep him safe. I also felt he was being selfish.

He told me before he left on his ride that my thoughts and concerns had almost deterred him from going. He stopped to seriously consider my misgivings and had questioned himself as to why this ride was so important. Up to this point, he had dismissed all the qualms and reasons others had expressed as to why he shouldn't make the ride: illness, weakness from cancer, getting lost in the mountains never to return, even literal craziness–to him, they were minor concerns.

Naturally, I felt otherwise. My main thoughts went something like this:

I believe each of us comes to earth to accomplish certain things, first and foremost to reconcile oneself with God. After Dad's diagnosis of cancer, I felt that God had given him a window of opportunity to make sure he accomplished this objective. Here, in the dusk of this life, he had time to evaluate, and, if need be, prioritize. I worried he was wasting his final years by choosing to go into the mountains alone, probably never to return, rather than spending that precious time with us, his loved ones. I also wondered if he was running away.

In the end, dear reader, you must be the judge. Was my father's last journey *worth it?* Did he find and reconcile himself with God *amid* the journey? And that window of opportunity... was it ultimately wasted, or was that an opening by which God could insert Himself into my father's life's journey?

GWT & CHUCK'S ROUTE

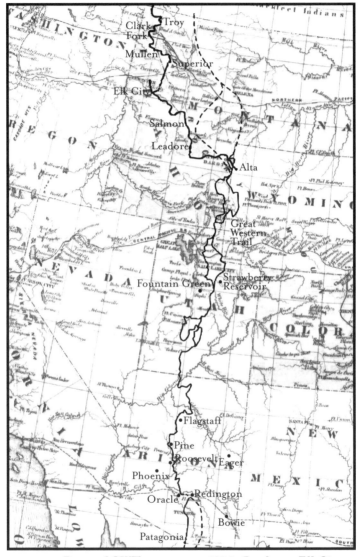

--- Proposed GWT
1991 - Alta to Mexico
1993 - Alta to Leadore

1994 - Leadore to Elk City
1995 - Elk City to Canada

CROSSROADS

Chapter 18

SATURDAY 9 NOVEMBER 1991

I write tonight not knowing if I should continue or abort my ride. I feel broken and beaten.

As I rode the trail this morning, I felt Defeat. He had been at a comfortable distance days ago, even out of sight at times, but he was gaining on me. By early afternoon, he matched me step for step, quick to fill my footprint before the grass had time to bounce back. This evening his shadow is not attached at my feet, stretching long behind me as the sun set, but now, he stands upright behind me, inside my shirt, holding me fast in his tight embrace. No longer is my breath confident and clear, but stifled and shallow. Defeat's hot breath singes the hair on my neck and the tips of my ears. His foul breath quietly circles in my mind, burning each synapse it touches, leaving a wake of shriveled, charred tentacles as his whispered caress asks, "What are you doing? Why are you doing this? Do you have something to prove? Just quit."

Doubt and Despair gnaw at places in my mind Defeat has not yet touched. I feel empty. For the first time since beginning this ride to Mexico, I have no hope. Hopelessness is an ugly feeling, a lonely desolate place. Maybe it's time to let my dream go.

Dripping wet, I awoke this morning flat on my back, protectively cradling my cracked rib. Sweat beads rolled down my temples as I crawled from my soggy sleeping bag. The outside of my bag was wet to the touch, despite its "moisture releasing" shell, clear skies, and dry air. My underwear was twisted and stuck to my body in damp bunches from the nightly sweats that continually plague me. Rats! If my bone marrow cancer, multiple myeloma, had an odor, I would imagine it to be that of a rotten potato, whose ghastly smell means internal rotting.

It wasn't the sweats last night (though I'm ever so tired of waking dripping wet) or the continual buzzing of cars that travel the Arizona Summerhaven highway, or even the cracked rib that disturbed my sleep, it was the anxiety over my pack mule, Sam, and my frequent need to get up to check on him. What if Sam doesn't make it? I fear my friend is dying, and I worry that tomorrow will prove me right.

Sam, my sturdy pack mule who I thought would make the ride without any problem, is sick. My guess is he has a twisted gut or suffers from severe colic. The colic could be from parasites he's picked up along the way, possibly from the cow chips he's been eating, or it could be the painful buildup of stomach acid, since there's been no food to digest.

Teton, my once-plump packhorse, now shows his sharp hipbones and ribs I can count. He stumbles frequently from fatigue. I'm worried about him going down and not getting back up. While the mules eat cowpies in the mountains and aren't so picky, Teton just doesn't eat.

The only animal apparently unaffected by the ride is Teancum, my three-year-old saddle mule, who many thought couldn't make it because of his young age. "He'll get leg-weary and just quit on you," the experts said. But Teancum's temperament hasn't changed since leaving home. He never tires of his daily game of "puff belly." As I tightened his cinch this morning, true to form, he did the deep, ritual inhale. The power play has begun. Usually I give a knee to his ribs, followed by an affectionate low growl to encourage his exhale, but he just grunts and becomes more resolute. But I'm more stubborn than he. I watch his ribs for any slight exhale, or wait for his ears to flick forward indicating a crack in his determination–then I quickly yank the cinch tight!

Sometimes Teancum thinks he's won when I turn and walk away, but I always win when I return a few minutes later and catch him distracted and quickly tighten the cinch some more. This morning, however, I couldn't even give him a feeble knee to his ribs. I stood, feeling the pain of my own cracked rib, and knew that by lifting my knee, I'd add to the injury. With ears turned backwards, waiting, Teancum sensed I wasn't playing. Dropping the ritual, he exhaled. No fun in the game if both don't play. He quickly forgave my disheartened apathy with a nose-nudge to my shoulder and an extended jaw, inviting a scratch, one of his favorite things. I ignored him, worrying about what would unfold today. Teton long ago gave up "puff belly." Sam is as adept in playing the game as Teancum is, but the last few days he, too, has stopped playing.

I rode hunched in my saddle most of the day, attempting without success to shield my rib. I'm jolted by each of Teancum's steps; the rib belt I wear, a corset of sorts, seems to do little good. A day of continually clenched teeth and knotted muscles has left me exhausted.

Today while traversing the trail, with my frequent backward glances at Sam, it was hard to appreciate the strikingly beautiful rock country with its gigantic, rounded boulders stacked one atop the other. I had packed him as light as I could, tying several cloth bags onto Teancum's saddle to lighten Sam's load. I didn't dare load any extra on Teton.

I occasionally walked and led Sam slowly up the trail, allowing him to stop as he wished. He plodded along close to my shoulder. Teancum followed behind Sam, with Teton bringing up the rear. Descending west from Mount Lemmon, Sam stumbled along the steep and rocky path as I held my breath. Evidently it hadn't been cleared for horses in quite a while, but Sam managed to stay upright. He would lay down often; luckily, it wasn't on the steepest part of the trail. He'd groan, drop to his knees, and attempt to roll onto his back, an action prevented by the pack boxes. Teancum would pause and patiently wait for Sam to get back up. Teton, with head hung low, glad for the rest, would pull up behind Teancum. I'd cluck encouraging words to Sam, "You can do it boy," or "Hang in there; you're okay," but I had a hard time believing myself.

The going was slow as we made our way past sheer rock walls and giant rocks that partially covered the trail. The spectacular view to Romero Pass went mostly unnoticed. Sights that would have brought such joy days ago, now looked cold and hard. Slumped in the saddle, with my left arm wrapped around my rib cage, I descended Sabino Canyon. Then it was again up to Camp Canyon, to Sycamore Canyon, and finally to Molino campground, where camp set-up was tedious and lengthy.

Molino campground bustles with campers and hunters. A lanky, loose-jointed cowboy, with a waxed handlebar mustache and quick smile, just left my campsite. He'd approached me with a smile and pleasantly asked, "Howdy, where you comin' from?" As he extended his hand, I set down my plate of spaghetti and stood up.

"Hi there. I've ridden down from Wyoming, headed to Mexico."

"You've come all the way from Wyoming?"

"Yup."

"Whew," he whistled. "That's quite a ride."

I nodded, gesturing for him to sit if he'd like. Shaking his head, he said, "No thanks. I just wanted to offer you some water for your animals. I know it's hard to come by around here. We packed in plenty for our stock; you're welcome to it, if you'd like."

I smiled gratefully, and my spirits rose. "Thank you. I'll take you up on the offer; there hasn't been much water up in the mountains."

"Is there anything else you need?" he asked, taking my hand and shaking it gently.

"I've gone through several sets of horseshoes and am low on nails. Do you happen to have any extra?"

"You bet. Just a minute." He returned shortly with a handful of nails.

"You sure you wouldn't like some spaghetti?"

Wagging his head, he declined. "Are you alright? Looks like you've hurt yourself."

"Think I cracked a rib. I'll be okay," I replied, straightening up to prove myself fit.

"Holler if you need anything; good luck with your ride."

I finished my meal alone, half-heartedly pondering what to do. Now, I'm trying to put to paper my thoughts and feelings. I sit erect, supported only by my rib belt. The bulky pack box behind me appears to be a support, but a thin air strip separates my back from the box. It's less painful to sit upright than to lean against anything.

The animals are tied for the night. I worry about Sam as he continues to groan, lying down flat, only to stand, then lay down again and roll repeatedly back and forth, while keeping his feet in the air, trying to relieve the pain in his belly. Then he repeats the cycle. He hasn't eaten or drunk anything today, and I've fretted over it all day long. Poor Sam! I led him in circles this evening in hopes that if the problem is a twisted gut, the kink would straighten, but no luck. No doubt the shortage of water added to his problem. But now when we have water, he isn't interested.

Dusk is approaching, evidenced by lengthening shadows (except mine that holds me hostage). Insect chirping seems magnified and flies pester. Defeat confidently bides his time.

After swatting at a few flies, I notice one fly waiting patiently along an ant trail. An unsuspecting ant, burdened by the weight of a piece of spaghetti noodle, hurries toward the suspected thief. The much bigger fly looks to be the champion, but the stronger ant scares the fly away, retrieves the noodle, and hurries on. Is there hope?

Please, Lord, watch over Sam.

HEADING SOUTH

Chapter 1

Monday 5 August 1991

They never thought I'd make it this far. I was too ill. But here I am, my first day out, riding my mule to Mexico. I've saddled up, taken a leave of absence from teaching the gifted and talented, kissed and hugged my family, and am headin' south to the border.

Some have accused me of losing my sanity, not unlike Miguel de Cevantes's *Don Quixote*. In the novel, Alonso Quijana, an old country squire who'd read too many books filled with tales of knights and knighthood, went insane. After renaming himself Don Quixote, the self-proclaimed knight sets out to traverse the countryside, fight the foe, and seek adventure.

Like Don Quixote, I, too, have read many books, studied too many maps, and dreamed of adventure. My dream is riding my mule from Wyoming to Mexico—then from Wyoming to Canada while I fight my foe: cancer, or multiple myeloma. The sanity part, of course, may still be in question—eh?

Disbelief, then scepticism, were the reactions I received when I shared my dream with family and friends. My plan was to divide the trip between two summers. I'd start from my home in Alta, Wyoming, and ride down to Mexico; then the next summer, I'd complete the ride from Alta up to Canada. The reason for breaking the journey into segments was two-fold: First, I'm a teacher and, while grateful I'd been given a leave of absence until January, I knew a longer period of time would push the envelope. Second, I didn't want to get caught in the snow.

In preparation for my ride, I'd surmounted my first two of three hurdles: crawling onto Teancum's back and coming to terms with a few family members' disapproval. The third hurdle was to convince the schoolboard to give me a leave of absence. The school year of May 1991 was ending. Passing through the double doors of the red brick middle school building in Driggs, Idaho, only a few miles from my home in Wyoming, I attended the monthly board meeting where I'd requested to be on the agenda. One year had passed since the diagnosis of multiple myeloma. No doubt the board members wondered why I was coming. I'm sure some thought I might be retiring.

In the center of the gym, board members sat at tables arranged in a large semi-circle. I sat with other community members on bleachers, listening to proposals, budget concerns, and discussions about half-day kindergarten. Before opening the meeting for questions, Chairman Davis turned the time over to me: "Chuck Christensen, you have the floor."

Maybe a bit of explaining is in order. Every time I go before the schoolboard, several of them will ask me what crackpot thing I have in mind this time—what field trip I'm wanting to take, what unit I'm wanting to teach that semester. I take it as a compliment, though. Learning is doing, not just listening and reading. This time, however, was different. As I stood before the board members, Mr. Smith sat directly in front of me, eyes half-covered with fleshy lids that seemed too heavy to raise. Next to him sat Jan, her dyed-brown hair designed to neutralize the orange and red roots at her scalp. Looking for data, she continually shuffled the stack of papers in front of her. Upon finding the sought-after information, she smiled in relief until the next search began. Mark, needing no notes to jar his memory, sat on the other side of Mr.

Smith. Though there were other board members, I knew from past experience that these three were the ones who would ask most of the questions.

"Thank you, Mr. Chairman. I'd like to request a leave of absence starting this fall, September 1991 through December 1991," I said, turning to look at Chairman Davis, who sat next to Mark.

"May we ask why?" asked Mr. Smith, all eyes turning to him. From past history, I knew he was the one I'd battle.

"I'd like to ride my mule to Mexico." I met Mr. Smith's gaze as his lids raised briefly, revealing the entire pupil, then flapped down to mid-pupil again. Jan's hands had ceased moving and now rested on the papers in front of her. Mark had no reaction, only a question: "Aren't you ill?"

"I'm feeling much better after the radiation and chemotherapy," I said, straightening to show strength. Mr. Smith, putting lips into motion before brain, asked shrilly, "Are you crazy?" No one moved. The ceiling fan seemed to get louder; shoe rubber squeaked uncomfortably against the gym floor as feet shuffled; then, all became silent. A sheet of paper from Jan's stack fluttered.

"Some think so," I replied, willing my jaw muscles not to tighten, telling myself not to become defensive. Jan began smoothing the stack of paper, pinning the escaping sheet.

"You'll never make it to Mexico!" Mr. Smith snorted, plowing forward, wagging his head, jowls wobbling.

The cliche *I'll die trying* flitted through my mind. A literal cliche, thought some. Each word Mr. Smith had spoken seemed a complete drawn-out sentence, barbed and aimed at my heart. I had heard these words before: "You can't..." Something inside me clenched. Few words motivate me more. If words had ever determined a course of action, these pointed me in a fixed and unchangeable southbound goal.

"Are you really feeling that much better?" Jan asked,

trying to lighten the mood.

"Yes," I said, immediately noticing Mr. Smith inhale, preparing for another question. I raised my shield, ready to spar.

"Do *you* think you'll make it?" Mr. Smith asked, adding an eye roll to his skepticism. Soliciting support for his point of view, he searched the room. But all eyes were on me, awaiting my answer.

"I hope so," I said quietly, letting the tension go, lowering my shield a little. Despite the snorts and eye rolling, I needed Smith on my side.

"We'll do what we can for you," Mark said quickly. His son Jake had been one of my gifted and talented students. One of Jake's favorite classes had been Dutch oven cooking in the school parking lot. Mark then pointed out the field trips and adventures I'd planned for the students–trips that took personal time and showed my dedication to the students and their learning. He told of snow-cave camping at the foot of the Tetons, a trip to Salt Lake City for vocational work, visits to businesses, doctor's offices, and Hill Air Force Base, where students learned about aerodynamics and planes. Trips to the museum at Craters of the Moon, watermelon picking in Hagerman Valley, and the sand dunes by Mountain Home were also mentioned. The schoolboard had given me a lot of latitude before, and I was hopeful they would do so now.

"This trip is what he does. It's who he is," Mark said, looking over at me and smiling. Chairman Davis took control of the meeting and we discussed details. I stood, as if on trial, waiting for the decision. In the end it was unanimous. Whether they thought that I wouldn't or couldn't achieve my goal, due to the cancer, or just felt sorry for me, or that I'd be dead before the scheduled leave time, they gave their consent. Some board members felt like they were signing my death warrant, but they gave a dying man his wish. Even Mr. Smith begrudgingly was on board, although he wanted it down for the record that he would be poised and ready with, "I told you so."

I exited the school building with my mind tumbling through the lists of what needed to be done to get ready. My body floated to my car. I was really on my way. I felt light, fluid with anticipation, except for the small clenched muscle inside.

The next two months rushed by quickly. Then, suddenly, it was time to leave Alta and time to say goodbye.

"Be careful, Grandpa. You'll have a safe ride; you'll come back and ride with me next summer..." I turned from packing the trailer this morning to find Brittany, my nine-year-old redheaded granddaughter, waiting patiently, first in line to say goodbye. Tears rolled in silence down freckled cheeks as she reached up to tenderly hug me.

Anita, my daughter-in-law and Brittany's mom, stood close, speaking softly. "Britt has been praying night and morning for the past week, asking the Lord to watch over you and bring you safely back to us."

"I did, Grandpa." Tears filled my eyes as I felt Britt's head nod against my shoulder. I patted her back. She'd started my own river of tears, which continued flowing through all my goodbyes.

"Thank you, sweet girl," I said, releasing her and wiping my eyes. This was the hardest part of going–saying good-bye. As brave as I'd been declaring my intentions to ride to Mexico, I was also a realist. Behind all the plans and bravado, there was a piece of me that worried I might not come home. Wiping the steady course of tears from my cheeks, I began working down the line of well-wishers and loved ones.

I came to LeAnn, my second oldest, who was visiting from Virginia. "Sweetheart," I said as tears filled her eyes. I opened my arms; without hesitating, she fell into them, nestling close. She'd been one of the reasons I almost cancelled my ride. I closed my arms, trying in vain to still the racking sobs that escaped her lips.

"Dad." Her voice was muffled against my collar.

"I have to go," I tried to reassure her. She nodded, resigned. Her tears wet my neck. Mine wet hers. She'd fought me all the way. She thought I was wasting limited time and that I would miss the window of opportunity to set my affairs in order. *Was* I wasting valuable time by being alone in the mountains? *Was* I running away? I had easily dismissed other concerns of being too sick, getting lost and dying alone, or just being crazy. But her spoken fears had made me pause. She felt I was being selfish. And I worried she was right. Maybe we both were selfish: me by being alone, her by wanting to keep me safe.

"I love you, sweetheart."

"I love you, too, Dad. Be safe," she said, lingering in our embrace. Her sobs had quieted, but she was still inconsolable, convinced this was the final farewell. I continued down the line, receiving hugs, promised prayers, good-luck wishes, and an abundance of tears.

Lastly, I bade a tender farewell to Sally, my wife. "Be careful, and let us know where you are," she whispered with a gentle hug. A questioning look with a fleeting trace of sadness tugged at the creases around her eyes. She put on a brave, supportive face. But it was a false face. Like LeAnn, she, too, wondered why I was doing this, but had resigned herself to my wishes. Maybe she just knows she can't reason with pigheadedness and quit trying.

"I'll call home every chance I get," I assured her while returning the hug. "Love you," we both said in unison with a final squeeze. I'm grateful for her quiet strength and support. If I didn't have it, I wouldn't be going.

Nothing brings me more joy than my family. I value

my role as husband, father, grandfather, brother, and friend. Some think it flies in the face of reason that I'm leaving them when I may not have much time left. Others think I'm grasping for one last powerful thrust at life, while overlooking what gives life value. What seems to some as enough, seems to me to be giving up. How do I explain my need to go? A deep, burning need to go. It's a need like that of holding ones breath under water and enjoying the uniquely colored fish, the beautiful corral, and the complete experience of ocean life. But to survive, eventually one needs to break the water's surface and gulp in air. Once my burning lungs are full of air, then I can dive deeper, live better, and love stronger. For me, it's that kind of need. The mountains are my air. My family doesn't understand. I'm not even sure I do, nor am I able to adequately explain my feelings to them in a way that would take away their worry. Maybe I am a selfish man and missed the mark. I just know I have to go. I'm keeping this journal partly in an effort to help my family come to understand why. I'll splash my thoughts down as they come.

Leland, my oldest, waited patiently by the horsetrailer for the farewells to end. He wrestled with his wiggly twenty-month-old son, Hunter, who insisted on helping me pack all morning. I hadn't the heart to discourage him, even though at times it added more work.

As I left home, a final backward glance showed loved ones bunched together, some tall, others short, all with hands waving over a sea of red, blonde, and brown heads.

With the little one in tow, Leland drove me to Pole Canyon, the starting point, south of Victor, Idaho. Hunt, as we called him, wanted to help unload horses. I gave him a bridle to carry. He'd taken it to the heap of items piled next to the trailer and was circling around for another load, when Leland intercepted him and rechanneled the boy's efforts by giving him a flashlight to look for bugs. After twenty minutes having only seen an occasional ant and beetle, he lost interest. But by then we had all the animals saddled, with the exception of one, and Hunt was content to sit in a saddle on the ground and watch us finish packing up. My heart began to splinter again as I stooped to kiss Hunt's head. One of my teardrops landed on his forehead, which he quickly brushed away with his sleeve.

"Sad, Grandpa?" he asked, reaching up to hug me.

"No, I just love you so much and will miss you." I took him gently in my arms as he placed a wet kiss on my cheek and wiped at my tears.

"Put kiss in pocket," he said, repeating a phrase he often used, his little arms barely reaching around my neck.

"I will." I patted the pocket over my heart to show him where it would be. Leland joined us in a three-way hug.

"Grandpa has to go now," Leland said, placing Hunt in the truck and climbing in beside him. As they drove away, Leland called out, "I'll see you at the Grand Canyon," while Hunt waved frantically out the window, yelling continuously, "Love you, Grandpa, love you!" until I could no longer hear him. But I could still see his little arm fluttering like an out-of-control windshield wiper until they disappeared from sight.

They were gone. I stood still with scrambled emotions. I needed to pull the kiss out of my pocket right then and reapply. It helped slow the tears. My chest was constricted and hurting, yet my heart was flying free. A man torn. I couldn't help but think, "Can I really do this? Will I see my loved ones again?" Euphoria followed immediately. "I'm really on my way!" I thought of Anita's parting words: "We'll be anxiously waiting for your calls to check in with us. If we don't hear from you close to the time you've estimated we should, we'll get a helicopter out looking." I don't doubt for one minute that she'll keep her word. Actually, it brings great comfort. It's also reassuring that family will join me on part of my ride.

Teancum shook his head, his bridle clanking, anxious to get underway. I smiled inside and wiped the salt tracks from my cheeks. I, too, am anxious to apply mountain balm to my soul.

"Are you alright?" my nephew Jubal asked, walking up to stand by me. He'd stayed back in the shadows up to this point while I said my goodbyes, letting me have my day. He'll ride the trail with me to Logan, Utah, where he and his wife live while he attends Utah State University studying health and medicine. I have guesstimated he'll be with me for two weeks. This morning I heard family members ask him in hushed voices to watch over me. My family thinks that Jubal's skills as an EMT and a Search and Rescue Squad volunteer will be put to good use.

"Peachy," I replied. "Let's go." I placed my hand on Jube's shoulder and gave it a gentle squeeze. Jube smiled his trademark smile, the one his sister, Angie, says attracts the ladies. I remember Angie's belly-laughs as she told of going to the mall with him. Right after entering a novelty shop to try on sunglasses, three girls about age fifteen gathered at the counter to the left of the rack. Jube, unaware of their whispers, pointing, and sideward glances, kept trying on sunglasses while Angie gradually became unnerved by all the attention.

"Jube, do you know those girls?" she whispered, subtly tipping her head in their direction.

Jube peered through the dark lenses at the gaggle of girls and gave them a charming smile. "Nope," he said turning away. Angie swears she heard an audible sigh. The brave blonde who appeared to be the leader, blushed at the smile, and with the nudge of her friends, sauntered over with her posse in tow.

"May we have your autograph?" she asked, still a little pink.

Jube looked around, surprised, then pointed to his chest.

"Mine?"

All three nodded in unison. One began digging in her purse for paper and pen. Seeing Jube's confusion, "Blondie" asked, "Aren't you Keanu Reeves?" She pointed at his chest, waggling her finger, "From the movie *Speed*?" Jube removed his sunglasses and asked, "Who's Keanu Reeves?"

By the time Jube and I had left Pole Canyon it was late afternoon. It sprinkled on us a little on the trail as we passed over Fogg Hill and down to Palisade Creek. We averaged about three miles per hour and only rode for four and a half hours before it got too dark to continue. One mile below Lower Lake we saw the outline of a cow moose in an oak grove and decided this would be a beautiful place to camp our first night out. We tied horses, set up camp, and ate in the dark using "braille." Tomorrow night we'll stop before dark so we won't have to camp right on the trail.

Now, I'm sitting with flashlight in hand finishing this long, day-one entry. My ribs are hurting, but the spirit is still high and hopeful. I'm protective of my ribs, continually afraid of them popping, loosening from my sternum. While riding, I adjust the rib belt that reaches from nipple to navel. This belt is stiffer than canvas and made of a white ribbed material that I velcro snugly around my middle. It fits like a girdle, protecting and supporting my ribs. Maybe I should have brought along my plastic brace, which opens like a clam for even more protection. I guess time will tell.

For part of the time, I'll be traveling the Great Western Trail (GWT), as well as proposed sections of the trail, and am anxious to see how it unfolds. Hopefully I can be of some assistance determining the route in those undecided areas. The Forest Service started the GWT idea in the mid eighties. Many agencies–the Forest Service, State Parks and Recreation, Backwoodsmen, various horse clubs, hikers, etc.– all had different interests, and so the idea stagnated. Then in 1988 a couple of backpackers from New York City hiked from Canada to Mexico and inspired the vision of the GWT, which would benefit all outdoor groups. A government feasibility study was then undertaken to determine whether or not a trail from Canada to Mexico was even possible. The study showed it could be done.

The GWT is planned to go from Banff, Alberta, to Montezuma Pass on the Mexico border, eventually stretching more than 2,000 miles–though alternate routes almost double the available trail. It will pass through Arizona, Utah, Idaho, Wyoming, and Montana, and will make use of public trails, when possible, with plans to cut new trails connecting existing trails. The GWT will try to stay on top of the Continental Divide, a western version of the Appalachian Trail.

Utah and Arizona already have proposed GWT trails on their maps; the other states are still in the thought process with no official GWT mapped. These states have suggested trails that *might* work for the GWT. The possible trails in Montana, Idaho, and Wyoming are what the Forest Service has mapped out for me to follow. I declined an invitation to spearhead the Idaho section of the GWT. It's a big job, and my plate is full right now.

Enough explaining. I'm tired but happy. Will write more tomorrow.

"There is nothing that a mule and a mountain won't cure."

TUESDAY 6 AUGUST 1991

Waking this morning to the rustling of aspen leaves and the smell of pine trees was heaven. Jube rolled out of bed with a Grand Canyon smile and started rounding up the animals. I started breakfast–fried onions and potatoes. They smelled awfully good, but occasionally while stirring I felt nauseous, a residual effect I guess of the chemotherapy I had a few days ago.

Jube clearly enjoyed breakfast. Mouth full of fried potatoes and slurred speech, he said, "These are great, Uncle Chuck." His spoon was more shovel than utensil.

"Good. Did the cowbell bother you last night?" I asked between careful bites, sucking in air to cool the hot spuds and taking inventory on how it settled on my stomach.

"Naw, I was glad to know the horses were still at camp and not bolting for home. Do you ever have to worry about the mules leaving?" Jube seemed oblivious to the steam that rose from his fork.

"No, they'll stay with Teton; that's why he wears the hobbles and the bell."

After a few bites I'd decided I couldn't eat too much and encouraged Jube to finish the pan. He hesitated, then nodded and dug in, scraping the fry pan clean and eating less vigorously than before. "Well, my horses stayed close, too. So far, so good," he said, keeping the conversation light.

"Yup, we'll keep our fingers crossed on that one," I said, knowing it was just a matter of time before we ended up on a pony retrieval mission.

After breakfast I suddenly realized I'd forgotten my toothbrush, along with a shovel, the purpose of which was to "leave behind no trace." Humph! I made do with a stick to dig a latrine hole. I then joined Jube and removed my dentures of thirty-seven years as Jube passed me the salt and we both brushed, me with teeth in hand, him with finger in mouth. Apparently he'd also forgotten his toothbrush. He flashed his easy smile, showing off his naturally perfect teeth—which brought to mind the summer I had all my upper teeth pulled.

It was spring, between college sessions. I was twenty-two years old and tired of all the cavities. I told the dentist to pull all the top teeth and make me a set of upper dentures. He argued; I prevailed. I literally went from the dentist's office, sore and bloody, up into the hills to heal while herding sheep.

The sheep didn't mind my slurred words between wrinkled, pursed lips. By the time classes started in the fall, I had my false teeth.

Currently, I'm too weak to tote anything over ten pounds, so Jubal does all the lifting. I'm quite concerned about this. I can't lift the full panniers to put them on the packsaddle. Of all the things that could stop my ride, lack of strength hardly seems at the top of the list. I have until Logan to either buff up or figure out a way to pack the mules myself, or this trip will be shortlived.

My saddle mule is black with light brown circling his eyes, crossing his nose, and outlining his ears. He's named after my favorite *Book of Mormon* character, Teancum. I've packed plenty of oats for Teancum because of his young age. Horsemen cautioned me against bringing him on this trip. "His legs will give out and he'll be done." I hope they're wrong. I'll have to keep an eye on him.

Sam, my other mule, is tall and dark, but not quite black. I'm packing him. I originally named him Uncle Sam because he was born on tax day, April 15th; it did occur to me to name him IRS, but Uncle Sam was better. I eventually dropped the Uncle part and now he's just Sam. He's big and strong; he'll make the trip just fine.

I brought Teton to pack too, a sorrel Morgan gelding whose registered name is Teton Flyer. He was bred to race, hence the fancy name and papers, but the breeders found he had no desire to race and wasn't a fast horse anyway. We got him for a good price. His gentle temperament is ideal for kids. Most of my children at one time or another have crawled under his belly and between his legs, or have run and jumped over his hind quarters, with both hands springing off his rump for forward thrust, landing on his back–just like Roy Rogers–all while he nonchalantly kept eating. The only problem with him is his snack attacks. He's a little round and when kids ride him it's common to see their little legs kicking frantically, and to hear them complaining, "I can't get him to stop eating and go!" We'll work some of the excess off him.

Jube packs Sandy, a small palomino mare with stovepipe legs, due to deformed tendons that continue down to her hooves. Jube packs her light. Her pack is topped off with Jube's guitar tightly tied. Sandy's temperament is opposite of Lady's, the five-year-old golden Appaloosa with no spots that Jube rides. Lady seems a bit of a prima donna with her hatred of mules. (Not as pretty as she is, I guess.) She looks at Teancum and Sam with her ears pinned back and her teeth showing like she wants to use them for floss. If she's got her backside toward them, her tail is swishing, her head raised and slightly turned for a good kick view. Horses are like people—some sweet, some not so much.

I can lift my saddle and the packsaddles, if they are stripped down to bare bones. I had a special lightweight saddle made that has extra cushion to help my back. I remove the breast collar and breeching strap and anything else that unbuckles or unties to lighten the load; then, I reattach them after the saddles are in place. The hard part is raising my arms above my waist to put the saddle on. My strength is nil and I have to be careful not to bump my ribs. I rest the saddle on the side of the mule, gently wedging it between him and me; then I "walk" it up over the back by alternating each end. Teton isn't bothered by the procedure at all, especially if he's eating. The mules stand pretty quiet for this, as well. It can take some time, though.

"Uncle Chuck, let me help. I can do it," Jube offered quickly after watching me struggle with my saddle this morning.

"No, thanks," I panted. "If I can't saddle my own animals I might as well quit now." Leaning into the saddle as much as I dared, I paused to catch my breath.

"If you need any help, let me know," he nodded, respecting my stubborn streak and retreating. He busied himself packing items in the panniers and keeping watch over me out of the corner of his eye.

"I'll holler if I need you," I gasped, continuing the slow process.

By the time I finished saddling the mules (horses, ponies—any of these titles affectionately include all my four-legged riding animals), Jube was about done packing the panniers. I held the ponies while he lifted the heavy panniers onto the packsaddles.

Despite the slow saddling, we got away early this morning. Riding west of Palisade Reservoir we noticed the fascinating ecosystem below Lower Lake in the canyon, a mixture of cedars, jungle vines, oak trees, thickets, and lush foliage. Above the lake is much like home: pine trees, quaking aspens, open spaces, sagebrush, and lots of sky. The Lord's beautiful handiwork is everywhere.

Midafternoon we watered the ponies at a stream that runs parallel to the trail. All animals were leisurely drinking when Jube's packhorse, Sandy, suddenly jerked her head up, her nostrils wide and quivering. She yanked free from Jube, dragged the lead rope through the water and splashed across the stream. Instantly, Lady (Jube's mount) bolted on Sandy's heels. Being herd animals, Teancum, Sam, and Teton weren't but a millisecond behind Lady, kicking and snorting and adding their own water spray in a flurry of panic. It seemed to be raining. Jube and I managed to stay in our saddles, but looked as if we'd weathered a hurricane. Now on the wrong side of the stream, Jube quickly gathered up Sandy's lead rope as our five horses and we turned to stare back across the stream. All ears and eyes strained forward, waiting to see what ferocious animal had lumbered down the trail and caused such a scare. Nothing. Then, a twenty-inch rubber boa slithered across the trail. Are you kiddin' me? Where's the bear? Tons of horse flesh spooked by a pound of rope-like flesh reminds me of people climbing onto chairs to avoid spiders. The snake was funny-looking; both ends round, not pointed, with bright plastic-looking colors–much like a child's toy. We continued on our way, counting our blessings, grateful a rodeo hadn't broken out. Our ponies, however, had owl eyes the rest of the day, flinching at every rustle.

At the mouth of Palisade Reservoir, we stopped to visit Nivel Backle, a grizzled, certified outfitter, who guides folks into the mountains to fish and hunt. He looks, in every detail, the quintessential mountain man: a black beard peppered with gray patches, shaggy dark hair that hangs just below the pupil of each eye, and a leather vest decorated with feather conches. I've no doubt his clients feel they are getting the real deal.

"You're only using U.S. Forest Service maps?" he asked skeptically, looking up from the map I'd laid out in front of him. He pushed his black bangs aside with thick fingers that looked like they couldn't bend, revealing his crystal blue eyes. I told him that I'd asked the Forest Service in each state I'd be traveling through to trace their proposed GWT on the maps they sent me. I pointed out our travel route and told him I'd saved a lot of money not buying U.S. Geological Survey (USGS) topographic maps.

"Ah." He smiled, revealing a row of perfect white teeth. His head bobbed, hair falling back over his eyes. His schnauzer look returned. "You may wish you'd gotten those topographic maps. Your forest maps are extremely simple, not much detail in 'em."

I agreed. I knew I'd be able to find a flea's precise location on the USGS topographic maps, but he'd have to be a rich flea.

After Nivel had pointed out which trails were good to

travel southwest of Bear Creek, I rolled up my maps and placed them back in my saddlebag, secretly hoping the Forest Service maps would be enough.

We rode along the highway to Palisades Dam, but before crossing over, stopped at a small store to call home. I told Sally where we would be camping and asked her to bring a shovel, toothbrushes, additional rope and more grain. In the early evening, Leland and Sally came to Bear Creek campground, just west of Palisade Reservoir, and brought the things we'd forgotten. It's only been two days, but when they pulled up, my heart tore open. I felt my every heartbeat when Sally gently hugged me, then handed me my favorite No Bake cookies. Before they left I told them when and where I'd be able to call them next. I don't want a chopper out already. I'm writing as I finish off Sally's cookies. The lump in my throat makes it hard to swallow. More than just cookies, each bite warms me through.

We rode for almost seven hours today. My ribs are still sore, but the custom saddle I had made seems to be helping. Another glorious day.

"If you want peace, happiness, and quiet, go to the mountains."

Chapter 2

Wednesday 7 August 1991

"Hey, is anybody in camp?" My eyes flew open like they were spring-loaded. It was eight o'clock. Still rubbing sleep out of our eyes, Jube and I quickly crawled from our sleeping bags. There stood Brad Parkinson, my fellow trail-clearing partner and teacher friend.

Embarrassed to still be in bed so late in the morning, all I could say was "Oh." Jube was red-faced, too. He quickly dressed and went to get the horses ready for travel.

"I called Sally yesterday and she said you were here," explained Brad. "So I decided to ride with you awhile today. Is that alright?"

"You bet, you bet. We're glad you came. You kinda caught us with our pants down though," I said sheepishly, pulling on my pants and boots. Brad unloaded his horse from the trailer while Jube and I saddled ours. We skipped breakfast and Brad helped us pack up, getting on the trail about an hour after Brad woke us up. I've had friends and family tell me they want to ride part of the way with me, but Brad is the first to join us. We rode up Bear Creek to Deadman and saw some deer and elk, then south to Big Elk Mountain Pass.

Teton's pack rolled off center four times today–aaargh! We'd packed them too top heavy with the extra grain sacks Leland and Sally brought. The rigging ring broke once, letting the pack fall clear down around Teton's ankles. Mild-mannered horse that he is, he just stood still and waited for us to come and fix it up. Thank you! No rodeo again. It seems like we're dodging bullets.

During one of those pack rolls, we lost the shovel that

Leland and Sally brought just yesterday. We also lost our tent. One would think we're greenhorns! The tent must have rolled under a bush out of sight as we repacked, or it slid out of its casing. We need to be sure a tarp is tucked and lashed around those kind of top loads. In lieu of my lost tent, we'll use a "fly" (my pack tarp and ropes). That should work.

Brad started back to his trailer and left Jube and me before we started down Wolverine Creek. We quickly lost sight of the trail and had to start bushwhacking, ducking branches, and dodging brush as we cut our own trail. The descent was slow, the side hill steep. Teancum was doing well in the lead. I stayed busy swiping branches out of my face, gently releasing the branch so it wouldn't whip Teton in the face. He stayed close behind us in Teancum's tracks. Sam, tethered to Teton, snaked behind not deviating from our broken trail. Sam and Teton knew how to bushwhack. Jube followed, riding Lady and leading Sandy, who wasn't as used to breaking trail as my ponies. She learned quickly, after wrapping around a tree or two, that the easiest trail was the one Lady had just traversed.

Teancum, with attentive ears pointed forward, carefully picked his way along. We approached an opening in the brush. Appreciative of the break from swiping branches, I relaxed a bit, glancing back to check on Jube. No sooner than I'd turned around in the saddle, Teancum's legs sunk out of sight, as if they'd been cut from beneath him. Mud poured up over my boots before I had time to realize what had happened. I lurched forward, grabbing the saddlehorn in time to keep me upright in the saddle. Teancum had plowed into a bottomless mud bog. Taken by surprise, with mud up to his belly threatening to suck us in farther, Teancum panicked. He tried scrambling out, lurching and floundering, only to try over again, squealing with fright. It was as if I was riding a bucking bronc. With Teancum lunging, I clung to the saddle; Teton's lead rope pulled tight. Like dominos, Teton, then

Sam, toppled into the bog almost on top of us. Teton frantically began using Teancum as a steppingstone, scrambling up over his hind quarters. Meanwhile, Sam began using Teton as a ladder, crawling up his back. Afraid of being trampled, I bailed off into the soft mud, which immediately sucked me in up to my thighs. I flattened out and army-crawled to the edge. Teton scrambled over Teancum's back, helping to pull Sam over Teancum as well, and out of the bog. Teton and Sam, mud-covered, heads hung low and nostrils flared, stood sucking in air, but seemed alright.

"Chuck!" Jube yelled. "Are you alright?" He'd pulled Lady up short before she fell into the bog.

"I'm fine," I called back. "I'm worried about Teancum, though. I'm afraid he may have some broken bones." Up to the point where Teton and Sam stomped on him, he'd fought hard to escape the bog, but after his trampling, Teancum was silent and still, encased in mud. His head pointed downhill. His eyes were closed, but his red ringed nostrils were wide and quivering. Worried his head would sink under the mud, I began crawling back out to him.

"I'm going to ride above the bog, Chuck. Wait for me and I'll come help with Teancum," yelled Jube. He dropped Sandy's lead rope and kicked hard as Lady crashed through brush.

By the time Jube made his way around the bog, I had Teancum's head cradled in my hands as best I could so his nostrils were above the mud. He opened his eyes wide with fear. "Shh, shh, shh," I soothed, as I wiped grime from his nose. "You'll be ok." He didn't move, but kept his wide eyes on me. Jube threw me the end of a rope, which I tied to the mule's halter. All the while that Teancum's eyes tracked me, his body stayed perfectly still. Jube quickly cinched the other end of the rope to Lady's saddlehorn, then backed her up a few steps to take up the slack. Teancum's head slowly rose out of the mud. I swallowed hard and patted his neck. Before Lady put her weight into the pull, I crawled to the edge of the bog, out of the way. Lady strained, pulling the rope taut. But Teancum was stuck, pure and simple. He'd been pounded like a post into the bog. At Jube's encouragement, Lady doubled her efforts. The added pull from Lady gave Teancum the willpower to try again, though he was exhausted. A sucking sound accompanied his feeble struggle as Lady strained at the rope. Half dragged and half crawling, Teancum oozed from the bog, lying at the edge of the mud, his legs tucked under him and his sides heaving.

I untied Lady's rope from Teancum's halter. But before he could stand, he slid on his side about thirty feet down the steep hill. His descent came to an abrupt end when his head wedged between two trees, his legs pointed uphill. I worried there would be a broken neck to go along with broken ribs.

Jube and I made our way down to Teancum and found his front knees wedged between tree roots, which surely must have helped stop his slide. He was immobile. Once again his eyes found my face and followed my movements as I checked his neck. It seemed alright. We thought that rolling him over on his side might help wriggle him free. One of us would have to push; the other would lead Lady. Jube, once again, handed me Lady's rope, which I tied around Teancum's saddlehorn. Knowing my low strength level and possibility of a rib popping, Jube quickly volunteered to push. I led Lady off to the side of Teancum. She pulled steadily while Jube knelt and pushed on Teancum's wedged knee. After one knee was freed, I circled around, tugging on the other side while Jube strained and freed the other knee. Lady and I then headed back up the hill while Jube pushed on my mule's head. At last Teancum managed to get his legs under him, and he shakily stood. He was free.

"He looks ok," said Jube, as I handed him Lady's reins.

Nodding, I ran my hands over the mule's entire body to make sure he really was alright. I was sure he would have broken bones or internal injuries after the trampling he'd taken. Luck, answered prayers, and a genuine miracle were on our side. Even with the trampling and the slide, he'd only suffered superficial cuts. I wished I had some gasoline to pour on the cuts, like we doctor at home, but I made do with some Bag Balm I'd thrown in my saddlebag at the last minute. Figured that the ointment used to help cow's udders stay soft and help heal cracked bags would help Teancum, too.

"I think he's alright," I said, relieved. Teancum stood, eyes closed, blowing hard.

We had to get off the hill. Jube cut trail while I followed on Teancum at the rear. Bushwhacking and nausea had taken their toll on me, and when the adrenalin rush left after I received assurance that Teancum was alright, I was exhausted. As soon as the terrain leveled out, we stopped. Indifferent to the caked mud that covered me, I dismounted and lay down with Teancum's halter rope still in my hand. I closed my eyes and said a prayer in my heart, grateful Jube was with me to help. Had I been by myself, I don't know how it would have turned out. Jube has the right temperament for a crisis. Calm under pressure, he once convinced an attacker to drop his knife as he stood over his victim and was threatening the paramedics who'd arrived. I'm glad to have him with me. Before I faded, I vaguely remember him saying something about his being tired.

I must have dozed off shortly after my prayer, but not before I felt Jube's eyes on me. After what seemed like seconds, I awoke to Jube brushing dried mud from Teancum, the leather gloves in his back pocket gently swaying with each stroke. Teton and Sam had also been cleaned up. Jube had softly taken Teancum's rope from my hand and tied him to a tree, to let me sleep. Revived by my rest, I summoned sore muscles to constrict and willed each to move. The mud on my clothes, dried and curled like cornflakes, cracked and dropped to the ground as I stood up. I noticed the rest had done Teancum some good, too. He tried to nibble Jube's gloves.

Jube climbed a hill and used his binoculars. It turned out that we'd missed the trail. It was east of us all the time. We were relieved to have found it and glad to realize we were within sight of McCoy Creek Valley. With Caribou Mountain looming large on the southern horizon, we're finally confident in our route.

Only an hour had passed since our battle with the bog when my weak limbs failed. I stopped in the middle of the trail and dismounted again.

"How ya doing, Chuck?" asked Jube, pulling Lady to a stop.

"Just need to rest for a minute or two." Still holding Teancum's halter rope, I lay down slightly off the trail. I knew this wasn't the best place to stop, here in the dirt and rocks, while just a little further up the trail was a grassy spot, but I was about to fall from the saddle.

Claiming fatigue, Jube also dismounted. "It feels good to sit down." For the second time today he gently removed Teancum's lead rope from my hand and tied him to a bush, and also secured Sam and Teton.

The rest did me a world of good. After eating a piece of jerky, I felt I could continue. Remarkably, I'm considering my condition at near full strength. I finished taking my chemotherapy pills for the month this morning and am looking forward to getting my full appetite back, as well. I underwent chemotherapy intravenous (IV) drip right before I left on this trip, and I plan to stop in Salt Lake City for my next dosage. I'm hoping my white blood cell count is up so I can start a full dose of pills. My urine shows high levels of the M protein, and our objective is to lower that level.

We set up camp along Wolverine Creek, north of McCoy Creek, below a herd of sheep. The sky looked clear, so we didn't bother setting up the fly. Dinner was Ramen noodles and canned pears, which I was able to keep down. After taking care of the horses, we climbed into bed. The saddle pads under my bag are still a little muddy and smell of horse sweat, but it felt good to lie down and unclench my skeletal muscles. Only after bedding down each night do I realize that I subconsciously keep these muscles in a continual knot to compensate for weak bones.

Tired, but the continual barks of the intimidating white Pyrenees dogs that guard the sheep, and the return yapping of coyotes, are keeping me awake. I wonder how riding in the Pyrenean mountains in Spain and France, where these dogs have guarded sheep for centuries, differs from the Rocky mountains where I now ride.

Sweet dreams. Good night.

Chapter 3

Thursday 8 August 1991

Only three days out and wouldn't you know it: I need the pantyhose! One would think that an old-timer like me, who's been riding his whole life, would have skin like leather–or at least callouses on his behind. But I've got two saddlesores the size of quarters, right where the bone sits on the saddle. I've literally got "rode" rash on my behind!

This morning, I rifled through the panniers and found the small bag that contained my personal items. Pushing aside the bar of soap, comb, and toothbrush Sally had dropped off, I pulled out a pair of wadded up pantyhose from the bottom of the bag. I shook them out, then removed my pocket knife from my back pocket. Jube looked on curiously as I folded the foot of the pantyhose over the blade and swiped, removing the lower part, making them similar to long johns. Puzzled, he asked, "What are you gonna use those for?"

"I'm getting all dressed up." I winked and ran my hand down a leg of the hose, checking for holes.

"Dressed up?" Wide eyed, Jube wrinkled his face in confusion.

"Yup, I'm puttin' on my fancy pants," I chuckled, barely able to contain myself.

"Oh–you're gonna wear 'em." His eyebrows drew up in understanding.

"Yeah, it's an old trick to cut down on the friction between rear end and saddle. The pantyhose slide just enough to prevent sores, or at least help lessen the sores. They're also supposed to prevent leg hair from rubbing off. Remember Fritz?" Jube nodded. "He suggested wearing pantyhose when riding long distances. Claimed they're as necessary as gloves, hat, and a rope. I'm beginning to believe him."

"Mmmm," Jube murmured, bobbing his head.

"I've got several pair. You want to give 'em a try?" I extended both my hands toward Jube, one with knife handle first, the other with another pair of hose. "You make your own, custom fit, depending on how long you want 'em. Sometimes I cut mine below the knee like long biker shorts."

Wagging his head and raising his hands to my offering, Jube smirked, "I'm not man enough to wear 'em, Uncle Chuck. No thanks."

"Suit yourself. Holler when you want 'em." I pocketed my knife and stuffed the tailored hose into my front pocket until I could put them on, and returned the extra hose to the bag. Hmmmph, I guess he's pretty enough already!

Our camp last night was a beautiful spot about two thirds the way down Wolverine Creek. The coyotes teased the sheep dogs the entire night, and the dogs woof-woofed back. The skeeters are big and plentiful here. With the dogs barking, coyotes yapping, and mosquitos buzzing, we had a real symphony going all night. Our eyes this morning were a little baggy as a result, but we're still happy—still loving life.

Breakfast was sure good this morning: fried spuds n' onions, delish! I'm feeling much better after a night's rest, and the stomach is doing well. We'll be eating lots of potatoes; they require no refrigeration, won't squash, and cook up easily in my aluminum Dutch oven, which sits atop my aluminum Coleman burner. I brought along a fancy fold-out kitchen pack, but it takes about an hour to set up. Forget it! It looks impressive, like a five-star camping kitchen, but not worth the work it takes. I can't lift it anyway; it's too heavy. I'll leave it in Logan with Jube.

We got underway about 11 a.m., after washing dishes and organizing cupboards. Because of Teton's packs rolling yesterday, we spent a little more time mentally weighing each stowed item. The oats went in the bottom, followed by a pan here, and a stove there. Every so often, Jube would heft the packs to see if they were roughly the same weight. We did better today; packs stayed put.

We crossed McCoy Creek Road, where fenced cattle ranges lined both sides of the trail, and beautiful pastoral scenes sprung up as if right out of a Will James novel. James is the cowboy artist and author who wrote and illustrated *Smoky*, which won him the Newberry Medal of Honor. It was one of my favorite books growing up.

We continued east of Caribou Mountain–HUGE!–and paused in Caribou City, a historic gold-mining town. Piles of rock still lay here and there in an otherwise beautiful forest. The trail was extremely steep, so Jube and I dismounted, leading our ponies. I tried to teach Teancum to tail me. He was so nervous, he either climbed in high gear, running over me, or he kept turning off the trail. I'd growl when his head appeared over my shoulder and his hooves nicked my boots; then I'd cluck encouraging words when he stayed on the trail. He got the idea.

At Anderson Gulch, we came across a massive lodgepole pine that rose into the sky, green on one side, dead on the other. Half dead like me, I guess, but I'm feeling good and my ribs aren't so tender anymore.

We were accompanied by a group of hummingbirds today. They hovered within fifteen feet of us, just looking us over. Their tiny wings were beating so fast only their bodies were visible. Beautiful, amazing little birds.

We arrived in Jackknife Basin, south of Caribou Mountain, and set up camp by two shepherds. One from Mexico and the other from Peru, they didn't speak English, so there was a lot of smiling and nodding. In an attempt to socialize and ease the awkwardness, Jube and I made a Dutch oven cobbler with walnuts, raisins and fruit cocktail. But we had too much fire and the bottom burnt–grrrr! We finally gave up on communicating and turned in.

FRIDAY 9 AUGUST 1991

After breakfast this morning we began breaking camp. Working at a heightened speed without being obvious, Jube tried to stay one step ahead of me in an effort to do the "lion's share." But I was on to him. I'd gotten up and started earlier. We packed in record time.

Following the Peruvian herder's gestures, we left Jackknife Basin and headed down Teacup Trail, hoping we'd correctly translated his hand signals and facial expressions. It turned out that we had. I rode by a fawn mule deer who still had all his spots. He stood like a statue, immobilized in granite about thirty feet off the trail in a wash. Beautiful animal.

Five days have passed, and wow, do I need a bath! My eyes and nose tell me so. We are heading into Afton to spend the night with cousins, so it was a gift when we came upon a beaver dam, clear green water pooling at its base, then easing over the branches and rippling downstream. The water looked enticing and harmless and, being two days ahead of schedule, I eased Teancum to a stop. "Jube, I'm going to take a quick dip."

"It's a great place, Uncle Chuck," Jube replied, always agreeable–though he didn't offer to join me, preferring to cat-nap by the horses while I bathed. After dismounting and tying my horses, I found clean clothes and picked out a spot in the river that was about waist high. The water felt therapeutic to clenched muscles. The baths of Rome couldn't have been better. After scrubbing my dirty skin 'til pink, my clean, crisp blue jeans felt like they'd just come from the store window, my shirt off a mannequin. I felt brand new. Rolling up my dirty jeans and stuffing them into my saddlebags, I was ready to visit company.

"Jube, it was wonderful. You should give it a try," I said, shaking the water from my hair, then tipping my head to drain the water from each ear. He sat up, got to his feet, dusted off his pants and reached for his hat. "Naw, I'm ok. I'll wait for a bonafide shower." He still managed to look relatively fresh; however, we both needed a shave. I shrugged, then smoothed down my wet hair and gently placed my felt hat on my head, chancing that my hair would dry with a bad hat ring.

"Suit yourself," I said, adjusting my hat with my pinkies high in the air, as if I were drinking English tea.

Jube smiled his signature smile. "You're feeling better, huh?"

"Yup." He'd summed it up just fine.

We arrived on the roadway at half past one, still ahead of schedule, and unloaded at Pinebar Campground, grateful for the corral at this campsite. A tall Kentuckian school teacher and his fourteen-year-old son were curious about our animals and came over to visit. "Mind if we pet your horses?" asked the boy, his hair and skin the color of a tomato.

"Go right ahead. Any of them will welcome it," I replied while Jube removed the panniers and I stripped off Sam's packsaddle. Teton began tugging at his halter rope, his finger-like puckered lips straining to wrap around a few strands of grass just outside his reach.

"May I give him a carrot?" asked the boy as he stroked Teton's neck. As if Teton knew food was involved, he retracted his lips, lifted his head and turned to the boy.

"You won't be able to get rid of him if you do," I replied."But you're welcome to give him some." I stacked pack items in a neat pile by the corral and tucked in the edges of the tarp I'd thrown over them. Jube chuckled as he led Lady and Sandy into the corral, muttering something about a jelly-belly horse.

Teton must have smelled the carrots because his nose beat the boy's hand to his pocket. "Looks like you've both been in the sun," I said, turning to the man standing behind the boy.

"My son and I started on a camping trip for a week and enjoyed it so much we kept on going. We're in our second month now." (My kind of people!) The man smiled, causing his sunglasses to ride up on his nose. "But we didn't bring enough sunscreen." For a time, we talked school teaching, camping and such, and he explained that even though they were from Kentucky, neither had been around horses much. But he offered to watch our animals overnight.

We made sure the animals were settled, then stood out along the road with our thumbs out. With my store-window jeans on, I was hopeful. How could any cars pass us by? Several did. Must of looked scarier than we felt. It took three different cars to eventually get us to Afton, Wyoming. We asked around town and everyone knew Leonard and Lori Wilford. Leonard is the local veterinarian. Lori, his wife, is a cousin of ours from Alta. They had gone to the county fair, so we stopped by and ran into several old friends.

We found Leonard in the livestock pen, admiring the steers. "Chuck!" he roared, shaking my hand vigorously and preparing to thump my back with the other hand. Just before impact, though, he must have remembered my frail health, so his hand stopped just short. He held no reservation for Jube and thumped his back like he was trying to restart a heart. Jube exhaled with a grunt after each thump and gulped for air after the vigorous welcome. When I mentioned we were hungry, Leonard directed us to the concession stand. I was starving and my stomach felt well, so I had three hamburgers and two pops. Delicious! Jube had the same. With arched backs, we guided our bellies to the local rodeo and presented tickets Leonard had given us. Afterwards, he took us to his home. Our burgers were beginning to digest when we arrived at the Wilford home. Lori made large banana splits for us. Our eyes bulged, but we managed.

Lori offered to do our laundry. Whew–much needed. As she began sorting in the other room, it got quiet. Smiling to myself, I yelled, "It's ok, Lori; they're to help me ride without getting sores!"

"Oh, I'm not wondering at all," she called back, but I could see right through her.

Leonard drove us to the store and helped us get more groceries and horsefeed for the trail. Later in the evening, a German shepherd with embedded porcupine quills in her muzzle was brought in to see Leonard. He was worried her swollen muzzle would cut off her air supply. The dog whimpered and whined when Leonard got close. He ended up sedating her to keep her still. I watched as he removed the quills. Using pliers, I had removed quills from dogs, not sedated. Leonard's removal showed much more finesse. Some of the quills broke off and he had to go fishing for the hooked end. Remind me to stay clear of porcupines!

A real bed feels so good. After warm baths, we fell into bed at midnight. Whew!

Saturday 10 August 1991

The bed did feel wonderful. Much softer than saddle pads and dirt. All was well until around 5 a.m., then my world just fell away. Minions grabbed my guts with knife-like fingernails and wrung them with Herculean strength. I bolted for the bathroom. My guts felt turned inside out. It seemed my body wanted every soft organ extricated. Violent diarrhea and vomiting soon reduced me to dry heaves at both ends. Was I ever sick! I figured it was from tanking up on three hamburgers, two cans of soda, and a banana split. Yesterday I hadn't eaten since breakfast, so I thought I'd just overdone it. Leonard, though, diagnosed it as giardia, contracted from bathing in the beaver pond. I came to learn that beavers are natural hosts of giardia. Leonard called a doctor friend and described my symptoms. He came by and did the pinch test on my arm and said I was severally dehydrated. The pinched skin took a long time to resettle, so I am to drink one gallon of Gatorade and lots of water. Also, diagnosing my illness as giardia, he gave me some pills, saying that just a few protozoa on my lips, when ingested, were enough to do it–spooky! I have pills for six days. I hope they do the trick.

All this morning, I have laid around in the fetal position and hugged my belly, my stomach cramping, the minions still at work. Thinking back to the beaver pond, I felt like a fly that had been drawn to the deceptively beautiful and deadly Venus flytrap. Bogs and beavers–things are not always as they appear.

About 1 p.m. I started feeling better. I showered and cleaned up. Leonard then drove Jube and me to the store for a water filter. I was prepared to pay whatever it cost. Before, I never worried about drinking stream water in the mountains, even with all those sheep around. "On guard for giardia" sounds like a slogan. But now I am a believer!

At last, Leonard drove us back to our horses at Pinebar Campground. The animals had faired well overnight alone, and were glad to see us. The boy had fed Teton several apples and carrots. As if an imaginary string connected him to Teton, every way the boy turned, Teton shadowed him.

Teancum nudged me several times as I stood by him rubbing his nose. "Hey, buddy, how'd you do last night?" I accommodated his nudging by weakly scratching his jaw line. He lifted his thick head and stretched his neck for easy access. Stay away from his ears, but scratch his jaw all day long.

As I squatted to lift my saddle, my legs quivered, threatening to buckle. I hadn't eaten anything up to this point. Didn't dare. With saddle in hand, I straightened up and leaned into

Teancum, panting. I hadn't the strength to raise the saddle and walk it up onto his back. Jube, saddling Lady, watched me out of the corner of his eye and let me try until I realized I just couldn't do it. Then he quickly sidled over and gently took the saddle from my hands. "Let me do it, Uncle Chuck. Just sit down and rest a while."

"Thank you," I quietly replied as I shuffled over to a flat grassy patch, shaded by pine trees. I sat down and watched Jube go about getting packed up.

He saddled my ponies, then checked Sandy's stovepipe legs. Lady stood guard, "smiling" at the mules. She's learned to keep her distance. Out on the trail, Sam has landed some well-placed kicks when she's tried to bite him. Now she only "grins" defensively, not aggressively. Jube's bunch and my bunch do a dance in the corral; one group approaches, the other leaves, and vise versa. Teton floats between the two groups, but sometimes by the law of association, Lady lets him have it. Mostly it looks like they've come to an agreement: You leave us alone and we'll leave you alone.

The fourteen-year-old Kentuckian was sad to see Jube packing. "If I give you an apple, will you give it to Teton later?" he asked, with both front pockets bulging.

"Sure, he'll think he's got it hard now after all the spoiling you've given him." Jube smiled, looking into the boy's peeling, lizard-like face. The boy pulled from his jean pocket a large red apple and handed it to Jube. While Jube packed, the boy hovered, continually petting and whispering to Teton. I lay watching with my insides slowly building up, threatening to erupt like Mount Saint Helens. I felt better after a trip to the bathroom. Jube stretched his packing to two hours, then about a quarter passed 4 o'clock, we finally got underway. Looking back as we rode from camp, we saw the pink-faced boy standing by the corral, chomping on a large red apple, waving with one hand, both front pockets empty. I wondered if the boy's dad would suspect what became of his apple.

I braved some jerky on the trail; it set well on my stomach and gave me needed energy. The giardia pills may be working.

Lost the trail early this evening; had to bushwhack. Maybe we should've purchased some topographic maps! Found the trail; came to a bridge over running water. The wooden floor slats were spaced so Teancum could see water passing underneath. After *much* snorting, shying, backing up, and hullabaloo, I finally led him, wide-eyed, across. It wasn't much later that he was feeling so cocky, he wouldn't even cross a trickle of water. So we stopped and had mule school. Sometimes this requires a thick halter rope across his behind to get his attention as we go back and forth across the creek, again and again, until he no longer balks. Sometimes school is short, sometimes long. Later in the evening, we held mule school again. I hope he's learning. While Teancum is in school, if it looks to be lengthy, Jube dismounts, ties Lady and Sandy, then lies down to watch and rest. I believe he napped during the second session of school.

Mule School Rules:
1. Never allow mule to be contrary.
2. However, let him be afraid; be patient.
3. Let him smell the scary item.
4. Praise him for positive movement.
5. Spank with reins or halter rope.
6. Repeat as needed.

At 7:30 p.m. we set up camp just north of Suicide Pass on Brush Creek Divide. If my memory serves me correctly, teamsters driving horses or mules, with wagons full of salt to be taken to mines on Caribou Mountain, named Suicide Pass for its difficultly in crossing. The pass is steep, rocky, and can be icy. The teams sometimes gave out, leaving the wagons dangerously perched on the trail, poised and ready to fall. The route was harrowing and it must have seemed like suicide to attempt the pass. Had macaroni and tomatoes for supper. It tasted good; my stomach feels a bit better.

Philosophy for today:
1. "Clean" in the mountains is a matter of smell. Covered from head to toe in dirt, you can technically still be clean; it's the unwashed laundry and bodies that determine dirty.
2. "Being lost" is a frame of mind. Ofttimes we don't know where we are in relation to the trail or map, but we can find our way using common sense.

Three things were learned today:
1. Beaver ponds are not for bathing.
2. Mountain water is to be carefully filtered.
3. Those praying for my safety are to be well-thanked. Had giardia hit me when I was alone in the mountains, I would have been in serious trouble.

Chapter 4

SUNDAY 11 AUGUST 1991

Mount Saint Helen blew, almost into my shorts. I managed to stay in bed until daylight, but the diarrhea finally drove me out of my sleeping bag. Running and spraying, I had almost waited too long. The spewing started as a 4th of July sparkler and ended up a bursting Roman candle. It felt like Satan's spawn was raking my guts with a red-hot poker.

There went my town bath! But I did feel better after I was empty, even if I didn't smell better. Grrrr. Day two of taking giardia medicine. Wish it was working faster.

We slept out under the stars last night. What an impressive heaven! It's easy to feel closer to the Lord when you are in His vineyard, admiring His handiwork.

We started this morning by singing some hymns. One in particular especially hit home: "Amazing Grace." The line of "once was lost but now am found" ran true to our day. We spent the day lost. Luckily, so far each "lost" has ended with being "found," causing me to both celebrate and reflect on the richness of lost and found metaphors in scripture. Believe me, a person feels the same joy and relief each time he is "found."

Once again, I wonder if I should have purchased the topographic maps. I wonder how often I'll write that on this trip.

We rode six and a half hours today. Spent the day bushwhacking. We left the trail early in the morning because it went where we didn't want to go, and we thought we could cut through. After surprising an elk and spotting a deer, we rode up on a hilltop to get our bearings and see the lay of the land. Across the canyon in the middle of the forest was a dump truck and backhoe. They looked out of place. When we bushwhacked our way over to the vehicles, it turned out the U.S. Forest Service was clearing a road right through the middle of the dense forest. Just before we got to them, we crossed the Oregon Trail in Terrace Canyon. We could still see the ruts the wagons had carved. It reminded me of the covered wagon my brother Barrie and I built back when we were younger. It would've been neat to clock back some 140 years to watch and visit with the Oregon Trail travelers.

We found a road-crew man by the backhoe and asked for directions, but he didn't know the country. We got to Diamond Flat, then to Diamond Peak, and started bushwhacking again. Finally, after lotsa worry and wonder, we came across a trail and, lo and behold, it was where we wanted to be! "Found" felt good.

While bushwhacking, Sam must have been snoozing. He went around the wrong side of a tree twice and really skinned up his nose. So unusual of him. Bag Balm came in handy again. Also, Teton lost a shoe and I lost my camera. No pictures now; maybe I can pick one up at the next town stop.

Being lost most of the day, bushwhacking our own trail but not having to meet anyone's expectations, can still be conducive to peace, beauty, and enjoyment. Jube is clearly enjoying himself as he brings up the rear of our caravan. "Attitude determines altitude," he once called up to me, looking like a boxer doing a "bob and weave" as he dodged tree branches rebounding from Sam's pack. Not thirty seconds after that, Jube found himself on the ground, swiped from the saddle when Lady decided to do her own trailblazing. "I guess I can't beat Lady after what I just said," he smirked. He held true to his words.

My heart warms when I think of how much Jube has helped me on this trip and what wonderful company he has been. He's as uncommon as his name, which he got from a

1958 Western movie filmed in Jackson, Wyoming, called *Jubal*. In the film, Glenn Ford played Jubal Troop. Melissa, Jube's mother, fell in love with Glenn Ford, so "Jubal" it was; just Jube to most.

Tonight we're camped south of Diamond Peak. With some daylight left, I did my laundry in the creek. It needed to be done due to the spraying this morning. I feel and smell better all the way around.

We're hoping for a clear, open trail tomorrow.

MONDAY 12 AUGUST 1991

We've been out one week today. Thinking back to when I first became ill, I'm glad I'm here and made the decision to do the radiation and chemotherapy. The decision wasn't easy.

In early May 1990, I hit a low in the middle school faculty bathroom during lunch. I was discouraged, hopeless, and felt physically tortured. As I staggered into the bathroom I began to feel light-headed. I stood in front of the urinal, and the room began spinning; before I knew it, floor tiles rose up to meet me.

The next thing I remembered was Craig Kunz, the principal of Teton Middle School, banging on the bathroom door. "Chuck, are you all right?" he shouted. He sounded so far away. I could tell I was sprawled on the floor, but didn't know how long I'd been there. I just knew I hurt all over. "I'm coming in," Craig bellowed. The door squeaked open and, through my eye lashes, I glimpsed a pair of shoes approaching. I lay curled up under the urinal, my left cheek flattened against the cold tile, eyes closed, pain racking my body. The stench of urine filled my nostrils. "Chuck! Chuck! Are you all right?" Craig called out again. Squatting by me, he looked into my face and touched my cheek with the back of his fingers.

Without opening my eye, I gasped, "Just let me die."

"I'll call the doctor."

"No, I don't want a doctor. Just let me be," I whispered. Opening my eyes, I focused on the discolored grout under the urinal.

"Can I help you up?" he asked, resting his hand on my back.

"No," I groaned, wincing. "I hurt all over. Don't touch me."

He carefully knelt down by my face. "OK, Chuck, what do you want to do?"

"Let me do it myself," I answered. Summoning the strength to slide my left elbow under me and roll up onto my knees, I managed to crawl over to Craig and sit next to him with my back against the wall. We talked about the frustration of not knowing why I was so ill, the possibility of cancer, my not wanting chemotherapy, and about Sally, each of my kids, my dreams, my fears. I needed the listening ear.

"Chuck," he said, " I thought you were dead on the floor when I came in. Don't give up. The doctors will figure out what's wrong. Your family loves you and I'm sure they want you to fight this as best you can. You can't feel any worse than you do right now. Don't rule out chemotherapy if you need it."

"Ok," was all I could muster. With Craig's encouragement, I decided to try to stand.

"How can I help you?" he offered. Tucking my legs underneath me, I got on my hands and knees, facing the wall. "Where can I touch you without it hurting?" he asked.

"Under my arms. That's the only place that doesn't hurt," I replied. Craig squatted behind me and, placing his hands under my arms, began to gently lift me as I used what little strength I had to walk hand over hand up the bathroom wall.

"Let me take you home, Chuck," he said, offering his arm. Nodding, I took his elbow.

Up to this point I thought the side effects of chemotherapy would be worse than my pain, which centered in my back and was compounded by the soreness of my ribs. I often felt my ribs "pop" close to my sternum. Ribs attach at the spine and come around the front to the sternum, held in place with about two inches of muscle to allow the ribs flexibility. The muscles connecting the ribs to my sternum were loose, which often caused a rib to feel like it had popped out of place. This would happen during simple actions such as coughing, rolling over in bed, or lifting my arms. Despite all that, chemotherapy still seemed worse. I'd seen how sick some of my friends who'd undergone chemotherapy had been, and I didn't know if I wanted to go through that. But after the school bathroom episode, I was willing to reconsider. If, in fact, I had cancer.

By late June 1990 I'd been diagnosed with multiple myeloma and had decided to try radiation and chemotherapy. The radiation was to alleviate the pain on the brisket, the center torso. I took radiation for three weeks, Monday through Friday, then started chemo, a small first dose because my blood volume was four units low. The chemo was at first administered intravenously, followed by pills for four days, twenty-six days off, then repeat the cycle. The oncologist said we'd do that between six to eighteen months until we got a maximum kill on the cancer cells. Then we'd quit and monitor to see when they started gaining on us. Then we'd start chemo again. I'd lose my appetite for a few days after each chemo drip, the treatments taking two to three hours. I always wear a "cold cap" or hydrogen cap, so I haven't lost any of my hair. Eventually, the cancer cells will acquire an immunity to the medicine. Then we quit chemo, fold up, and go home. Won't change the end, but hopefully buy some time–relatively good, quality time.

My biggest problem during the first few months of chemo had been controlling my thoughts and attitude. It was easy to start feeling sorry for myself, whining, blubbering, then turning belly-up to the sun to await a premature, unfair death. I began to feel vulnerable, afraid of doing even the simplest things. I visualized the cancer cells as a type of vermin, chasing, cornering, and devouring my defenseless healthy cells. Hopelessness surrounded me. I enjoyed nothing. Dwelling on the cancer and fearing death held me hostage.

It was at this point when loved ones played an important part in my decision to wring every drop of living out of life. There'd been so many offerings of love, encouragement, support, and "others have made it" that my loved ones literally pulled me back from despair. Dang near impossible to wallow in self-pity when someone hugs you and says "I love you," or "Remember when we..." or "You're too precious to give up" and "We need you." It's surely joyous to be reassured by so many so often. So, I decided to let go of the fear. I started counting my blessings. Soon there were so many precious things to be grateful for that my problems shrank considerably–a lesson to learn.

When August 1990 came around, others wondered if I'd be teaching. I knew I couldn't stop teaching. If I did, I'd shrivel up and die before the cancer could kill me. Craig was one who encouraged me to keep at it.

I could get out of bed with help. And I could take care of my personal necessities, but that often exhausted me. I'd had a couple months of chemotherapy, and would continue every month, but I still had considerable pain in my back. I felt brittle and weak. Sally would help me pull up my pants, snap them, put on my clam-shell body brace, and button my shirt. I could last the day teaching with the aid of the body brace, which both helped support my frame and protected my fragile ribs and back. In order to stand up straight, I'd lean against a wall, hook my thumbs in my front pockets and lock my elbows, or I'd support my body with my hands on a desk.

After the bathroom incident, Craig often checked on

me in my classroom to see if I was alright. Several times he found me teaching while lying on the floor in the back of the classroom. Craig was one of my greatest supporters. It meant more to me than he'll ever know.

After a full day teaching, I'd come home, remove the brace, and usually go right to bed. My family had constructed a high plywood bed in the living room, topped with a sponge mattress, which would stabilize my back and allow me to still be part of the activities. The height allowed me to roll on and off the bed, with help. It was raised up on 50-gallon plastic barrels. The white barrels had been used in my butchering business. I'd given up butchering shortly after hurting my back while throwing hay bales in January 1990.

Teaching during the fall of 1990 was physically painful. I was hopeful I'd feel better and gain more strength as the months went on. But the words of my oncologist, "You'll never ride again," echoed in my ears and were tattooed on my heart. As time passed, I worried that he might be right.

By October 1990, the pain in my chest and back had lessened. My bones were still fragile and my ribs easily popped around my sternum, but I felt better and stronger than I had for months. I'd even managed to gain a few pounds back. The monthly chemo seemed to be making a difference. It was during spud harvest break when, with time on my hands, one day I sidled over to the hat rack by the front door and took down my well-worn felt hat. One of ten, it was tan with a braided horse-hair hatband, bowler style. It felt so good on my head, a custom fit. I'd made it so by dousing it in the stream behind our home, then plopping it on my head and allowing it to dry. Bowler hats have a dome style crown and their brims usually curl; mine has a flat brim. It's my favorite riding hat because I can always get its form back. It's been stepped on, run over, and rained on more times than I can count. Afterwards, I punch the crown up with a fist to the cavity and straighten the brim, and it's like new again. You can tell a lot about a man by his hat.

Now, hat resting on my head and Sally gone, the coast was clear. I took the body brace from the closet, undid the velcro on one side, and gently slid into it. The giant clam shell closed over my chest and I carefully secured the straps under my arm. I hadn't worn it lately; the radiation had helped with the pain. Now, I usually wore a canvas corset. I thought I'd be prudent (ahem) and wear both shell and corset for this planned exercise. My winter coat went over everything.

Heading out to the barn, I found Teancum in the corral, white puffs exiting his nostrils with each expelled breath, and enticed him over to me with a bucket of oats. "Here, boy, look what I've got for you." I snapped the lead rope onto his halter. Wanting to minimize his wiggle room, I tied him with a hitch up close so his frost-covered chin hairs pressed up against the post. I clucked over him like a mother hen. I'd missed riding him. I knew the saddle was too heavy, so decided I'd try it bareback. But I needed something to stand on. Placing an empty five-gallon plastic bucket upside down on the ground next to Teancum, I softly rubbed my hand over his back, neck, and hindquarters. "That's a good boy," I cooed.

He was young with not much experience, and the bucket must have spooked him a bit. His ears stood straight up. He began blowing hard and rolling his eyes, as he side-stepped away. "No need to be scared; it won't hurt you," I soothed, patting and reassuring him until he calmed down. I again slid the bucket over by him, pinning him against the fence. He couldn't move away from me now, but if he got scared he could kick the bucket over. This was more exercise than I'd had in months. I moved slowly, then stopped altogether until both Teancum and I were breathing evenly.

With the end of the lead rope in my left hand, I gingerly planted my left foot on the bucket, grabbed hold of his mane and pulled like I would have with a foot in the stirrup. Teancum stood still. My arm muscles had atrophied and gave no support to my legs, but what little pull I had strained my sternum. My leg quivered. My ribs threatened to pop. I slowly stepped down. After allowing my heart to slow down, I tried again. This time, however, I used a wood block in front of the bucket as a stair so I could step on top of it without straining to pull myself up. Teancum still didn't move. Now, standing on the bucket, feeling more vulnerable than a baby bunny with an eagle flying overhead, I gently leaned against Teancum as if against an eggshell, and lifted my right leg to swing it over his back. More precarious than before, my left leg on the bucket shook so as to almost topple it. The image of me lying in the dirt with broken bones, waiting for someone to come find me, flashed through my mind. I carefully lowered my right foot back on the bucket. Once again I waited to calm my breathing, while Teancum stood like Stonewall Jackson. I still spoke softly to him, though now I was the one who needed calming.

This time I decided I'd half lie across Teancum's back, using stomach muscles instead of chest muscles, and hoping the two braces would protect my ribs. Then I would slide my right leg up and over his back. It worked! I was on. What I had never given any thought to before—an act that was usually completed in mere seconds—had taken me thirty minutes. But here I was, finally sitting atop my mule's back. My throat constricted and tears rolled quietly down my cheeks. I'd climbed my Mount Everest.

The quiet tears turned into heavy rain. I bawled like a schoolgirl. The only things on Stonewall that moved were his ears, which he swivelled side to side, listening to the strange, loud sucking noises that came from his back.

I sat there as long as it had taken me to climb on, deciding then and there that cancer was not going to determine who I was. I vowed to ride as far and for as long as possible. Mexico was the farthest I could think of; Mexico it would be. I had to go this summer, though, since my doctor thought I might not be here the next.

Wiping my cheeks with open palms, and my nose with the back of my coat sleeve, I stayed on Teancum, floating. Then after awhile, I started feeling cocky and decided to go for a little ride. Leaning forward, I tugged at the end of the lead rope; the knot easily came undone. The gate was a bit of a challenge, but we managed. Approaching the house, I spied Sally through the large kitchen window; she'd returned home and was busy oil painting. For a split second I wished Teancum and I were in camouflage, but I rallied courage and prodded him to step out. If it were me sitting in the house, I'd probably have stepped out and yelled, "What in the hell are you doing?" But Sally just shook her head as I waved meekly. With a wide grin covering the bottom half of my face, I rode past the house.

Sally shared her journal entry with me later that night. Only one word was written on the white page: *Unbelievable!*

Several days after climbing on Teancum, I was still dreaming of *the ride*. I thought back to times when I'd been called a dreamer. Once at the county fair, an old guy who was kind of a circus performer/traveling magician gave me a personality reading. He lured me into his tent with, "Come inside and learn your future." Then, gazing deep into my eyes, he intoned with the sincerity of a preacher, as if the prediction was mine alone: "You are a dreamer." He may as well have included, "You desire wealth" or "True love guides you." Even as a fourteen-year-old, I could recognize his shotgun prediction. He could have been describing all those at the fair that day, everyone in the country, on the globe, and every life form in the galaxy and beyond, past, present and future. I guess that's how fortune-tellers keep clients coming back: tell them what they want to hear, validate their wants and wishes. However, it's true. I am a dreamer. I returned his unblinking gaze and gathered myself right out of there.

Another earlier episode also gave me pause when a high school English teacher wrote on my report card that all I did was look out the window and dream, and that I must have so many dreams that, if stacked, they'd reach the sun and back. Of course, the majority of that many dreams would be unfulfilled wishes, impossible to accomplish. My dreams might only reach the clouds, but I must say that I've fulfilled every one: whale hunting, skydiving, mountain climbing, and building an underground house, to name a few.

This ride may be a dream that is subject to things beyond my control, but here I am on my way. We'll just see if I complete this one. I'm sure Sally thinks I'm half pit bull, who locks my jaw around an idea and never lets go. This stubborn streak in me, I guess, I've learned from my donkeys. I've heard Sally say, "Oh no, he *said* it; now he thinks he has to *do* it."

Dreaming about the ride was followed by joyous months of planning, working, and anticipating the journey, which are every bit as precious as the trip itself. Cecil Jensen, a Forest Service friend, and I began to map out the ride from Wyoming to Mexico. An old cowboy, he'd made the trip during the forties along a different route. His fond recollections did much to spur me on.

Cecil told me about a Great Western Trail designed to traverse the Rocky Mountains from Mexico to Canada. I sent letters. I made phone calls. I collected maps. As the time got closer, Cecil's family talked him out of coming with me. After all, he's eighty-four years old. I'm the youngster at fifty-nine and in better health than he. I guess I'm also more pig-headed, too.

I volunteered to clear forest trails in prep for the GWT ride, taking former and current middle school students along with me. I had a few months to toughen up the mules and see what I was in for. Because Teancum is a relative youngster, I had to find something for him to do each day. Remember: *"Idle mules are the devil's workshop"* (or something like that).

There was cause for celebration today: Jube and I were on the trail the whole day–yahoo! It was reassuring! We left Yellow Jacket Trail mid-morning and passed another herd of sheep resting in the shade on a nice trail that led all the way into Smoky Canyon. We met ten Forest Service office personnel out doing a feasibility study to burn forest for elk feed rejuvenation. The Forest Service maps I've got have the GWT traveling for twenty-seven miles on gravel road from Smoky Canyon to Georgetown. Bright sun overhead, we rode part of that stretch today. The gravel made even the horses cranky. Lady landed a kick on Sam and left a horseshoe print. He got even by taking a bite out of her. It was hot, dry and dusty, with not much water. And I've got a sore behind, despite the pantyhose.

Midafternoon, we stopped at a roadside stream for the horses to drink, and I heard an "Oh no!" from behind. Then clatter... splash... thud! Turning in my saddle, there stood Lady, devoid of rider and saddle. Jube and his saddle, meanwhile, lay sprawled in the stream, soaking wet. Jube came up angrily sputtering, "I guess Lady needs a breeching, too!" Sheepishly reaching for Lady's reins and slopping out of the water, he shook himself off like a dog. Lady had put her head down to drink, Jube explained, and both saddle and he had slid over her head into the water. Free of her burden, Lady had then neatly stepped out of the saddle and continued drinking.

I wrapped an arm around my ribs to stem the chuckle. Ever capable Jube, who'd declined using the pantyhose, had finally fallen (literally). In truth, it soothed my pride to see him weather a little challenge of his own. Practical breeching at last trumps sleek finesse.

After letting Lady get her fill of water, Jube led her to the side of the road and resaddled. He didn't admit it, but I think even his behind got sore on this part of the twenty-seven-mile stretch. His wet jeans surely rubbed a rash. Still couldn't convince him he needed the hose, though.

I can't imagine this road is the best route. The GWT needs to use other trails, or cut a new one and stay off-road. But, we were glad to stop here in Georgetown Canyon and set up camp by a wonderful cold spring. Heard thunder and pitched a fly, but it didn't rain.

All day we'd snacked on dried fruit and jerky, mostly out of boredom, but we were ravenous for dinner. My stomach held; the pills are working. The can of peaches, some Dutch oven potatoes, and a can of chili were decadent! The chili fell short of our usual homemade chili, but when one is camping, almost anything tastes good. Jube and I have competed in Dutch oven cook-offs, and I must say that we mix up a pretty mean pot of chili. We've even won a prize or two.

With a little daylight left after dinner, Jube, using my gun, enjoyed some target practice. He's getting to be a good shot. My son Leland, a deputy for the sheriff's department in Jackson, Wyoming, insisted I bring a gun. I chose an eight-inch python .357 magnum. However, I don't have anything worth stealing, and we haven't seen any threatening animals, so I don't anticipate using it. It just adds weight. We've seen many broods of chicks along the trail. Got me thinking about chicken and dumplings. But if Jube used a gun that size on a chicken, all that'd be left would be the feathers.

After shooting practice, Jube pulled out his guitar, rolled a fat log to the side of the fire, tipped it end up, and sat on it, teetering, oblivious to the uneven bottom. At times his entire body rocked to the vigorous strumming. With both feet lifted off the ground, he appeared to be balancing only on a jagged edge. Other times, with his eyes closed, only the tip of his boot toe tapped as he crooned a lullaby. He sang of ghost riders, mountain homes, cattle rustling, and endless sky. I lay nearby, eyes shut, and let the music take me square dancing, branding cows, or smelling wildflowers. His music washed over me and made me feel like John Denver–glad to be a country boy.

Philosophy for today: Camps are so comforting that it's hard to leave them, but there is no progress on the trail without departure. Camps are needed for rest, water, and food, but we must step out and leave comfort to accomplish and achieve.

"Increasing age and knowledge gained has reassured me that dreaming is not only okay to indulge in, but also the breath of life for me personally."

All is well, and we are surely blessed with things happening right. Good night.

Chapter 5

Tuesday 13 August 1991

Today when we stopped to snack and rest along the road, all ponies stood hip shot, dozing. Teancum was bored, and opted for mischief.

"Check out Teancum, he's loose," Jube said, looking up from his water bottle and glancing over my shoulder.

The mule had nibbled at his halter rope, bolted, and was eyeing the road. I stood up slowly, the mood of the day still with me. "Hey, boy, where are you going? Come here; come on." I dusted off my pants. He stopped and gave me a distrustful stare as I approached his tail. Patting his behind, I began working my way up his back. Then he exercised his agency to stay just out of reach of my fingertips. As I reached for his halter rope, he casually turned in the opposite direction and took a few steps away. We continued our dance, me reaching for halter rope, him stepping away. We gradually progressed down the road in that manner, him being coy, me beginning to fume. Thirty minutes later, I was rabid, salivating for mule stew, and dreaming of mule-skin boots.

"Hey, Chuck, you want me to get on Lady and go get him?" Jube called after me.

I stomped back to Jube, blood pressure high. "Let him go, the ornery bear bait," I growled as I plunked down and reached for the apricots. But no sooner had I retreated than Teancum, realizing the gig was up, discontinued his forward steps. Pausing for a moment as if deciding, he then meandered back to where the other horses were tied and began to graze. I stewed, watching him roam and drag the halter rope. Then when it was time to leave, Teancum stood like the tamest milk cow that ever was when I reached for his halter rope. Blasted beast. Sometimes I wonder why I prefer mules over horses.

Indeed, there are horse people and there are mule people, and the disagreement over which animal is better, continues. Sam Egbert, a shepherd and good friend, introduced me to mules. Sam would take his mule fishing. He'd sit on the mule in the middle of the creek and fish from the saddle. He convinced me to give mules a try. I was sold.

It seems mules are able to carry more weight and generally have more stamina than a horse. They're smarter, and won't founder on grain, or run or work themselves to death like a horse will. Nor will they put themselves in danger, which often makes them appear stubborn. This is where Sally points out my similarities to mules: "Guess it takes one to love one."

These facts may be disputed by horse people, but most everyone agrees that mules out-shine horses in high jumping. Sam, my pack mule, is the master. He can jump a chest-high fence from a standstill. While my horses stretch their necks over or under the fence, Sam can travel from one grassy patch to another in a single bound.

While they have nothing against mules, my family prefers the beauty of horses. However, for me, the thick head, distinctive Roman nose, long ears, and compact body grow on a person. I guess I won't butcher Teancum yet.

After taking a rest, we rode into a canyon filled with a gigantic abandoned phosphate mine, a maze of huge buildings and old machinery. Impressive. Humongous power lines, water treatment plant, railroad, and ten-story processing behemoth, all rusty, dilapidated eyesores. A man driving by told us it had operated in the mid fifties and shut down because of low demand in the phosphate market.

The peaceful feeling of the morning fled as we approached the phosphate mine. Teancum's ears were locked forward.

He spooked at the bridges, the railroad tracks, even at my fluttering map when I was map-reading. But for a three-year-old and it being his first time out and about, he's doing well. The ponies no longer were bored but were sidestepping this way and that; Sam was tight-lipped and leery. Lady snorted continually as if a bug had flown up a nostril. But sweet Sandy and mild Teton followed along quietly without fanfare.

We rode into Georgetown, Idaho, at 1:30 p.m. and spied a quaint, old-fashioned soda fountain. Jube and I tied the animals to a telephone pole and went in. Burgers and shakes were our options. I have to admit, my mind flashed back, if only for a second, to Satan's spawn and red-hot poker, even though I knew they hadn't come from eating burgers and ice cream. I reasoned through it and ordered what were the best cheeseburger and raspberry shake I've ever tasted. Stomach still solid.

Georgetown happens to be famous for its raspberries. It also has lots of dead fruit trees that some loving pioneers once planted and younger generations had not valued or watered. It's sad that sometimes one generation's treasures are not appreciated by their posterity.

We called home to check in with family and give a projected next-call date. Then we rode to a forest west of Georgetown and camped for the night by North Stauffer Creek. We pitched the fly; rain looked probable. I'm thinking we may yet wish we had that tent.

Before dinner, Jube took up the gun and disappeared into the brush to try his luck. Before long I heard a shot. Looking up from the sheet of poetry I was memorizing, I saw Jube step through the brush, holding a dead wild chicken by its feet. He typically radiates humility, but I thought on this occasion I almost saw him with his thumbs in his lapel, strutting toward camp like an old-time gunslinger, and then blowing smoke from his gun barrel.

"I got one, Uncle Chuck, can you believe it?" He held the chicken high and grinned so broadly his teeth took center stage.

"Wow, a head shot?" I set the poetry down and rose to my feet to get a closer look. Nodding, he laid his kill on the makeshift log table we'd erected. "A good clean shot. The practice has paid off," I gushed. He just smiled, flushing slightly, and proceeded to gut his prize and pluck its feathers. He singed the pin feathers over the flame from the Coleman stove, while I cut onions and potatoes. The smell of fried chicken and potatoes n' onions was almost too much, so forget the dumplings! We felt like Pavlov's dogs salivating at the bell. Eagerly, we hovered over the Dutch oven (as if that would help it cook faster). As much as I enjoy spuds, there's much to be said for variety, and tonight we had it. We felt like stuffed turkeys afterwards, as Jube plucked out tunes on his guitar and sang softly. Then I went back to memorizing poetry.

We finished riding the twenty-seven miles of road today. The country was pretty, but roadriding lulls you into apathy. Ponies plodded. Teton relaxed with deep breaths and a few sighs. Sam's lower lip flapped with each step. Teancum's ears flopped back and forth. We sang in the saddle, but time snailed by. Still, we covered more ground on the road than in the mountains. Timewise, one mile in the mountains is equal to about three miles on the road. But I'd rather do a quality mountain ride and cover less ground than a quantity ride, any day.

WEDNESDAY 14 AUGUST 1991

Today is Jube's 26th birthday. We celebrated with more riding.

It didn't rain last night, but I soaked through my bag. Night sweats haunt me continually. Having the tarp up added peace of mind. During the night I was awakened by soft chewing. I couldn't find the flashlight, but could make out an ominous silhouette just outside the tarp. My imagination went wild. Finally I fumbled upon the flashlight and shined it into a large eye–a rather goofy looking one, actually. Teancum had found my hat and was nibbling on it. I rescued it and shooed him away. Luckily I caught him before he'd taken a chunk out of it. He might be after the salt from my sweat. I'll pick up salt for the animals next store stop.

This morning Jube and I discovered that our animals were altered. Seems like the mules got their revenge last night. Lady's mane was bitten off at the hairline in two places. I didn't hear the scuffle; it must have been swift and silent. I also saw that Teancum and Sam are getting breast collar sores where their short hair is rubbing off. So I loosened the collars by a hole, dropping them down below the sores. I'll keep an eye on that. Teton's longer hair is a better buffer.

Beautiful riding today, with sunny forests and huckleberry groves with lots of big berries. They are my berry of choice. I couldn't help but picture a table topped with huckleberry pie, ice-cream, pancakes, jam, and muffins. Can you believe we admired them, but rode on past without stopping to taste a single one? In hindsight, what were we thinking? A lesson to learn: Focus on your goal, but stop and smell the roses–and eat the huckleberries.

In Emigration Canyon, Idaho, we crossed a high-way, which was once part of the main Oregon Trail from Montpelier to Fort Hall. The campgrounds were filled with vacationers and motor homes. Glad we can see the country from horseback instead of through the big windows of a mo-tor home. We rode the High Line Trail from Soda Springs, Idaho, to the Utah state line this morning. The trail was pretty, and it was reassuring to know where we were–on a trail marked on our maps. Teton had thrown a shoe, so we stopped on the hilltop to let our ponies graze, re-nail the shoe, and have lunch. A man with grey hair curling around his ears and wearing a black Stetson rode up on a strawberry roan gelding. "Need some help?" he asked, tipping his hat back to reveal a freckled, pink crown. Turns out the gray hair around his ears was the only hair on his head.

I set down Teton's front foot and replied, "Just putting on a shoe. I'm Chuck Christensen," and reached up to shake his hand, then introduced Jube.

The rider bent down and took my hand. "Reb, Reb L. Bishop," he said, pumping my arm. I could tell his parents had had a sense of humor. I wondered if he thought so, too. I smiled, hoping he understood it was because it was nice to meet him. Smiling a little bigger than usual, Jube nodded a hello. It didn't take long to find common ground in a mutual friend. It turns out that Reb knows Ron Allen from Hyrum, a disbeliever whose words were something like, "Mayhem and death await you." I guess Ron needs to see with his eyes instead of his heart. Reb agreed to take this message to Ron: "I'm on my way to Mexico."

After lunch we packed up and promptly lost the trail. So much for being reassured. We bushwhacked for a couple of miles and finally hooked into the trail in Horseshoe Basin. If this is to become part of the GWT, the route will need signs hung at the logging road turnoffs. It's unclear as to which is the trail and which is the logging road.

The only water along the ridgetop was in cattle tanks that are set in the ground and hold thick, green water with the look and smell of urine. So we had to dry camp above Paris Flat. The animals are thirsty and I feel it a personal failure to not have planned better for them. We will have a water location drill tomorrow morning, first thing.

I am so tired; the bed feels good. My ribs are sore from brushing against tree limbs while bushwhacking, but I'm relieved they are only sore and not popped. I've been faithfully wearing my rib belt, and it is helping.

We're glad about how well things have gone so far, considering we could've had trouble at several different spots. My first thought was that we've been lucky; then on second thought, I remember the promised prayers. I hope loved ones don't tire of petitioning for our safety.

Thursday 15 August 1991

Camps without water make for sleepless nights. I was up half the night worrying about the animals, and the other half dreaming of mules with dry, stiff, chicken-like tongues. But they seemed fine this morning. We got up early and skipped breakfast to be on our way, with the plan to water the animals at Bloomington Lakes, six miles to the south. I was thinking about water all the time and all but ignored the beautiful scenery along the way.

About an hour after leaving Skyline Trail, we came to Bloomington Lakes. Two are more like puddles, but the other is a gorgeous mountain lake set against towering blue-green limestone ledges. Watered the horses and replenished our empty canteens. With water, I was able to finish off the last of the giardia pills. Grateful I didn't have to swallow it dry. They seem to have done the trick. Since the second day, I've had no bouts of diarrhea, and I feel a lot better. I've still got antibiotics, just in case I need them.

We then headed south to Egan Basin, named for Howard Egan, a horsetrader and Pony Express rider. Past Gibson Basin to Sink Hollow Canyon and down the canyon trail to Highway 89, we crossed the road east of Logan, Utah.

We are four days ahead of our itinerary. It's time to do some tidying up. We left the horses tied in a grove of trees, went to the side of the road, and stood with our thumbs out. We hadn't had a bath since Afton, Wyoming, but I was confident I'd done adequate cleaning-up after the blow out. We hoped that our unshaven faces and dirty appearance wouldn't prevent drivers from offering us a ride. And as hoped, within minutes, a white food van pulled over amidst a cloud of dust and lurched to a stop. We hurried to the passenger side window and stretched our necks to hear the young, dark-haired driver ask, "Where're you headed?"

"Are you going through Logan?"

"Yup, jump in," he said with a jerk of his head. We climbed into the empty van. "I drive for a food vendor; that's why there are no other seats."

"That's alright; we just appreciate the ride," I answered.

"Yeah, thanks a lot," piped in Jube.

No sooner had we crouched down on the floor behind the driver than he floored it. Jube and I looked at each other, our eyes wide as we were thrown against the side doors. We raced around curves and actually caught some air as we topped one hill. I steadied myself by wedging my feet under the driver's seat, bracing one hand on the floor and wrapping the other around my ribs. Jube sat with his back against the side of the van, knees bent, feet and legs spread, hands bracing himself. The driver told us he'd just had his money pouch stolen earlier that morning. I couldn't believe he stopped and gave us a ride when he'd just been robbed. You'd think he'd be gun-shy. But his attitude was "so what," it wasn't his money. His only interest was driving home in the shortest possible time. Screeching to a stop right in front of Jube's house, he turned in his seat and glanced over his shoulder at us. "Good luck with your ride," he said.

White-knuckled and pale-faced, Jube and I crawled out the door. "Thanks for the ride," croaked Jube. My stomach was in my throat, but I swallowed and managed a "Yep, thank you."

"Sure." With that, he floored the van and sped out of sight. We were grateful for the ride, especially since he'd dropped us at our exact destination, but we were even more grateful to be alive.

Jube turned to me. "Chuck, are you feeling alright?"

I nodded while running my hand over my face. "I about lost my lunch going around one of those corners. I prefer a cantankerous ol' mule rather than the two-wheeled, Indy 500-driving we just experienced."

"Me too, me too," he replied as we staggered up the sidewalk to his front door.

Laurel, Jube's wife, was surprised to see us. She wasn't expecting us for four more days. So far we've ridden two hundred itinerary miles in ten days. Teton is losing his roundness and doing well. The mules, though, are getting breeching and breast collar sores. The pantyhose are keeping me from the same fate. They're priceless, and my ribs are doing pretty well. I'll hole up in Logan a few days to let the mules' sores heal, and to brainstorm on how to lift the packsaddles so I can continue on by myself.

One of Jube's friends, Wayne Bell, drove us up the road this evening to retrieve our horses and gear. Teancum broke away before I could load him in the trailer. Darn mule. I thought for sure he'd run off and we'd lose him. Fifteen minutes later, I'd tolled him back with Teton's cowbell. He loped up to me with a "Ho, hum, let's go" expression. Aaargh! I fell on his neck and hugged him as if the prodigal son had returned. We penned my animals at Jube's brother Jason's place. The pen was dusty and weedy, with some weeds over seven feet tall. Grateful for the hospitality, but the dusty pen is a poor second compared to the wide-open spaces and green mountains. Wayne gave me some hay.

I'm sleeping on a thick foam hide-a-bed with a dropped center—interesting. I'm not sure if the dropped center is intentional or not. I'm curled in the pocket like a hibernating squirrel. Glad for it, though. It's good to be here.

Chapter 6

Sunday 18 August 1991

Ahhh… flushing toilets and hot showers! And with a
belly full of meats, breads, and fruits, I've felt like a king in
a castle the last couple of days. I even had a nap or two, but
have also been productive. We came up with a good idea for
lifting the packsaddles alone. On Friday I watched Laurel
hoist a ten-pound sack of flour onto the counter when she was
making rolls. This reminded me of when I was a boy and used
cloth flour sacks as small packs. A brain-child was born!

Later that afternoon, Jube and Laurel took me to Ogden
to a supply shop, Cross Western. My eyes goggled everywhere
I turned. Each item appeared made for the mountains. But
I'd come for a set of Ralide boxes–large, lightweight plastic,
bright hunter-orange boxes that I'll hang empty on the packsaddle. Then I'll stuff cloth bags each full of ten pounds of
food and gear to put into the Ralide boxes. I bought a scale
to weigh each cloth bag so the boxes will be equal weight.
I also picked up a salt block for the horses, a replacement
for the lost shovel, and a "mohair" cord to reduce pack mule
sores (Authentic mohair, the fleece of Angora goats, is out
of sight, price-wise, and difficult to find. The small rope or
cording available in farm and western stores is an acceptable
substitute). I decided against replacing the tent. The tarp (fly)
is easier to set up and gives a closer feel to nature.

With my items on the counter, I checked my back pocket
for my checkbook, then began patting myself down as if I were
a policeman searching a suspect. The patting gained momentum as I remembered Leland's caution not to take it along.
By the time I twice completed the search, I was convinced I'd

lost it. I could hear Leland's recriminations about taking the checkbook, and I began to feel like a middle-schooler preparing to meet the principal. The sales clerk calmly watched me dance, then she smiled, and pointed to my hat. Blood rushed to my face as I remembered I'd stuck it in my hat band last night after it had fallen out of my pants. Whew! On Saturday morning it was off to the fabric store. Back at Jube's home, Laurel and I measured and cut remnant fabric, and Jube sewed the cut pieces. We now have twenty-four fine, multi-colored ten-pound-capacity bags. The bagging system looks like it will work.

With the bags sewn, I turned my attention to fashioning two breast collars from the soft mohair cording. A longer twenty-inch strap on each side of the hope ring, along with the saddle pad, should help lift the hope ring so it won't rub the mules' chests so much. I also replaced the web breeching on Teancum and Sam's saddles with leather breeching. I hope this does the trick.

After shopping, sewing, and tying the breast collars, I laundered the big saddle pads and my sleeping bag. Fresh once more! I also bought an automated Fuji camera and shot a roll of prints. I guess I'm anxious to recoup the first ten days' loss of photos. Waiting at Jube's for me were letters and packages from Sally, family and friends. Their love filled my tank. I made calls to check in and report. Anita, Brittany, Hunter and their "firecracker," Simone, will ride with me for three days across Ben Lomond Peak to Huntsville Reservoir. My throat constricted when I heard this. Nice!

I talked to a mule concessionaire from the North Rim of the Grand Canyon who said that crossing the Grand Canyon is fourteen hours of hard going. So I'll plan to camp at Phantom Ranch in the bottom of the canyon, but will need to go through all the bureaucratic folderol for the privilege. Would you believe when you dial the Grand Canyon telephone number it gives a twenty-item directory, but no person to talk to? I felt automated, robotted, and filed. But I finally got things squared away.

Evening came and I collapsed to watch a video at Jason's home about refugee journeys from Vietnam to Darwin, Australia. Some people's lives–and deaths–are almost totally predetermined by where they are born or live, or by the policies of their government. The video made my eyes weepy when I thought of all I have. I felt humbled and grateful for having choices of spouse, career, and dreams. I can choose to have a pig's head and a donkey's behind–and it's *my* choice, not the government's. What a blessing freedom is.

I'll depart Logan tomorrow mid-morning. On the trail I'll meet up with Doubting Ron Allen, who has to see to believe. Looks like "rebel" Bishop delivered my message. Ron will ride with me for two days to Avon.

Philosophy for today: Ofttimes we consider opposition evil. What if it's an eternal principle to produce strength and power? Inertia and apathy are two aspects of comfort. Opposition and adversity are the good side of force. We need to rethink our relative feelings about hard times and struggles. Prosperity is more to be feared than famine, because of the laxness it produces in the multitudes.

The fact that this trip so far has had so many things happening exactly right makes me marvel at the power of prayer in my behalf. My journey... it's really going to happen, and it's going to be glorious, even the opposition part of it. Thank you, loved ones, for your ceaseless supplications in my behalf. I hope to repay you in some fashion.

MONDAY 19 AUGUST 1991

This morning Jube tried his hand at horseshoeing for the first time. I coached over his shoulder. Teton stood like a perfect gentleman. Jube's a natural; the shoe fit like Cinderella's slipper. Preparations complete, I gathered my animals and Jube drove me up Logan Canyon.

"Thanks, Jube, for all your help, but mostly for your company. I'll miss you," I told him as we unloaded the horses.

"It was a great trip; I'm glad I could go." I detected more than a touch of melancholy in his voice. "I wish I could ride farther with you."

We tied the horses to the trailer. It seemed quieter without Lady's grin. "You're welcome to join me anytime down the trail, if you can manage to get away," I offered, my voice subdued. "I'll keep you posted as to where I am, or you can call Sally and she can tell you where I'll be."

"I'll see if I can."

We saddled my animals, then Jube watched me load and weigh each cloth bag. I could tell he wanted to help, but he let me do it alone. I placed the filled cloth bags into two piles for each horse, coming within a half pound difference for Sam's pack. Teton's was exact! No pack rolling now.

"That's gonna work," he nodded.

"Yep, I think so. Thanks for sewing the cloth bags; they're great," I said. He nodded again. His shoulders drooped as his gaze shifted from animals to tree line. I put loose grain in the bottom of the Ralide boxes, then covered it with the bags of plunder. Since leaving my "kitchen cupboards" with Jube, my biggest concern with weight now is the eight-inch .357 magnum. The gun is too weighty–about eight pounds in addition to the shells. Together they are my heaviest items. I had bare-boned the packs down for each animal, from one hundred and seventy-five to one hundred and twenty pounds total. Sixty pounds on each side.

"I'll be with you in spirit," Jube said, rallying himself. I eased up into the saddle and he handed me Teton's lead rope. "Bye, Uncle Chuck. Be safe." He tried to smile, though it wasn't his typical grin.

"I will." I leaned down and gripped his forearm; his returned grip was firm but gentle. He lingered, then nodded once more. Turning Teancum, I started out toward Card Canyon Trail. Looking back at Jube, still standing by the trailer, made me feel like I was leaving my right hand behind. I hollered, "Live and laugh!" Hands cupped to his lips, he shouted back, "You, too." He watched until I rode out of sight. He'd kept his promise; I was still safe.

The new mohair breast collars on Teancum and Sam now rest in different places than the original collars did. The sores have already begun to scab over. The down-time also helped them heal.

I met the disbeliever Ron up at Card Canyon Trail, whereupon he saw, believed, and joined. He rides a pretty bay mare who holds her head high and fluffs her tail a lot. He'll ride with me to Porcupine Dam near his home in Hyrum, Utah. A local guy, he can take me on trails instead of roads that I'd otherwise be riding.

We rode up Card Canyon, through Richards Hollow, into Blacksmith Fork and Pig Holes. Interesting names. In Richards Hollow, Ron spied a large timber rattler near the trail, but I rode past unaware. I need to sharpen my perceptions! We rode though Pine Basin, Scary Canyon and down to Porcupine Dam. It was beautiful, even when we had to bushwhack a little.

"Chuck, you scare me," yelled Ron from behind.

I'd taken the lead to bushwhack; that's what I do best. I pulled Teancum to a stop and turned in the saddle. "What do you mean?"

"You seem to enjoy this."

"Oh, isn't this fun for you?" I asked innocently.

"Fun if you like a needle in the eye," he said, pulling a pine bow within inches of his face to demonstrate. "Or a sharp branch in your ear." He'd been forced to stop with a branch literally tickling his ear.

Smiling, I turned back to bushwhacking and thought, "This is part of what makes the ride so fun. The challenge of finding our own way."

Just before dark, we met up with a government trapper out looking for coyotes to tag. He had two dogs for chasing coyotes, to make them circle back. When the coyotes appear the trapper shoots them–but not with a gun. He carries something he calls a shooting stick, kind of a giant slingshot with two ski poles hinged at the center with inner tube rubber, forming a big X. A piece of rubber loops across the top to cradle the tranquilizer. The poles double as a walking stick. He'd snared three bears within the past week. We'll need to keep our eyes open.

Camped tonight southwest of Hardware Ranch–all ponies loved the salt. After Sam and Teton had wandered away from it, Teancum lingered, his long tongue wrapped around the salt block. I thought I saw his eyes roll back in his head as his lids closed.

Rode seven and a half hours today.

TUESDAY 20 AUGUST 1991

A couple hours into our ride this morning, we jumped from a pleasant walk to a stampede. One second ears flopped and lips hung loose; the next, tails swished like airplane propellers and ears were pinned against necks. The ponies tore up the trail as if they'd been prodded by an electric shock. I dropped Teton's lead rope and grabbed for the saddlehorn. Teton, almost on top of Teancum, didn't need me to pull him along. He all but had his nose up Teancum's behind, pushing us. Who ever said Teton wasn't fast enough to race was mistaken! Teancum had to only raise his hooves and he was flying over the trail like Pegasus. Sam likewise offered no resistance to Teton's flight, galloping along like a racehorse. Hanging on for dear life, I heard bees buzzing furiously around us. Strange how one's senses are heightened and things slow down during times of danger.

After regaining my balance from the shotgun start, I clutched my ribs with one arm and swatted at bees with the other. The ponies kept up their mad dash while the bees clustered, and Ron and I squirmed in our saddles, waving our arms like crazy men. After about a fourth of a mile the bees thinned out. But one of the bees had gone down my collar. Its frantic buzzing sounded like a chainsaw bouncing around my back. It ended up down my sleeve. The buzzing was more disturbing than the sting I'd received. In fact, only after I'd unsnapped my shirt cuff and let the bee go, did I feel the burning on the tender backside of my arm, just below my shoulder. By the time I'd gathered up Teton's lead rope, Sam's upper eyelid had begun to swell. He'd been stung just above his top lashes. When we stopped for lunch, his puffy lid was pulled up and back, revealing the red veins underneath–not unlike those kids who can turn their eyelids inside out. Bees hit the horses again about an hour later, but fortunately no one got thrown. Whew. Ron came through peachy, but had three dead bees stuck in his hat band.

The new packing system with the cloth bags works well. By the time I find a tree branch to hang the scale on, then carry items back and forth, the process takes only a little longer than before. I anticipate, with practice, being able to cut down on packing time. If I'm careful with the scale and weigh within a pound or two, the packs ride perfectly! They stayed put even during the bee attack.

Today we saw lots of deer and many elk tracks. Ron, an avid hunter clearly anxious for hunting season, couldn't help himself; he'd branch off following tracks for a few hundred yards, then trot to catch up to me and make a guess as to how big the animal was.

We rode ridgetops almost exclusively. There were forty one-acre house lots up on the mountaintop. Desecration! Many houses were beautiful, but some were dilapidated and abandoned. Too many roads marred the beauty of that country.

Shortly after lunch, Teancum, without warning, suddenly veered under an overhead branch. Caught by surprise, I was swiped right out of the saddle. Ron, following pack mule Sam, reacted quickly, yanking his horse to a stop.

"Chuck?" Having had the air knocked out of me, I couldn't answer. Ron leapt from his horse and pushed Sam and Teton aside. Whitefaced, he knelt by me as my mouth opened and closed like a fish out of water. Air refused to go in or out. Ron froze. To reassure him, I raised my forefinger, silently asking for a second. He nodded, relieved. After a few seconds (but when air is stuck, it seems much longer), I caught my breath. Ron gently helped me sit up. "Alright?"

Groaning, I took a quick minute to assess my bones, then nodded with relief. I emptied my lungs and expelled my own worry. "That rascal did that on purpose," I grunted as Ron steadied me to my feet.

"Your hat stayed on, though," Ron teased with a forced chuckle, attempting to relieve the tension. "That's the important thing."

"I can't tell you how many times I've been asked my secret for keeping my hat on, mostly after a wind or a rodeo with one of my mules," I said, forcing my breathing to calm and dusting off my pants. Didn't want Ron worrying. I reached for Teton's halter rope. He'd stopped immediately after I'd fallen, waiting for me to get up off the trail.

"What do you tell them?" asked Ron, waving a horsefly away from his face.

Tugging my hat down straight on my head, just above my eyebrows, I smiled. "I tell them if they have to ask, they'll never know."

"Yup," Ron replied, stroking his own tan, weathered Hackberry (named after the world's greatest one-legged cowboy), the dead bees having fallen from its brim. I approached Teancum, who had paused to graze on some grass close to the trail, and patted his rump. "Why did ya go and do that, ya buzzard?" Turning to look at me, his big brown eyes blinked innocently. Gathering his reins, I stepped up into the stirrup and swung my leg over his back. "Let's go," I growled. Innocent of any wrongdoing, he obediently moseyed on down the trail.

"Maybe you need to trade in that mule for a real ride," Ron ribbed, encouraged that I was back to my old self. He kicked his fancy mare to step in behind Sam.

"He's just like riding in a rocking chair," I threw back over my shoulder. "He's just what I like." But we hadn't ridden five minutes when Teancum pulled up, lay down on the trail, and tried to roll over with me on him. Aaargh! What was he trying to do, agree with Ron? Stepping from the saddle before he rolled a second time, I yanked him up by his reins. I wasn't about to let him break my saddle.

Ron, looking on with amusement, couldn't let it pass. "It looks like he's rocked you right out of the saddle."

"You've got to break in any good rocking chair," I responded, trying to sell Ron on the benefits of patience. Teancum shook vigorously, sending a powder of dust in every direction. I stepped back into the saddle and leaned toward my stubborn mule's ear. "You're not helping me any here," I whispered through clenched teeth. Ron continued ribbing me endlessly about mules. But I'm proud of how well Teancum is doing. He's showing no signs of leg weariness.

We bushwhacked the last couple of miles through a steep, brushy draw descending from the ridgetops, totaling another seven and a half hours of riding today. Ron had prearranged for his truck and trailer to be left for us at the bottom of the draw, where we loaded our horses and drove to his home in Hyrum. His wife Marsha made a fabulous dinner of steak, corn on the cob, and potatoes, with raspberry shortcake for a late-night dessert. Good thing I only have those meals periodically! The friendly banter over mules and horses resumed during dinner. I'm sure it wasn't my imagination, but when Marsha mentioned two mules were for sale in Malad, Idaho, I noticed Ron perk up his ears. Hmmm… perhaps I'd not only converted Doubting Ron about my ride, but also planted seeds to grow mule ears!

After dinner I shared some cowboy poetry with Ron and Marsha. I enjoy poetry, and memorization comes easy to me. I've traveled to poetry festivals in Utah, Wyoming, Idaho, Nevada, and even to South Carolina. I've even tried my hand at composing a poem or two.

Early evening I called home to check in. Anita and the grandkids are coming tomorrow to ride with me for a few days. I called Jube to ask if he'd bring his horses for them to ride.

Undressed tonight and found a tender bruise that ran the length of my thigh bone, must have happened when I landed on the trail. Grateful for only a bruise, I said a drawn-out prayer of thanksgiving.

Chapter 7

WEDNESDAY 21 AUGUST 1991

This morning Ron and I met Jube with his truck and trailer at the pavement's end of Avon/Liberty. Jube sprang from his truck wearing his winning smile that could charm the meanest librarian. In a few long strides, he stood beside me. "You look good, Uncle Chuck," he said, eyeing me head to toe to make sure it was true.

"I *am* good," I said, patting his shoulder, appreciative of his concern. "Thanks for bringing your horses." Anxious to help, he'd bounded around to the back of his trailer and had his horses out before I even got there. Lady and Sandy joined my ponies in Ron's trailer. Squeals and snorting ensued, the reunion causing the trailer to rock with excitement.

"The Hatfields and McCoys reunited," grinned Jube, clearly wishing he were once more in the fray. As Ron and I drove away he beeped his horn in farewell. Jube, his image reflected in my rearview mirror, stood by his truck until we were out of sight.

Ron drove me twenty miles from Avon to North Fork Campground, near Liberty, Utah. By the time we arrived there, around ten o'clock, Ron had talked me into bushwhacking for a more scenic route. This entailed traveling an additional four miles south and one mile west up Eight Mile Canyon. We unloaded and he pointed to a steep, brushy climb up a gully. "You like carving your own trail, don't you?" he said, more a statement than question. "Then go one mile west through some oak thickets, and you'll top off in some beautiful meadows."

Leading four horses isn't difficult on a trail, but it can be challenging when bushwhacking. I put Lady in the rear, tied to Sandy, who was tied to Sam, and I led Teton. I wanted to keep Lady away from the mules to lessen the possibility of friction. But as it turned out, the problem wasn't attitudes; it was leading multiple horses through no-trail thickets. The horses got tangled up several times going around trees.

As we climbed the brushy gully, I began to think Ron was trying to teach me *not* to bushwhack. Scrub oak thickets are good places to stay out of, but, as promised, we finally emerged at the edge of a string of beautiful hilltop meadows, only a bit more scratched and cobweb-covered than before. I watered the animals at a cattle tank, then it was easy going down the flat canyon to the road. I traveled for four hours and got to North Park Campground, locating the horse corrals, park, and large pen complex with its restrooms and water tank. Wow, how's that for camping? Today was my first day of riding alone since the start of my journey. It went well despite oak thickets. In fact, thickets helped keep my mind off my tender bruise. Blessings can be found in unlikely places, if we choose to look and see.

Billy Harris, a friend who wants to ride with me, arrived at dusk, hay for the animals and his riding schedule in hand. He'll join me either Thursday night on Ben Lomond Peak or on the trail Friday. As we unloaded the hay and visited, up pulled another friend and former college roommate, Doug Carpenter. He'd brought some maple nut ice cream. What a treat! We enjoyed ice cream and visited before they both left.

I'm anxious to see Anita and the grandkids. I've set up camp and cooked some onions and potatoes in the Dutch oven. I'm waiting for them to join me for dinner. Just finished checking Sam's eyelid, it's turning right side out and the swelling's down. And I've lost the burning feeling where the bee stung me. In a couple of days we'll both be good as new.

Anita and the kids just arrived! She turned the engine

off, but the car continued to rock as if it were traversing rough terrain. In the rear window a head popped up, then disappeared. It was followed by an elbow suddenly appearing, then disappearing. Then a foot kicked at the window and was yanked out of sight. How wonderful to see them! The girls hopped out of the car one by one, first Brittany, her red curls flying and her grin so broad that her freckles connected. Stout little Simone, age six, followed, with her wavy brown hair in a loose ponytail and arms flung wide open. "Grandpa, Grandpa!" they shouted in unison.

"No python hugs for grandpa, only butterfly hugs. Remember?" Anita called after them.

Struggling to stand, I didn't have time to straighten up before they got to me, so I stayed kneeling. Then it was as if they hit an invisible wall. Both stopped abruptly, inches away. Then they encircled me with *oh*, such sweet little arms, so gently wrapped around my neck in soft butterfly hugs as they gave me tender, wet kisses. "We missed you, Grandpa; we love you," they whispered into my shoulder.

My eyes began to leak. Brittany pulled back and looked me in the face. "Grandpa, you've ridden so far!" she exclaimed excitedly. Then she expressed such simple faith by quietly adding, "I knew you could do it, Grandpa; I knew you could." That turned the water works on full force.

Meanwhile, Anita hurried around the car with Hunter squirming in her arms. "Grandpa, Grandpa," he cried, opening his arms and wiggling each little finger, as if they could pull me over to him. He was blurry, a boy under water. I released the girls and stood. Using the backs of my hands as tissue for my nose and eyes, I let those little fingers pull me in.

We relished our Dutch oven dinner amid squeals of delight, laughter, and questions. I forgot all about my bruise. After dinner, Anita and the kids helped me clean out the water tank and refill it. It was slimy and dirty, with lots of floaties. It surely looks better now. Tired, but glowing, we finally bedded down just before midnight.

Anita had come away with only one sleeping bag, in which she stuffed all three kids. She wouldn't accept mine, insisting that she'd tough it out with a sweater and coat. This is the first night I wish I had a tent instead of a fly. Not a peep or complaint, just smiles and, "We're glad we're with you, Grandpa." They make my heart feel like my belly after Thanksgiving dinner: full!

THURSDAY 22 AUGUST 1991

I got up early and rode down to Liberty to call Doug for another sleeping bag. By the time I returned to camp, he was already there with the bag. He also brought his daughter to drive Anita's car into Odgen so she could pick it up on Saturday when she and the kids will head home.

While in town, I found a man who sold me twenty-five pounds of oats for the horses. The mules do well with the help of the oats, but I have to watch Teton so he won't founder. He needs an off button. Even with oats, he's losing some weight, but still doing alright.

We gradually got packed up and started out around noon. Wow, they've got lotsa stuff! Diapers, multiple changes of clothes, food galore and gobs of wipes. I'd forgotten what it's like traveling with children. Still, it was wonderful to have them and Anita was great help packing up and lifting.

As we rode, Anita and the girls sang: "Miss Lucy Mack," "The Ants Go Marching One by One," "Down by the Bay," and countless others. More than once Simone yelled ahead to me, "Grandpa, you wanna sing with us?"

Each time I'd shake my head no and call over my shoulder, "Thanks, but I like hearing your angel voices; just keep singing to me."

Undaunted, she'd jump right back into verse with sister

and mother. Between songs, Anita would point out a fluffy sheep cloud, a large rock formation, or a scurrying chipmunk. Once, pointing to a group of flowers, she asked, "Why do they call those Blue Bells?"

"Shh, girls, listen. What do you hear?" Anita whispered ahead to the girls as she untangled Hunter's fingers from Lady's mane.

"What're we supposed to hear, Mom?" asked Brittany.

"The breeze in the trees, if you're listening," Anita replied. She shifted the sleeping Hunter to lean more evenly against her.

"Who planted all the trees?" asked Britt.

"God did," Anita answered. The simple truth gave me a lump to swallow.

We made it up to the divide on Ben Lomond Peak in about three hours. The trail was awfully nice for width, tread, and slope. That part of the trail is well developed, as evidenced by the dozen or so hikers we passed.

Stopping at a nice spot overlooking the valley, we were lucky to find some water about a hundred yards off the divide. It came seeping out of the ground, just enough for all the thirsty horses to get their fill. We set up camp and watched the night come on as it covered the Salt Lake Valley. Breathtaking!

My, do we change colors the longer we're away from soap and water! I think I've seen every color possible on the faces of my grandkids. Me, too, probably, except I'm behind my complexion and can't see my own face.

It's a cool evening. I am glad Anita has a sleeping bag tonight, apparently a large beetle had harassed her all last night. She hardly got any sleep.

Friday 23 August 1991

At daylight we were still mostly unconscious when along

79

came two guys on their mountain bikes. Dressed in camouflage with hunting bows strapped to their backs, they stopped their bikes at the edge of our camp. "Hello at camp," one of them called.

"Hullo, hullo," I answered, sitting up and running my fingers through my hair.

"We're just passing through and didn't want to scare you," one biker explained.

"You're fine. Thanks for letting us know. Good luck hunting," I answered, crawling from my bag. They started up the trail and were gone. Anita and the kids slept through the noisy exchange.

Invigorated by the good night's sleep, I dressed quickly. The cowbell on Teton had lulled me to sleep last night and kept me dozing comfortably all night.

Anita woke with puffy eyes, yawning. "Wow, that cowbell was loud. I've been awake most of the night; heard each clang and clank."

"Sorry it kept you awake; it does just the opposite with me. Were you warm enough?"

"Oh the bag was great! Much better than my coat," she said as she reached over and slid it on. She yawned again as she emerged from her cozy cocoon, being careful not to wake sleeping Hunter, who'd shared her bag.

Shortly after breakfast of instant oatmeal and hot cocoa, another bow hunter on a bike rode into camp. He was younger than the other two. "Did two guys on bikes come this way not long ago?" he asked as he stopped to catch his breath. "One's my dad and I'm trying to catch them."

"Yup, you're about forty minutes behind them," I replied, pointing up the trail.

He thanked me, lifted his weight to the high pedal, and sent dirt flying from his tires as he sped away. I've never been bow hunting, and am afraid my window of opportunity to try is closed, not enough strength.

We got off a little after nine o'clock, taking in the magnificent view along the ridgetop south of Ben Lomond, where we could see into both the Salt Lake and Ogden valleys. When we rode down to the bottom of North Ogden Pass, Billy Harris and his son Gunner met us to guide us back to their camp. Billy's dad, having driven to our rendezvous point, was also there with watermelon, pop, and assorted snacks. The kids silently ogled the goodies. "Dig in," he said. The kids needed no more encouragement, only occasionally glancing up at us to show teeth covered with treats.

Billy's mare has a nursing colt. Gunner rides a buckskin. We rode three miles south to where Billy had his camp set up near a beaver pond (Had no desire to bathe...). It was a beautiful camp with grass and sparkling water, but through my jaded eyes, the water looked like hell glassed over.

Today on the trail we heard jokes between songs. "Knock knock" jokes were followed by numerous explanations of why the chicken crossed the road. The girls eventually started making up their own jokes. "How's the best way to catch a horse, Grandpa?" Brittany called up to me.

"With a big bucket of grain?"

"No, with a really big glove," she snickered.

Simone wouldn't be outdone. "Grandpa, what's big, takes people places, and goes with gas?" she asked proudly.

"A bus?"

"No, Teton!" This got them both hee-hawing. Apparently, Teton's hind end had been making some noise.

Then the rhyming games started...

When at last we stopped for lunch, the kids kept busy exploring. Hunter stuck close to Anita. Brittany, much to my delight, was my constant shadow, and always quick with questions. "Why are you doing that?... How do you feel?... Can I help you?... Why are Sandy's legs so fat?..." My heart swelled as I explained things to her. Such an inquisitive mind. Simone, more in a world of her own, continually talked to birds, bugs, and herself.

Billy had brought supper of shepherd's stew and cooked scones for us. Wow, second big treat today. The scones were made from frozen bread dough and shaken in a bag filled with cinnamon and sugar. Delish! Could've rivaled any bakery.

Two of Billy's friends rode up to say hello, then headed back out. We ended the glorious day with some cowboy poetry and Anita singing "Danny Boy" and "Ireland." Heaven.

Billy and Gunner have a nice tent; we have our fly tarp–just as happy.

Saturday 24 August 1991

Sprinkled on us last night. Fly did just fine.

The kids slept between Anita and me. Simone's little fist tickled me awake during the night as it brushed against my chin. I gently put it back over her tummy, but it just flopped back onto my chin. After several tries, I gave up and fell asleep with my rough, calloused hand wrapped around her soft fist.

At first light I was jolted awake as Simone yanked her fist from my hand. "Bugs!" she screamed, burrowing down in her bag–joining Britt, who was already wiggling in the bottom. The nylon bag churned like a writhing cocoon. It turns out that, sheltered from the breeze, we were inundated with gnats. They hadn't been bad during the night, but they gathered with a vengeance at first light. Aaargh! I noticed Anita was lying with her sweater over her face. Hunter must have burrowed, too. I pulled my handkerchief up over my nose and grabbed for my hat to protect my head.

About that time I realized the cowbell was getting faint. Gnat infestation forgotten, I bolted from bed and did my best to run in an attempt to turn the ponies before they headed down the trail. I turned back to call Anita, but she was already sprinting after me, open sweater flying behind her. Last night we'd hobbled all the animals, with the exception of Billy's footloose colt, who'd decided to head home, its mare crow-hopping in hobbles close behind. And on their heels were Billy's other horses, Jube's two horses, my two mules, and Teton.

Billy, being the fastest, managed to get in front of my ponies and turn them, but he couldn't catch his or Jube's bunch. Anita and I at last wrangled Sam and Teancum. I offered Teton's halter rope to Billy. "Take Teton. He'll do fine with a halter." I stooped to remove Teton's hobbles; hopping and dancing around, he was afraid of being left behind. Billy grabbed Teton's mane and jumped like a circus trick rider onto his back. Dirt clods flew from Teton's hooves as they disappeared into the trees.

Returning to camp, Anita and I started breakfast, while the human jumping bean, Simone, climbed up on a log, then jumped off, over and over. Hunter dug in the dirt and Brit watched over him like a birddog pointing to pheasant. Billy had brought pancake mix, syrup and frozen sausages.

The sounds and smells of sizzling sausage were filling our campsite when Billy and the horses returned. "They were about a mile down the trail before I got around them," he said as he slid off Teton. We tied up the horses then wiped down Teton, who'd worked up quite a lather.

The sun beat on us today and wilted our bodies, but not our spirits. More song and chatter accompanied the plodding ponies. At one point, Simone mourned a bird whose "ingredients" were outside its body.

Cheerful chatter continued down to Pineview Reservoir. We took care of the horses and got Anita's gear separated out and loaded in Billy's truck and trailer. Billy will drop her and the children in Ogden, where they'll head home.

Oh, farewells are so poignant. Precious memories flood,

tender feelings surface, heart strings stretch, and tears flood. Brittany waited until all goodbyes were said, then, handing me a small blue flower, said, "I picked a flower for you."

I doffed my hat and placed the bloom in my hatband. "I'll keep it close," I said, trying to keep a stiff upper lip. I bent for a hug.

Britt circled my neck with her butterfly wings. "It's a forget-me-not," she whispered in my ear.

My resolve cracked and I lost sight of the flower. Rapid blinking did not stop the tears. "I won't forget." I hugged her as tight as I dared.

Anita, Simone, and Hunt joined the hug, arms softly entangled. The caress magnified my every heartbeat. I stooped as loved ones added their own blue flowers to my hatband. I could only nod and wipe the tears away. Only then did I remember the letter I'd written to Sally, and gave it to Anita. As Billy drove away, I had to pull out Hunt's kiss again. I watched, even after the dust had settled. It was so quiet. I removed my hat to enjoy the flowers and gently smoothed the dents out of the dome. Though my feet have wandered, my heart never has; I thought of home.

Jube and Laurel came to pick up Lady and Sandy within 30 minutes of Billy and Anita's departure. Not wanting to waste a chance to swim in the reservoir, they'd come prepared. Jube in his cowboy boots, a brightly-colored plaid swimsuit and a farmer's tan, stepped out from behind his truck, wearing his trademark grin. That outfit on someone else might have been cause for ribbing, but on Jube it was endearing. Laurel wore a flowered swimsuit, flip-flops and shorts. Her grin matched his. They scampered to the water's edge, stopped just long enough to kick off boots and flip-flops, and jumped in. Through all the splashing, shrieks, and giggling, I dozed in and out–but I vaguely recall hearing the theme music from *Jaws*, the beat gradually growing faster and louder.

Swim-time over, Jube loaded his horses and gear and headed back home, such a precious family. It's three o'clock and I'm waiting for Gary Watson from West Jordan to pick up me and my horses. I need to restock. Gary arrived with his son, Mat, to load us up and take us to their home. We drove through a terrific windstorm. Surely glad I was in the truck cab instead of on the back of a mule.

We pastured the ponies in a grassy lot, then enjoyed a relaxing bath and wonderful supper. Such warm, friendly people. Just like home.

Ah. This mattress is ever so soft. Good night.

Chapter 8

Sunday 25 August 1991

Early this morning I drove out to check on the ponies. They were in "fat city" with lots of grass. Then I drove out on the lakeshore, where thousands of birds in many varieties flitted along the shore. Wow! Thrilling sight for all, especially for birdwatchers.

Church was great. My ragged riding clothes didn't draw any comment. Folks were gracious; in fact, several horsemen wished they could ride with me. I invited them all. We'll see.

Sue, Gary's wife, fixed a scrumptious Sunday dinner of baked fish, vegetables, apple pie, and ice cream. Ah, the fish had been dipped in melted butter, coated with bread crumbs, sprinkled with garlic, salt and pepper, then topped with Parmesan cheese. Yum! Boy, after reading those last few sentences, you'd think I was tired of potatoes.

I checked on our animals again before bed. They're doing ok, but mosquitoes and horse flies are keeping them on the run. They won't get much rest if they're continually trying to out-distance the horsefly, whose bite is painful. Compounding things, the blood attracts even more annoying flies. Our ponies will be glad to get back up on the ridge.

Good night, all. It's stormy out and I may not get to leave early tomorrow morning.

Monday 26 August 1991

I'm already dreaming about the time when my sister Morrissa and her husband Ed will meet me to spend a day and night. Anxious to see 'em. Company sure is fun!

This morning's weather was rainy, cloudy, and windy,

so here I stayed, just fiddling around and running errands. Finally, about noon, the weather cleared, and I got serious about leaving.

Ponies were happy to leave skeeter heaven. I got packed up–including the several packages of wipes Anita left me–just in case she said–and departed at 1:40 p.m., following the "local advice" trail rather than Forest Service-suggested trail. It was steep but alright. Thick oak brush filled with demon claws tore at the packs. We got through the brush, topped out, straightened packs, but there was no trail. Still, it was fairly open ground, so bushwhacking wasn't bad. It was only a matter of time before I stumbled across the trail. The view of Morgan Valley, the Great Basin, and rock-strewn hillsides was beautiful. Because of open landscape, I could see bow hunters a mile away. I'm grateful for the bright-orange Ralide pack boxes. Don't want my animals mistaken for deer.

We summited at Francis Peak Radar and found water for the horses in a puddle on the road. At dark, I dropped into a canyon where the road takes off to Bountiful Peak.

This is my first night alone. My eyes were already heavy after caring for the animals, but still had to unpack. I was able to lift the cloth bags out of the Ralide boxes, then take the boxes off the packsaddle. I'm relieved the packing system works as well as it does.

Boiled water for Ramen noddles, ate, then flopped down exhausted on my sleeping bag. There must be a rock or stick under my left hip, so I can't lay flat. Too tired to care.

Tuesday 27 August 1991

Slept like "Rip Van Winkle;" dreamt like "Princess and the Pea." Woke with a bruise on my hip. Next time I'll take a minute to remove the object when I'm uncomfortable.

I couldn't find a suitable branch to hang my scale on, so I loaded each bag, then held the scale and placed the loaded bag on the hook. It lengthened the packing time, but I can do it by myself.

I got away mid-morning and rode past Bountiful Park, where the trail split. The Utah Forest Service knew I'd be riding the GWT. Not wanting to form a search party, they flagged the trail with signs so I wouldn't get lost. The well-built signs are so new, the paint even looks wet. The trail ranges from a well-beaten path to no path at all, so the signs are a welcome, reassuring sight. I rode ridgetops all the way. Surely glorious scenery in the Great Salt Lake and Morgan Valleys.

I met another shepherd from Peru–friendly and anxious to learn English, with a spate of instructional materials, audio cassettes, and a TV monitor to help. He winters on the desert outside of Delta, Utah. He invited me to a dinner of Tang and tasty fried chicken, then asked if I wanted to stay the night so we could "communicate," which was a struggle despite all the help aids. Concerned about the time, I declined, wanting to reach Emigration Canyon, Utah.

I came to where a huge gasline was being laid. A dirt road crossed over most of it, so I didn't have to maneuver between all the pipes and machinery. But the pipe openings we rode past seemed to be the size of Jonah's whale's mouth–could easily swallow man and mule. The donks snapped to attention at these strange, gigantic tubes that echoed when you called into them. Sam's loose lower lip and floppy ears tightened, and his tail hair fanned like turkey feathers. Teancum changed species entirely: owl eyes, squirrel tail, ant-antenna ears, and bloodhound nostrils. Teton, sensing the mules' anxiety, lifted his head slightly and became mildly engaged. I sat ready for a rodeo, but Teancum only snorted and danced nervously as we passed the scary machinery. *Sigh of relief.*

The afternoon was filled with rain and hard winds. I dismounted and backed under a tree. Teancum tried to follow me, but I already felt crowded and shooed him out. He kept pushing forward; I continued to push him out. Sam and Teton were resigned to wait out the storm and stood with heads down, tails to the wind and rain. Eventually Teancum stopped trying to invade my tree-branch shelter and took his place next to Teton. But, all the while, he gazed at me with rain dripping from his eyelashes. It was as if we were in a stare-down. I believe in eye contact while conversing, but it was a little unnerving that he didn't even seem to blink. I'd glance around, only to return to his stare. I squatted as far down as I could and checked; yup, eyes still fastened on me. Craned my neck to one side; eyes still fastened on me. Resolved in my mind that there was no room in the inn, I settled in for a long stare-down. Teancum finally blinked, then stretched his neck far enough to place his lips against my cheek and nibble.

That did the trick. This Grinch's heart grew four sizes. "Come on, boy," I said, flattening myself against the tree trunk. There was only enough room for his head, but that seemed to be fine by him. I patted, cooed, and scratched his jaw line as he rubbed his head on my shoulder. Funny how "no room" can turn into *enough room* when the heart is softened.

With Teancum's body in front and tree trunk behind, I felt like I just might stay dry. But bent tree branches released stored water, and soon my hat brim had become an upside-down umbrella.

It was then that the wind started sending sheets of stinging sideways rain through the branches. My hat stayed on, in spite of the wind, but sometimes the brim turned up in front, funneling rainwater down my back. Occasionally, it turned down over my face, in turns dumping water onto my belly or on Teancum's face. I may have been drier standing out in the open, directly under the downpour. I chided myself for being a rookie and not packing my rain gear on the top of the Ralide boxes. Leland had insisted I take his nice National Guard rain suit. Next time it looks like a downpour is on its way, I'll have it handy.

When at last the rain slowed to a drizzle, I started riding again, but the clouds were down low and I wasn't sure of my direction. I took a chance and it turned out to be the right way. Whew!

I veered up around the head of City Creek and its expansive, garden-like basins and meadows. Sheep were scattered all over, looked like pretty loose shepherding to me. I met another herder from New Mexico who'd herded his entire life. Talkative, once he got warmed up.

Rode too long–'til dark. Had to camp right next to the trail on a windy exposed ridgetop. The fly whipped all night long. I was tickled it held fast, in spite of all the popping. Who needs a tent?

Made twenty to twenty-five miles of trail today, despite the off-and-on rain. Long day!

WEDNESDAY 28 AUGUST 1991

The law of opposites is powerful. Endured terrible winds and slashing rain through the night, but, at sunup, I found things calm, bright, and warm. How precious is the variety in the universe. I got underway a little after ten.

Enjoyed a clear, beautiful, sunny ride today, and a breeze kept the flies away. Had to bushwhack on two steep scrub-oak hills, but the sun's warmth kept me smiling. Each bush to step over and tree to go around were only temporary inconveniences. I felt the peace of nature the entire day.

Emigration Canyon, Utah, was closer than I thought, which made for a short ride today. Arrived there before noon. Teton had thrown a hind shoe this morning so, after unloading packs and setting up camp by Mormon Trail, I nailed on a new one. Hung up a rope clothesline to dry out my wet bedding, as I'd packed everything wet this morning because I was so anxious to meet my sister Morrissa (Ress) and her husband, Ed, this evening. While the Dutch oven potatoes and Vienna sausages cook, I've got leisure time to write.

Sally and I stay with Ress and Ed when I go to Salt Lake City for my chemo drip. They always make us feel like their home is our home. How can we repay shared love and repay those who expect nothing in return? I adore my little sister Ress, who accepts me, despite my faults. Growing up, she was always good and kind, even when our situation wasn't ideal.

Morrissa never knew our father, and I only remember bits and pieces about him. My father, Morris, died December 5, 1938, when I was seven years old, the result of an unsuccessful spleenectomy performed at Mayo Brothers Clinic in Rochester, New York. I later learned that an enlarged spleen is usually a symptom of some other problem, one of which might be blood cancer. I don't remember anything about my father's condition except that he was sick. The surgeons told him that if he lived for six months, he would be out of the woods. He died five months, twenty-seven days after surgery, while he was shaving. I'd been away playing with some neighbor kids. When I returned home, I saw the hearse come up the street, slow down, and turn into our driveway; that's when I realized it was coming for my father. Our mother was left with me (7), Jim (5), Barrie (2), and was pregnant with Morrissa, who was born two weeks after our father's death.

My stepfather was a kind, gentle man whom I loved, but he was always more like a visitor in our home than a father figure. Looking back, I know I needed a firm hand to guide and direct me. I have no doubt my biological father and I would have butted heads, but wonder what life lessons, good or bad, I would have learned from him. We are all teachers, not necessarily by profession, but in how we live our lives and how we interact with those around us. What kind of a man was my father? Am I like him? Did he have multiple myeloma?

Consequently, growing up without a lot of guidance, I grew up rough. I had a quick temper and was a bully. I remember a girl in grade school, named Emma Black, who sat right in front of me. Her hair looked like Medusa's. It was dark brown, tightly curled, and hung to her waist. She kept it under control in long, tight braids. But little puffs of tightly curled fine hair at the base of her hairline managed to escape the braids. Each day I found myself fixated on those little puffs of hair, and one day decided to do something about them.

The next morning I made sure my mother didn't see me slip the box of wooden matches from the cupboard into my pocket. I ran to catch my friend Jack on our way to school, and showed him the matches. "Chuck, you'll get in big trouble if you take those to school."

I didn't tell him what I was planning to do. After the Pledge of Allegiance, Mr. Flayley began writing math problems on the board. Slyly, I pulled the matches from my pocket and glanced over at Jack, a smirk on my face. Wide-eyed and shaking his head, he mouthed the word "No!" Undeterred, I pointed to the end of a braid, then to the little puffs of hair. I planned to first take care of the jagged braid end, then move up to singe the fuzzy balls.

Kids seated behind Jack looked on wide-eyed as I struck a match under my desk. Emma sat quietly, taking math notes, as I eased the flame under the braid end, which didn't merely singe, as I'd thought it would. Instead, the oily end instantly lit up like a candle. The braid end turned into little black, pinhead size balls. The stench of burnt hair filled the room. Mr. Flayley whipped around faster than you could say "melted nubbins." Screaming, Emma flew out of her chair as her desk overturned. I had just enough time to slap and blow out the flame before Mr. Flayley's fingers reached out and seized my own hair. He yanked me from my desk, lifted me up, and held me at eye level. With my legs flailing, I instinctively grabbed his wrists in an attempt to ease the pain. He roughly let me drop, then half kicked, half pushed me to his office to call my mother.

Later that evening my mother marched me over to Emma's home and I apologized to her and her parents. I was grounded for a month and was given after-school detention for a week. My mother gave Mr. Flayley a piece of her mind (though I didn't deserve her support), letting him know in no uncertain terms that he was never to mistreat me again, regardless of my behavior.

There were other times I was more than a bully, and even risked public censure. As rural communities went then, if you hadn't already heard it from the grapevine, you could read it in the local newspaper. The paper kept its finger on the pulse of the community through high school events, letters to the editor, the sheriff's report, and obituaries. When each weekly paper was delivered, I always first turned to the "Sheriff's Report" to see who was featured. My name never appeared in the report, but that didn't mean I didn't ever deserve to have it listed.

In high school some friends and I got caught up in the shoplifting habit, not because we were hungry or broke, but just to see if we could get away with it. We took a lot of stuff from the stores in town, "patronizing" several merchants. One time I shoplifted a block of Velveeta cheese at Stan Myer's store. The principal of the school, who also served as Scout Commissioner, witnessed the deed, but without a word, stared straight at me for about ten seconds, then turned and walked away.

Over the next several weeks the guilt got to me. Then while riding to Salt Lake City on a scout trip with Stan, slouched there in the cab of his pickup truck, I screwed up my courage to confess. "Mr. Myer, I stole some cheese and other things from your store. I'm sorry." It had taken me almost five hours to gather the courage to tell him. He remained silent for a few minutes, and I wondered if he'd even heard me. Finally, he turned from looking out the windshield and momentarily held my gaze. I couldn't stand looking at him; I was so ashamed. My eyes focused on my boots.

"How much do you figure the stolen items were worth?"

"Probably about eighteen dollars," I mumbled.

"Don't worry about it," he said quietly.

Near tears, I warbled, "I want to pay it back for my own sake." He told me that he and all the other merchants in Driggs, Idaho, knew all about our shoplifting escapades, but had decided not to take action because they knew our families and figured we would grow out of it. Hell, I felt wormy when I realized those merchants and family friends knew about our stealing and had still treated us nicely. That surely cured me of shoplifting.

Those merchants, along with extended family members and friends of my father, were men from the valley who could be lumped together as "many fathers." They taught me valuable lessons and helped me feel worthwhile. When I felt like the concern was sincere, I was responsive to their guidance, and I credit many of them for helping me to not become more of a delinquent than I already was. I know, or at least hope, that I've changed and am a softer, gentler person now.

They're here! Will write more tonight…

Like rays of sunshine, Morrissa and Ed stepped from their blue van. Morrissa shaded her eyes from the sun's glare and swept her head back and forth, searching for me. I stood up and waved my pencil high above my head. "Over here!" I shouted excitedly. Her wave was no less exaggerated as she ran to me. Ed sauntered over to where we stood, hugging, allowing Ress and me to have our gleeful reunion.

"Chuck, you look great!" she gushed. To show her I felt alright, I danced a little jig. It was a slow jig with shuffled steps, but she smiled and added, "Ballroom quality, too." Reaching around Ress, I shook Ed's hand. "So good to see you both."

"You too," Ed replied, returning his hand to his pocket and stepping back, allowing Ress front and center. Ed is quiet, but stalwart and solid. Ress is the flash and bubble, but he is the rock. She'd be lost without him.

After warming up the corn and scooting the peach cobbler to the outer edge of the coals, we sat down to eat and catch up on things, me feeling like a treasured chef with their *oh's* and *ah's*. Before long, two Salt Lake City watershed guys stopped by. "We want to make sure you aren't going to let your horses on the Salt Lake City side of the watershed," grumped the short, compact man as he tipped his head towards the horses.

"We're just makin' sure the water stays clean," added his dark-haired buddy.

"Would you like some dinner?" I asked in an attempt to soften them. I knew the smell of cobbler still hung in the air. They declined. After giving me "the talk" about the necessity of pure water, water rights, contamination, and job obligation, they turned to go—but then the dark-haired fellow stopped short, turned to me and said, "You've got some nice-looking mules there." The shorter man nodded. Ahh, I smiled, their Achilles Heal was showing. Then the dialogue began. We talked of mule shows, mule pulls, mule bloodlines… We ended with their deciding I was no threat and them showing me a water hole on *their* side.

Shortly after they left, two other men who had interest in the east side of the watershed stopped to verify that I wasn't going to trespass on *their* side. Lots of private property in these Utah hills, and owners are a little protective.

Ed and Ress slept in their van, near the electrical tower. I noticed that a heavy dew had settled on the grass; looked as if a rainstorm had rushed through. Last night's rain must be hovering in the air, waiting on cue to drop as dew. I set up the fly, laid out my sleeping bag under it, and carefully stacked all my gear around my bag, everything I wanted to keep dry. I wriggled into my sleeping bag and expected my eyelids to clank shut. Saddles stacked atop cloth storage bags, clothes stuffed in Ralide boxes covered with rain gear, and a cast iron kettle bumping against my feet made me feel like a kid surrounded by his homemade fort and prized possessions. Alas, my muscles finally began to relax as they received permission to give up their vigilant constriction. My eyes traced the makeshift roof, then closed, waiting for the Sandman to do his job.

I expected sleep to come quickly. I was mistaken. The carefree kid-in-his-fort allusion quickly fled as my mind jumped ahead to tomorrow. Though I lay there protected from wind and rain, I felt exposed. In my mind's eye, I saw white coats coming and going, lab results, too few white cells, urine laden with unnatural levels of protein; I heard sterile instruments clanking, rubber-soled shoes squeaking on polished floor tile, and a slow dripping that promised both life and death. These images and sounds were accompanied by antiseptic smells that made me wonder if brain cells as well as blood cells were dying. A tear escaped the corner of my eye. Do I dare hope that this time my body will be strong enough for a full dose of chemo? I want maximum medicine to blitz the cancer, not those weak remedies that make me feel like a wounded elk limping along, just giving the hunter time to close in. I kept my eyes shut as I tried to think of something else. Need sleep!

The next thing I knew I was struggling to escape the slimy saliva of an anaconda's mouth. I turned, trying to pull free from the constricting jaws, but they just wrapped tighter around me. I managed to get my chest free. I don't know if it was my feet kicking or the chilly air that woke me. My eyes darted back and forth, but registered only blackness. I fumbled for my flashlight. It was 3:00 a.m. My grogginess left me when, partly exposed to the night air, I began to shiver. My "snake skin" sleeping bag gripped me, twisted tight around my legs. I regained my bearings and realized my nightly sweats had begun earlier than usual and were more intense. My sleeping bag was soaked through. I was a little sore from thrashing, but my bones seemed okay. If I'd been at home I'd have changed my underwear, but in the mountains I just air dry. I pulled the layers of saddle blankets out from under me and laid them dry side up on top of my bag. Then, using them as both mattress and blanket, I sandwiched myself between them and waited for morning.

After about an hour of thrashing around and trying to sleep, I gave up. With a flashlight propped on top of my saddle, I decided to finish this journal entry. The sweats from the cancer are miserable. First I'm hot and sweaty; then I'm cold and chilled.

THURSDAY 29 AUGUST 1991

The morning couldn't have come soon enough. As the sky began to lighten, I extracted myself from the horse blankets, smelling too much like my ponies. I stood air drying when Ress, ever the early-riser, climbed from her van. Briskly entering camp, she called out a cheery "Good morning!" I waved back, smiling, lifted by her enthusiasm. She helped take down the fly as we prepared to leave the animals and gear in Emigration Canyon.

"Were you cold last night?" she asked, squatting to pick up my sleeping bag.

"A little," I said as I turned to throw the horse blankets

over the line to air.

"Why is your bag so wet? Weren't you under your tarp?" I turned and saw her wipe one hand on the back of her pants, then the other as she shifted the bag back and forth between hands, her forehead creased with worry.

"I got a little hot," I said sheepishly, turning my head so as not to look her in the eye.

Her eyebrows raised, wide eyes boring into my temple. "This is sweat?"

"Yeah," I muttered as I turned back to meet her stare. She stood frozen for a second, then melted as her eyes filled. We stood, eyes locked, as if posing for a portrait, until she dropped the bag, stepped closer, and gently wrapped her arms around me. As we wet each others' shoulders, I noticed Ed had gotten out of the van and discreetly circled behind it.

Later, after making sure the ponies were tied securely for the day, Ed and Ress drove me to their home in Salt Lake City, where I took a long, overdue bath, shaved, and got laundered. Felt like a lizard shedding his skin. Called Sally and got a letter from her as well. I sure am missing her. Ress took me shopping to replenish supplies: horseshoes, nails, grain, food…

Ress saved a poem for me written by John Updike entitled "Perfection Wasted." It touched a cord and made me bawl. It's about a person's special magic and how it is extinguished at death.

She also baked a birthday cake today. Yup, I turned sixty! Happy Birthday, sexagenarian. (Sounds dirty, but it's not. It means someone who is sixty years old or between the ages of sixty and seventy) Sixty used to sound so old–not anymore.

I celebrated by going to the University of Utah Hospital for my monthly chemo dosage. My white count is still too low for a full dose of chemo. The white cells in the blood are a major cell type responsible for the immune system. Mine are weakened. I have high levels of M protein in my urine. The white count needs to rise and the protein level needs to decrease.

I must have cried all my tears last night worrying about the levels of my white count and protein. When Dr. Feldsen told me we couldn't do full strength chemo yet, I was ready. In fact, I expected it, and was glad to get what I could.

After the nurse placed the hydrogen cap on my head, she hooked up my IV. I watched the IV drip and felt resigned, submissive to my cancer.

Hospitals and their various exam and therapy rooms are all *waiting* rooms; all the treatments that go on in a cancer ward can't help but teach its patients patience. While receiving chemo, I had several hours to think. I was reminded of Dr. Feldsen's office, the end of June, 1990, when he delivered the results of my initial oncology test. "You have multiple myeloma, a cancer of the bone marrow. Your white blood cells (plasma cells) that produce infection-fighting antibodies have become malignant and are attacking your bone marrow."

Cancer! My worries were confirmed. That word alone sent such fear pulsing through me. I caught my breath and tried to slow my rapid breathing. I became intensely aware of the bitter, metallic taste in my mouth and feeling my heart pulse in my ears. Sally paled. She sat closely on my right, her hand on my knee. When she heard the word cancer, she lifted her hand, straightened her back, interlaced her fingers tightly in her lap and began to rhythmically knead the backs of her hands. We'd hoped cancer wasn't the culprit behind the intense pain. Now we knew it was.

"How far along is it?" I asked quietly, gripping the arms of my chair and adjusting my back to ease the pain in my lower vertebra.

Dr. Feldsen scanned my chart, seeking a diamond in the rough. "Stage three, the last stage. Some of the symptoms are bone pain and skeletal fractures. This would explain your back pain. A few of your lower back bones are punctured with holes. One vertebra is disintegrating and collapsing. Your bones are like white Styrofoam in texture and toughness, due to the myeloma."

"Will I be able to ride my mule again?" I asked, anticipating his reply. Sally unlocked her neck and swung her face toward me.

"Chuck!" she exclaimed, in disbelief. What was I doing worrying about riding when I should be praying to live?

The doctor reached up to adjust his glasses. "Chuck, you'll never ride again. I'm sorry." My gut clenched around a small hard rock. "If you were to get kicked, thrown, bumped, or dragged, any of which would cause powdery fractures, there you'd be, in a heap, until someone found you." All of these scenarios were periodic, familiar events with my mules.

Sally's head swivelled back toward Dr. Feldsen, her eyes relocking into position as she resumed her rhythmic knuckle-kneading. I remember my mind momentarily flicking back to a funny cartoon from a series called *The Far Side* by Gary Larson. It was a drawing of a boneless chicken ranch, with chickens flopped on the ground, draped over the fence and tossed on the stairs, taking on the shape of whatever they were lying on. The cartoon didn't seem so funny now.

"How much time do I have?" I asked. I reminded myself to loosen my grip on the chair arms, as the muscles in my hands had begun to cramp.

"These things are hard to predict, but after radiation and chemotherapy and given your stage, I'd say between eighteen months to three years."

We left the doctor's office and made our way to the car with downcast eyes, silent voices, and ashen faces. Once inside, the tears came. Cancer. Multiple myeloma. Stage three. Only eighteen months to three years to live. So many stolen dreams.

The five-hour drive from Salt Lake to Alta was quiet and introspective. First we must call our six children and tell them the diagnosis. Next we need to plan for the return to Salt Lake for radiation, followed by monthly treatments of chemotherapy. Then what? The assumption was "yes" to chemotherapy. I didn't know if I wanted to try it, but I remembered Craig's words: "You can't feel any worse than you do now."

During the car ride home, in the quiet of my mind, emotions took center stage. Denial hopped on his pedestal and screamed, "I'm not that sick! I'll beat this." Bargaining waited for a few moments, then mounted his stool and loudly proclaimed: "If I eat better, live more righteously, pray more sincerely, then…" I tried to make room for Hope by envisioning healthy cells devouring the cancerous ones in an attempt at self healing. I silently prayed for the Lord to extend His heavenly hand and heal me. But it didn't take long for Depression, in all his dark glory, to enter and out-shout the others. Not bothering to mount a podium, he engulfed the chamber like poured acid, burning and eroding every other emotional base, leaving only barren ground. By the time we arrived in Alta, only Depression still held sway, intoning a deafening whisper that had silenced the other emotions miles ago.

In the days that followed I slumped into an emotional trough. Several close friends had earlier died from cancer. Watching it take over their lives and seeing them gradually become a hollow, miserable shell of themselves, left me with dread and revulsion. Now it was my turn.

Deeply entrenched in hopeless self-pity, I went to bed to die. I lay there on my home-rigged plywood bed. This was when loved ones came and literally pulled me back from the clutches of despair.

Prior to my true diagnosis, I had gone to several doctors

to try to find out what was wrong with my lower back. I'd been suffering from excruciating pain since January 1990. It began when I was feeding horses in the barn. Throwing a bale of hay out through a hole in the wall, I felt a stabbing pain in my back, and immediately had to lie down. It felt like an ice pick was being driven into my lower spine. I eventually made it back to the house by leaning on the fence, frequently lying down to rest, and crawling. It took me a good half hour to cover the distance that would have normally taken less than a minute.

My back got steadily worse over the next few days; the muscle cramps were agonizing. I couldn't walk to the barn to feed the animals. The kind husband of a fellow teacher came every day for several months to feed my horses. I ended up giving him a mule, I was so grateful.

Attempting to find the source of the pain, we went to a chiropractor in Rexburg, Idaho. He massaged my back, gave it electrical muscle stimulation, and did an ultrasound to help with blood circulation. My back felt better while he was working on it, but immediately hurt again when I sat down in the car, though I tried sitting sideways and cockeyed all the way home. I could lie down without it hurting, but, whenever I moved, I felt the ice pick. We went to the chiropractor a few times, but soon gave up on him.

We then decided to try a physical therapist. She was good at what she did, but it was the same story. Felt good while she was working on me, but as soon as I got home the pain returned. I lasted about six weeks with her.

One doctor I went to was concerned about my bone density. He thought I had osteoporosis and prescribed large doses of calcium tablets. That didn't help either.

Then I tried Ty McCowin, a friend and horse brother, who's also an orthopedic surgeon in Idaho Falls. He gave two bits of advice: get a body brace and get busy exercising.

He explained that bones are like muscles; they need to be used. Disuse results in atrophy. So we began combating the "vegetable" syndrome by doing exercises. At this time I was stooping over at about a forty-five-degree angle to relieve the pain on my lower spine.

Dr. McCowin had a body brace built for me, kind of like knight's armor in white plastic, extending from neck to buttocks. Velcro straps on each side allowed me to tighten or loosen the brace. It did help me to stand up straight and relieved some pain in my back. However, we were dealing with the symptoms and not the source. It seemed that each doctor treated for his own specialty, not really knowing what was wrong. I grew terribly frustrated. Nothing was working, but through it all, I continued teaching.

One Sunday in late May 1990, two friends, Lew Wilson and his uncle Merrill Wilson, an oncological surgeon, were visiting from Salt Lake City. They stopped me after church. Both were genuinely worried about me. Merrill told me that if I'd come to Salt Lake, he'd get the best doctor he could find to help us discover what was really wrong. We took him up on his offer and within two days climbed into the car to make the five-hour drive.

Sally and I hoped this time it would be different. I went to see an endocrinologist, who, after running a battery of tests, sent us to Dr. Feldsen. An oncologist, Dr. Feldsen drilled a hole in my hip bone to remove some bone marrow. The procedure was excruciating, but revealed the multiple myeloma. Later, at Dr. Feldsen's office, I met a man who also had multiple myeloma. Shortly after, he died as a result of broken ribs, caused by an unknowing friend's hug. This wasn't very encouraging to me.

Jolted from my reminiscing, I heard, "You're done, Chuck," as Dr. Feldsen reentered my hospital room. "How are you feeling?"

"Alright so far," I said, anxious to be through. While the nurse removed the IV and hydrogen cap, the doc and I discussed my ride.

"You really think you can get all the way to Mexico?" he asked, smiling.

I smiled back. "That's the plan."

"God speed, Chuck. It's patients like you who give others hope. I don't like the taste of crow, but I'm glad I've had to eat it," he said, shaking my hand. Me offering hope to others? Only a few months before, I lay on a bathroom floor wanting to die. Now I wanted to experience all life had to offer.

"Thank you, Doctor. I appreciate all you've done for me. I'm convinced those people who say they'd rather die quickly than slowly, aren't living life to its fullest. If you're dying, slow is alright."

Dr. Feldsen chuckled as he turned to leave. "I think so, too. Be safe."

Before exiting the hospital, I procured the prescribed antibiotics to have with me if I need them, and also a dose of chemo in pill form. Over the next month, I could take them and stay on schedule, even in the mountains.

Ress picked me up after chemo. We had time for a quick bite (well, she ate, I picked). Then she took me to a Great Western Trail meeting for the Utah and federal agencies where I met some folks who can help me finagle Idaho's end of the trail. Don England, a Utah ranger, showed me a new trail they'd built for the GWT around the west side of Timpanogos Mountain, a 4000-volunteer effort. They even handed out T-shirts promoting the GWT.

I also visited with a man named Camden who brought a nice bunch of maps showing trail routes. After the meeting, I asked Craig and Caroline Norton, GWT promoters, if they would board my animals. They graciously agreed, picked up my ponies from Emigration Canyon, then drove them up

Parley's Summit, where they have a stable. In turn, Craig and Caroline took me to meet Helen and Cyrus Howell, and Helen gave me a list of endurance race riders and trail riders down through Utah who'd ride with me or help me if I needed it. Helen, Cyrus, Craig, and Caroline will ride with me Saturday to guide me onto the trail and through private property. Craig and Caroline have even lined up television stations and newspapers to cover my ride. I'll be a star?

It's been a long day, what with chemo and the GWT meeting. Tired.

While I was journaling and getting ready for lights out, there came a knock on my bedroom door. I opened it to find Ress standing there, cradling a brand new sleeping bag. "I got this for you today. It's made with Gore-Tex, a material that breathes on the inside, wicks out dampness and moisture, yet seals out dew and rain on the topside."

It was my turn to stand frozen for a split second, speechless, before my hands covered my eyes. I reached out for her shoulders and pulled her close. In turn, her arms circled around me in a gentle embrace. We stood silent and still in another portrait pose, every line crisp except smudges at the shoulders and tear blurs on the cheeks.

Sorry for the crinkled paper and smeared ink. Thank you, Lord, for loving family.

Chapter 9

Saturday 31 August 1991

Whooee! Got to the animals this morning and news-people were milling all around. Newspaper reporters and TV personalities from channels 2, 4 and 5, all from Salt Lake City. They hooked mics on my collar, set up banks of lights, and took lots of photos for the evening news. As the camera-man wove in and out filming from every angle, I watched the camera cord inch closer to Sam's hind feet.

"How much is the camera worth?" I asked.

The cameraman shrugged. "Lots."

"You won't have it in one piece if the cord touches Sam's feet."

Camera and cameraman were spared. But after an hour and a half of being interviewed and photographed–which was great fun at first–stardom began to wear thin. Finally, Helen, Cyrus, Craig, Caroline, and I got away at 11 a.m. They led, I followed, riding up Toll Canyon, a private, beautiful trail. Then over to Guardsman Pass east of Brighton and down east to Bonanza Flat to camp. Brighton, at least in the late sum-mer, is surely a disappointment for all its publicity, but the trail was spectacular.

Labor Day weekend crowds were out in force! Passed on the trail: seventy-nine bikers, three hikers, four motorcycles. Some bikers were stealth riders, suddenly appearing next to us. I was busy tallying the bikers in my head when suddenly Teton's lead rope was jerked from my hand. Sam, at the back of the pack, had come unglued. Startled by a biker's sudden approach, he'd reared and jerked unsuspecting Teton to a stop. Then Sam trying to distance himself from the two-wheeled ghost who'd materialized out of thin air, had fanned out from the trail and pulled Teton off balance. For his part, Teton had stumbled almost to his knees, then recovered and planted his feet. But the bigger, stronger Sam dragged him off the trail.

The biker, meanwhile, continued his course, looking neither right nor left. To him *we* were the phantoms. Now, most bikers are considerate, but this one must have skipped Courteous Biker 101. He could have cleared his throat or given a "Hello," or even called out a blatant "Boo!" Damn near had a rodeo!

Along the trail, we gabbed up a storm. Craig Norton recommended that I procure a Fuji chrome 400 camera for the rest of the trip. It has a faster shutter speed, would give better color, and is easier to use. So far the camera I have seems to be working fine, except for when I bumped it and triggered a rewind. Lost most of my 24 exposures.

After riding with us for several hours, Craig and Cyrus had to head home. Helen and Caroline will camp tonight and ride with me tomorrow. We set up camp at Bonanza Flat, near Brighton, the ladies pitching their tent close to their horses. I tried visiting, but was too tired and bowed out early.

Sunday 1 September 1991

We rode into Little Cottonwood Canyon, tied our animals, and from a dirt road, caught a ride into Brighton ski resort. There I phoned Tess Crane, who wanted to join us. But we missed her. Ouch! The more people, the more commitments; the less people, the freer I am. Where to strike the balance? Do I allot certain periods for heavy commitments and other times for self?

Got away late, lost the trail, bushwhacked, and finally a lady lawyer from Brighton got us onto the trail. Then, it was nice riding. We met up with Tess five hours late. She and her husband had zig-zagged back and forth, looking for us. We rode out through Sandy Baker Pass on East Ridge Trail, then lost the trail again. After about an hour of doubling back, bushwhacking, taking off through the brush, and swiping branches from my face, Helen gave me an ultimatum: "We are not going up that game trail with you; desert us if you will!" It seems some folks get nervous, loud and demanding when uncertainties arise. But I couldn't blame her.

By then it had begun to rain, adding fuel to her fire, I'm sure. I decided it was easier to be graceful and go with the group. We spent a total of two hours trying to get out of a cul-de-sac. Finally, we stumbled upon West Ridge Trail. After we got back on the trail, Tess gathered her bearings and confidently led us to Mill Canyon Spring, east of Timpanogos, arriving after dark. Her husband was waiting for us. The three ladies, grateful, I'm sure, left with him for home. Tonight's camp is set up on Timpanogos Divide, right next to a Peruvian shepherd. Used the glow of his lantern for light.

Sure appreciate the quiet. What a long day!

MONDAY 2 SEPTEMBER 1991

Had a restful night. I was so tired after lying down that I just passed out. My body must have needed the sleep, because I was late rising this morning. Felt like I'd been to a stress detox camp, my body so relaxed I had to peel myself out of bed.

When I awoke, everything was damp, drenched in dew. My new sleeping bag worked like a charm. Thanks, Ress! Its fabric breathes, releasing body perspiration, and blocks dew. I'm warm even when the bag is moist. Its shell is so thin I can see light through it. What a wonderous, modern development. My! It's interesting how one thin layer will trap the dew. Is there a parallel here? Will even a thin hope repel despair?

I enjoyed breakfast, even though my stomach was still queasy. Birds chirped, insects buzzed, and the ponies grazed as I relaxed, the morning sun warming my face. Being alone is peaceful.

This morning while I was picking burs out of Sam's cinch cover, the thought came to me that this chore, when I was running to destinations and meeting schedules, used to be drudgery. Now it's joyful, because it will make Sam more comfortable. Hmmm.

By the time I started packing, most items–including my sleeping bag–were already dry. Truly wonderful. I no longer need the scales for the cloth bags, now that I know what items go where. I'm getting quite speedy at packing. Some hunters rode up this morning after I'd placed the last bag in Teton's Ralide box. They stopped to say they'd seen the article in the Provo Herald about me and my ride to Mexico and to offer words of encouragement. I hope I get to see the news articles.

I was tempted to ride the American Fork road into Provo Canyon because on the map it looks shortest. But Don England will be disappointed if I do. So instead I took a beautiful trail carved from the sheer side-hill into Mutual Dell Campground on Scenic Loop Road. At Timpooneke Campground, I paused to link into Timpooneke Trail. Several groups of folks came over, eager to visit. The Chapmans, a family composed of at least six school teachers, invited me to a delicious Dutch oven lunch. We formed an instant bond and enjoyed swapping stories. My, how nice to be a public figure! The media coverage has certainly eased the way for me. Skepticism has changed to encouragement. It's nice.

After lunch I went to see what the west side of Mount Timpanogos looks like. It's breathtaking. Two different trails lead to Mount Timpanogos, Aspen Grove Trail, and Timpooneke Trail. Horses aren't allowed on Aspen Grove Trail, so I took the Timpooneke route and traveled around the north and west side. The Indian trail on West Timpanogos makes me want to relive some Indian history. I wish there were information on it readily available.

On the southeast side of Timpanogos, I lost the trail behind Big Baldy, so I followed Dry Fork down toward Orem. Rode through north Orem in the dark and planned to head up Provo Canyon, but encountered bumper to bumper traffic coming home from Labor Day. Too dangerous.

Found a spot to camp by the side of the road, close to some power poles at the mouth of the canyon. Long day, but sunny and beautiful.

TUESDAY 3 SEPTEMBER 1991

Fourth and last day of chemo pills. Glad to be done for now.

Had a hard night. It's not much fun sleeping by the side of a busy road: hot, dusty, and noisy. The ponies stood, tied up short, in a dry weed patch all night. The traffic was still thick in the morning, so I rode to the closest mini-mart and called Mike Gooding, a friend and fellow teacher, who lives in Provo.

Mike's been working with abused kids at the state hospital. He's got a heart the size of Texas–not to mention a truck and trailer to rescue me. During the wait, I called Sally and touched base with her. Mike picked me up, took me grocery shopping, then hauled us to the trailhead in South Fork, Provo Canyon. Fun to visit with him. He's offered to help with the Idaho end of the GWT. Very nice man.

Got away at 12:40 p.m. and headed for Windy Pass. I forgot to water the horses. It's unsettling that I get so "gone oriented" that I fail to think of their welfare. We found water in Windy Pass. Whew. A fine trail has been constructed that winds around a steep slope and oak thickets. According to Mike, the Boy Scouts of America and convicts from the state prison jointly built the trail. The trusties from the prison could opt to work in the mountains or stay and work in prison. That's a no brainer, eh? They enjoyed working outside and received two dollars and fifty cents a day for their efforts.

Shortly after watering the horses I rode by an elk and her calf. They brought back memories of my hunting days. Within the hour a bow hunter came by on his bike. "Hullo! Coming by!" he yelled. I pulled Teancum to a stop to let him pass. Being warned, Sam just stood there and watched. Teton just took to foraging for food.

"Any luck?" I asked, resting my right elbow on the saddle-horn. The hunter, a young kid, stopped. Winded, he adjusted the bow slung across his shoulder. "Yeah, as a matter of fact, a four-point bull back by the water where you watered your horses." The pride in his voice was apparent.

"You were there?"

He gave a nod. "Hiding in the oak thicket about sixty yards from the water hole. I saw you water your animals and then ride by."

"Hum, I guess that's why you got the bull. We didn't see you either," I chuckled.

"That's the whole idea," he said, then maneuvered his bike carefully around Teancum and headed off up the trail.

As I watched him disappear over a rise, I felt the hair on my scalp salute. It's a little spooky being the one out in the open and not the one behind the brush. It was unnerving to know that the kid was so well-hidden neither the horses nor I spotted him. I couldn't help but smile, though; the boy reminded me of myself as a youth, hidden in the brush, hoping for an elk to step into the open so I could proudly return to camp with my trophy.

After my father died, my uncles and family friends stepped in, offered help, and included me when they could. My many father figures taught me how to shoot guns better, pack meat, and track and hunt in timber. I became an excellent shot and a good hunter; it surely did things for my confidence when I'd get an elk and no one else did. I felt valued and accepted in a hunting camp–a place I could shine.

Hunting was truly a major part of my path toward manhood and the adult community. Even now, being in a mountain hunting camp with horses is an instant transport into Nirvana. It's one place I feel I excel. Experiences in the hills and at the hunting camps helped shape my interests and abilities. Now going to the mountains with a horse is my way to compensate for any damage I might have done down on the flats. Being in the hills around animals has been therapeutic for me. This ride is no exception.

I wasn't sure of the trail that led down a pass, so when the creek turned north, I followed it. Lo and behold, I'm right where I should be–Little Valley, southwest of Wallsburg. Interesting sheep corral here in Little Valley; four-foot scrub oak stakes woven with wire. Looks very efficient.

Cooked half a box of rice and an onion for tonight's supper. Wow, lots of stew. Guess I know what I'll be having for breakfast.

I climbed into my sleeping bag, a heavy dew having come early. I can tell the sweats are coming, too. Trying to combat them, I'll fling open my bag to let in dry air, but soon I have to cover up when my teeth begin to click from the shivers. Back and forth it goes, sweating then clicking. The dew settles on the fly, but the humid air hinders my air dry. Lots of awake time. As a result, I'll try to write. Here I sit with flashlight, feeling like a soggy piece of bread.

The mountains are beautiful. I'm reminded of a book by Louis L'Amour, *Far Blue Mountains*. The setting is on the west side of Mount Timpanogos. Fancy Flew, Walkava, and his braves go on a six-week horse-stealing expedition to Sacramento and back. As I sit here, alternately slipping in and out of my sleeping bag, I can picture painted ponies, feathered warriors and raiding parties.

Oh, how I love books. Books have taught me many things: how to build a skin boat, an underground or earth-shelter home, and a cement-plastered straw-bale bunk house. From books, I've learned how to braid, tie knots, pack horses, and harpoon whales. I've been transported through time and distance; books have taken me from coast to coast, continent to continent. I've run with John Colter after the Blackfoot Indians stripped him naked, gave him a head start, and then hunted him. I've wept with the Cherokee people as they made the Trail of Tears march from Georgia to Oklahoma. I've traveled with Louis and Clark on their great Northwest discovery expedition. Out of books' pages I flinched from the "shot heard round the world" and wept while standing alongside the railroad tracks as the train carrying Lincoln's body passed by on its way to Illinois. I rode with Paul Revere on his famous midnight ride. At the request of Andrew Jackson, I helped pirates win the Battle of New Orleans. I cheered at Martin Luther King, Jr.'s "I Have a Dream" speech. I worked the salt mines of Russia and the rice paddies of Korea. And most of these adventures took place in the comfort of my own home. Yes, oh how I love books.

Presumed by his friends to be the source of Don Quixote's delusions, they burned his books—not only those telling of knights and their brave deeds, but, also, the ones featuring shepherds, for fear Quixote might regain his sanity only to have delusions of being a shepherd.

My family and friends haven't burned my books—yet—but Sally has on occasion asked with raised eyebrows, "So what are you reading about now?" When I showed her a book about building an underground house, all she could say was, "Oh, no," as she exhaled loudly, turned, and walked from the room. I truly believe if a person can read, he can become pretty much whatever he wants to become and do whatever he wants to do.

The importance of reading was impressed on me as a boy. In grade school, my teacher, Minnie Green, was to me the most beautiful woman in the world. I had a crush on her, and I wrote her a love letter. Minnie had her own library in her house; she reverenced books. I'd ofttimes go to her home after school and she'd lend me books to read. Two big bookshelves held dozens of Will James horse books, and I read them all. That was the first time I read *Smokey*. Minnie gave me *The Last of the Mohicans*. It was difficult reading, but I gave it my all because I felt I had a responsibility to Minnie. After all, she'd given it to me, I being her star reader. In the end, I just never quite made it through.

Early on, I loved to have *Boy's Life* magazine read to me. It was from *Boy's Life* that I first learned about Earnest Thompson Seton, who wrote about wild animals. Those pre-school years were the beginning of my love for animals, adventure, and travel.

Speaking of travel, I think I hear Teton's bell, and it seems to be traveling away from camp. . . Yup. I had to tie him up. His hobbles weren't doing the job. I cinched up Sam and Teancum's tie ropes, too, just for good measure.

Thinking back to the young hunter hiding in the brush by the water hole today, I wonder if my senses are dulled with age, or if I've become so focused on the finish line that I'm losing some of the enjoyment of the here and now.

Philosophy for today: While the final destination of Mexico ought always to be identified, is not the actual journey more important? Time, route, momentary trials ought always to be enjoyed during the time you're in them. Does the end ever justify the means? Or, do the means result in the end?

Time to try to sleep again. It's late and I'm still sweating, but if I don't get some sleep I'll be no good tomorrow. Good night.

Wednesday 4 September 1991

My sleeping bag isn't magic. This morning my bed again was soaked with dew and body sweat. I did get some sleep, though, so apparently the bag was breathing. It could've been worse.

The rice and onion stew wasn't as good for breakfast as it was for dinner last night, but it fed the growl. I lazied around, waiting for things to dry out. Steam was gone off the willows within thirty minutes of sunrise. Ponies are peaceful. It's difficult to envision the busy world twenty miles away, what with all this soothing sunlight, the green mountains, buzzing insects, and tolling horse bell—ah, heaven!

Gabe Lyons from Pleasant Grove came by with his backhoe and logs to close some old logging roads. The needed road repairs will help connect existing trails. Lyons wanted to buy my mules; made me glow all over!

Got away from camp right after lunch. I feel refreshed and eager. Passed several bow hunters riding along the ridge. I can now see Strawberry Reservoir with Mount Timpanogos in the background. Shepherd roads are confusing. I'm continually wondering, "Is this the trail or a sheep road?" Signs at major junctions would be helpful to travelers.

Rode through a herd of sheep, saw a deer grazing alongside its fleecy cousins, and met up with a Guatemalan shepherd who invited me to his camp at Buck Spring. I accepted. Then, ponies and I crossed the Strawberry ridge and spotted a round tankful of rainwater. I thought of bathing, but would have felt a little exposed up there on the ridge. A big buck appeared not a hundred yards from the tank. We moved on south and camped next to the herder in a meadow south of Clyde Creek. He shared some chips and salsa. Delicious.

My hand-held water filter works wonderfully! I don't worry anymore about drinking the water, even with all the sheep and wildlife around.

Thursday 5 September 1991

A dry night; comfy, in and out of the bag. Got away in good time. Rode all day along the Continental Divide. No water to be found. My map said a spring was there, but couldn't find it! The horses came close to foundering. When I pressed a finger above my mule's gums, he had a slow return to pink ratio. Prayed to find water for the horses. After more scouting, we came across a cattle trail and followed it to only a seep of water, but it helped until we got to Indian Springs, where there was a nice flow. Found more hunters and a shepherd there. Then on to a signed trail into the canyon. Great water! Surely makes life easier with posted signs and accurate water maps.

With the sun high, I stopped for lunch at an off-trail campsite. After finishing off the rice and onion, I delighted in jerky, dried apricots, and nuts. I'd learned a valuable lesson: only cook enough for one meal.

My appetite is back and I savored every varied flavor. As I held jerky in my mouth to soften it enough for false teeth to chew, I noticed an edge of paper sticking out, anchored under a rock. Folded twice, on it was inscribed the words to "How Great Thou Art," all four verses. I already knew the first verse, but the others were spotty, so I refolded the paper and tucked it in my shirt pocket.

Along the trail, with the hours of rehearsed cowboy-poetry sermons and singing, my ponies must have felt they'd spent a day at church. Cowboy poetry and hymns… does it get any better? Those ponies could have sprouted wings and flown to heaven, Pegasus-like. Teancum's ears would perk up and turn backwards as I'd practice "Amazing Grace." As time progressed, they periodically rotated back and forth to listen, then finally ended up flopping loosely. Either I got better at singing or he went deaf. Must have worn him down and lulled him to "relaxation"—I purposely don't use the word *apathy*, which wouldn't speak well of my sermons or singing.

Early evening we came to the road leading to Skyview, a part of Spanish Fork Canyon that features a nice horse pasture, cafe, and motel. There was no room at the inn, but the waitress, who'd seen an article about me in the news, let me into an employee room that wasn't being used, where I could use the shower. Turns out the kindly waitress could identify with my condition, as her dad suffered from pancreatic cancer.

I was able to leave the animals in the horse pasture. After a so-so rib-eye steak at the cafe, I walked down the road to the motel, called Sally to check in, and relayed that all is well.

A bed tonight—ah.

Chapter 10

Friday 6 September 1991

Not much to do today so I kinda dragged. The horses needed a rest anyway, and I needed groceries and horseshoes. Hitchhiked into Spanish Fork. Called Val, a relative from Teton Valley, who took me shopping in town, then back out to my animals.

Rainy, but I got busy. Sam had worn through both shoes at the toes. Tied his front feet up, one at a time, so he'd stand still enough for me to put new shoes on.

Ate dinner at the cafe again. Folks both there and at the motel were very hospitable and supportive. Perhaps they're hoping for Great Western Trail business later on as more travelers become aware of the route. I've been thinking of a "trail steward" idea that I believe is worth consideration. A volunteer, living near a particular section, would care for a section of the trail, advise on water and campsites, and provide "helper" lists of area residents willing to greet travelers, haul hay, etc.

Sitting in the motel waiting for the day to finish is the pits. I'm anxious to get going tomorrow.

Saturday 7 September 1991

This morning I called my son Leland, as well as Lamar Garrett, a fellow horseman and covered wagon-builder from central Utah, to line up transportation from Mexico to home. I mentioned to Lamar that I wouldn't be leaving the motel until mid-morning due to the heavy rainfall early this morning. So he and Don England, the ranger from the earlier GWT meeting in Salt Lake City, came up to see me. Don said he'd mark water and trailheads to help eliminate confusion. Lamar agreed to haul my animals and me back from Nogales, Arizona, to Provo, Utah. Leland will then tow us from there to home. En route, I'll set up GWT meetings in Provo and in Salt Lake City to plan the Idaho campaign and gather information for a booklet or magazine article. Don and Lamar have put a lot of work and dreaming into the GWT.

Shortly after my guests departed, the rain began to taper off and cousin Val pulled up with a bottle of his chokecherry jelly. What a treat for the trail! He helped me pack up and said that he wanted to go with me, but is obligated to a job.

I got away by noon and started on the highway to Tucker, then went up a *very* muddy road to the ridge. Rain fell off and on. It's nice to have Leland's rain gear on top this time. I passed a village of hunters camped in the mud, a collection of tents, campers, and mobile homes. Everybody—except this numbskull, yours truly—was holed up, waiting for the rain to stop.

Threw off to the roadside at about supper time, hidden from view by the fog. I expected the Headless Horseman to gallop by at any minute. The strong winds made for horizontal rain. I wrapped up in my raincoat. The brim of my hat, in place despite the wind, folds down to protect my face. A motel room looks better by the minute.

Tied the ponies close by so I could keep an eye on them, built a cocoon with my supplies and tarp, then hunkered down. Anticipating a long night, but hopefully a warm, dry one.

Sunday 8 September 1991

It was foggy and rainy all night. Some passing hunters reported that it had rained all day in Salt Lake City; explains why it's raining here, since the westerly weather travels this way. Miraculously, I didn't get the sweats last night and remained completely dry.

Sang some hymns, prayed, ate breakfast, and decided that, despite the rain, I'd head out anyway. Then it began to clear. Got underway before noon. Very pretty along the ridgetop; excellent graveled road.

Rode all day. Then, lo and behold, there appeared out of nowhere one Devon Mower, Laurel's father, Jube's father-in-law. He pulled over in his truck just waiting to say hello. Devon was to meet me as my contact person for this area. Turns out that he and his son were coming up to hunt elk, and spotted me. It was fun to visit, and since I'm a day early, we were able to move up our rendezvous date to tomorrow.

Soon after Devon left, a young couple from Sandy, Utah, pulled alongside Teancum and me and asked, "How's it going, Movie Star?" They'd seen me on a Salt Lake City TV station and wanted to visit. They peppered me with questions, generously shared their lunch of chicken, macaroni salad, peaches, and water. It's nice to hear the encouraging words of "Good luck. Wish we could go too; we hope you make it."

Got to Highway 31, crossing about five o'clock, but it had started to rain hard so I stopped and hurriedly set up camp to weather the storm. Gonna be a long ride tomorrow, twenty-four to twenty-eight miles. I'll try to get an early start.

It's surely been a restful, blessed Sabbath. All the people who've stopped to visit with me have been kind and encouraging, and have offered to help any way possible. Fuels my belief in the goodness of mankind.

Goodnight, Loved Ones.

MONDAY 9 SEPTEMBER 1991

Whooee! What a hailstorm last night! Just before midnight, the bottom of the clouds fell out. Hunkered under my tarp, I stayed dry and cozy. An eight-inch drift of hail was piled by my fly this morning. Clear but blustery, I tried to hit the trail early, but only got away by 9 a.m. Sam's got a withers sore starting, so I rode him and packed Teancum. I was a little worried Teancum wouldn't pack as well as Sam, but he did fine. The change in saddles should help Sam. I'd forgotten how nice he is to ride, a fast mover.

Passed six sheep camps today. One shepherd spoke English, another only partly, and the others not at all.

Windy, coming strong from the southeast, and cold. I wore a sweater, rain parka, and long johns. The road was terribly muddy with lots of pot holes, but we had a beautiful ride and arrived at my rendezvous point with Devon Mower about 4:30 p.m. He was already there, waiting for me. I tied my ponies at the state shed in Gooseberry, then went with Devon to his home in Fountain Green.

I saw only one deer today, none yesterday. Devon says the mountain lion population is alarmingly high, so deer are disappearing. Now the lions are turning to the sheep. There surely is an abundance of sheep here, though not meant for lion consumption. In an attempt to manage the lions, the number of government trappers has been increased to five. This district is about one and a half times the size of the Teton district.

Letters from loved ones were waiting for me at Devon's. Plucked my heartstrings. Called home to visit with Sally.

Figured out why Laurel is so nice; she's just like her family. They've offered every creature comfort possible. Wonderful people, wonderful ride, wonderful day.

TUESDAY 10 SEPTEMBER 1991

I bought a thick blanket for Sam; should help with his sore. Also, bought a barley and corn mix for the horses. The ponies turned their noses up at it, but I tried it, and liked it. Will try cooking it. The store wouldn't accept a check, only cash, so I couldn't get film. Devon and Roma– Laurel's mom—drove me back up to the ponies. Roma had wanted to walk along with me for a while, but the trail was too rough, rocky, and slick. It was far too cold and blustery, as well, so they unloaded me and said goodbye.

Got the ponies untangled and packed up. The biting wind cut to the bone so I put on my leather chaps, which are a bit baggy now. Seems like Teton and I are on the same diet. My butt's disappeared, so there's nothing to hang the chaps on. Obviously, I need suspenders, but can't risk pressure on my spine. I just need to keep them above my hip bones until I can get a smaller belt, since this one has no room to punch another hole. They stop the wind but don't have enough insulation in them to keep me warm. My teeth chattered most of the morning. The chaps keep the mud off me, but are quite heavy—only a problem when I'm getting on and off or walking. Teancum stood patiently, waiting for me to climb on since the extra weight slowed me down. We were underway shortly after noon.

Muddy, cold, windy... but beautiful country. South of John August Lake, I passed two more shepherds and a forest road crew. They were holed up and camping, due to weather.

Pitched my fly over a pole fence and beat the rain. Arranged my stuff under the fly for more wind and rain protection, then burrowed in. My bed is in the middle, surrounded by all the "furniture." As comfy as a hog in a straw stack. Sally sent me more poetry. I'll learn some for the Kanab gathering.

The ponies have nice grass. Glad.

WEDNESDAY 11 SEPTEMBER 1991

Howling wind and pelting rain last night, but I was warm and comfortable. The storm broke this morning; rain quit, but still windy. I lie east of Manti now.

Met several herders, two from Guadalajara, Mexico. Both spoke English. The first one gave me water, the second shared his lunch–wonderful browned mutton, ever so tasty. Afterward, we sat around his fire, warming our fingers and toes. As I wiped grease from my chin, the shepherd disappeared into his tent and emerged holding a coil of rope. "Need some rope?" he asked, smiling.

"Ah, yes," I replied, turning my back to the wind. I stood up, clutching my chaps, whereupon he sized me up and cut a length and handed it to me. Threading the rope between my belt loops and chaps, I cinched them up. Felt like I'd just stepped out of Dog Patch. Hoped I didn't have to run to the bathroom, but I was glad to finally have both hands free.

The herder sat back, watching. He smiled when I looked up with raised eyebrows. "Looks good," he chuckled.

I have fond memories of herding sheep. Lots of good people. I thanked him for the food and wardrobe addition, then shuffled to the ponies, feeling the weight of the chaps in my groin muscles but not my ribs. The wind break that the chaps provide compensate for slower speed. Glad I brought them.

Beautiful, open high country. Passed an 11,282 foot high point on Skyline Drive. Rode until nearly dark, then pitched camp south of Indian Lake and Blue Lake. I debated whether to fix supper or just fall into bed. I compromised; got water heating, added the horses' corn-barley mixture and some salt, and ate my supper in bed. Yummy. What's wrong with those horses?

A few snow pellets are coming down. The ponies look passive, but tough. I'm proud of how well they're doing–so well mannered.

So, so tired.

Thursday 12 September 1991

Bear bait, that's what they're gonna be! The knot-heads are gone! I realized in the wee hours of the morning that I wasn't hearing the cowbell. Aaargh! Teton and Sam, though both were hobbled, had wandered off before daylight, with Teancum in tow. I quickly pulled on my clothes and ran back down the trail. About three quarters of a mile down I found them hopping and munching as if everything was normal.

Reaching up, I clipped the lead rope on to Sam's halter. "What do you think you're doing, huh? Are you going to leave me alone up here?" I asked, frowning as I scratched Sam's thick head. I gathered up Teton's lead rope and called over my shoulder, "Come on, Teancum, let's go." He fell in line behind Teton as we trudged back up the trail. It was hard to be too upset with them. The sheep have grubbed off all the horsefeed and the ponies must have felt like they had to go scouring for their breakfast.

Last night the wind quit after I crawled in bed and all was peaceful. Absolutely calm this morning; beautiful warm sun. No heavy chaps today. I lay on my bag and flopped front to back, toasting both sides as if at the beach. Easy to see why some folks are sun worshipers.

Got away late morning. Nice riding. Ran into a herder from Centerfield, Utah. I think he is the first one I've met whose native tongue is English. He said he'd like to join me next summer, if I was still riding.

Red, yellow and orange are beginning to spot the trees, and white snow is banding the mountain's ridge. Spectacular! The trail needs markers at the intersections. I'm often unsure of which way to go. Family prayers are still in full force, seems like every turn has been the right one.

I lost a glove and it bothered me all afternoon. Unsettling. Ate lunch in the saddle–dried fruit, jerky, and almonds.

I made it to Interstate 70 at dusk, a half day ahead of schedule. Finding the road fenced, I threw off in a graveled turn-around. Discouraged that there was no feed for the animals, I tied Teton and Sam to some brush and staked

Teancum. With a bank of dark clouds swiftly moving in, I put up the tarp and set the pack boxes under it, leaving just enough room in the middle for my sleeping bag. The saddle blankets were damp and smelled of sweat, but I was too tired to care. Arranged them side by side, between the pack boxes.

My preparations almost complete, I glanced up at the sky, then threw my sleeping bag on the saddle blankets, hoping to beat the rain. I heard dogs barking, but didn't pay much attention to it–until Teancum let out a scream. Glancing up from my bedroll, I was alarmed to see Teancum galloping at full speed right at me, dragging his stake. Wide eyes rolled up in his head and his ears pinned back, two dogs were closing in fast, biting at his heels. Apparently some motorists had let their dogs out for exercise and, spying Teancum, they'd given way to their wolf instinct. Mules can be fierce fighters, and have even been known to kill mountain lions, but Teancum is only a three-year-old and still wants someone else to do his fighting; and on this occasion that "someone else" was me.

I scanned the area for a weapon. A branch about as thick and long as a baseball bat lay near where Sam and Teton, nervously tugging at their ropes, were tied. As I lunged for the stick, Teancum stampeded past me, veered behind me, and came to a stop, placing me between him and his pursuers.

Screaming like a banshee, I came up swinging the stick like a cutlass. "Get out of here, you dang dogs!" I screamed at the top of my lungs. "Leave my mule alone!" The closest dodged my first swing and jumped out of range of a second attack, backing away. Teancum looked on with interest, his ears twitching and attentive, secure in the safety of my protection. I turned on the second attacker, my weapon raised. Growling and sidestepping to avoid the stick, the dog made the mistake of getting too close to Sam, whose well-placed hind-kick launched him a good ten feet. With a pained yelp he sped off, limping back over the hill with the other dog at his heels.

Felt a little like a musketeer—man for mule and mule for man! I dropped the stick and quickly went to check on Teancum. Snickering, he lowered his thick head so I could rub his soft brown muzzle and assure him that, "No one's gonna hurt you, boy, not as long as I'm here." Squatting down to check his legs for bite marks, I was relieved to find only minor scratches and scrapes.

I didn't think Teancum would wander far tonight, so didn't bother tying him. Finished spreading out my sleeping bag and made sure everything was covered. As I moved about camp adjusting and covering items, Teancum dragged his lead rope and followed close behind. Like a devoted puppy, he hovered nearby and rubbed his head on my back whenever I stopped. It began to sprinkle shortly after I got everything stowed under a tarp, so I quickly tied him to the bush with Sam and Teton and climbed into bed between the pack boxes. My stomach growled. Hungry, discouraged, and worried about my animals, nevertheless, I tried to sleep.

Still lying here after forty-five minutes. Worried about how often ponies will be forced to scour for food. So tired. It's still raining. I've had no supper... Yup, I'm in the dumps.

Friday 13 September 1991

Long night. Woke up damp from head to toe, but to a bright, sunny morning. My spirits rose immediately. Seems to mirror the scriptures—after the trial, comes the reward.

Eddy, my son in college, wanted to come visit, but had a conflict. Instead, Jeff, a friend of Eddy's will come in his place. I took advantage of a little down time while waiting.

First, I had to scout for pony food, air drying in the process. Couldn't wander too far for fear of missing my rendezvous with Jeff, but did manage to find brown, dry clumps of dusty grass, enough that each pony got some. Returned to road camp. Looked like a washer maid's camp off the side of the road, with wet items hung all over the fence. Fed my hunger with fried spuds and onion. Sam needed shoes on his hind feet, but wanted none of it. He fought a long time and I finally ended up hog-tying him on the ground, his feet sticking up in the air; even then I only got one shoe on. He's got lots of battle scars, what with his stubbornness, and I was worn out.

Jeff and his wife arrived at noon, BBQ on a bun and corn on the cob in tow. Wow! We talked of family, friends, and my ride, and I invited them to come camp with my family in the Tetons next summer. They helped me pack up, then I headed out midafternoon, leaving no evidence of a washer maid having ever been there.

I wasn't paying attention while traveling through an oak thicket, and rode right into a tree spike. The branch glanced off my rib belt, went under my arm, and dumped me on my butt, or what's left of it anyway. I sat still for a moment to let my breath out slowly, while checking my ribs and back for injuries. Unhurt, I climbed back on Teancum and settled down on what couldn't hold up my chaps, but would still cushion a fall. Again, thankful for answered prayers for protection.

Made it to a nice campground on Gooseberry Ridge, an oil rig's dry-hole campsite. The drillers, along with the U.S. Forest Service, had fixed it up nicely. What really made me grin was looking over meadows of green grass. It would be a good night. My spirits are high, even after having to put on the chaps again for wind protection. If the ponies are happy, I'm happy.

I relearned "Army Mule," one of the poems Sally sent me. It's interesting how quickly I can memorize poetry that I like, and how slowly I learn something I'm indifferent to. I try to keep poems fresh in my mind so I can spout some when asked. So I'll ask Sally to send me some more of my favorites.

Saturday 14 September 1991

Wondered about tacking on Sam's last hind shoe; should I or not? Yeah, I did, though he still wanted no part of it. First, I put the packsaddle on him and tied a rope to his shoe-less hind foot. Then, I positioned the rope up over his tail, threaded it through the back X of the packsaddle, then down around his belly. Each time he'd kick, I'd pull up the slack. It held him good, but he fought and fought. Got it done.

While this tight-rope circus act was going on, a couple of guys from the campground came over to watch and chat. I met Randy Perry, a salesman of big commercial buildings and a guy who loves to hunt and has lots of top-grade hunting equipment. Fun to see his gismos and whistles. I also met Tony Cowper, who drives horsecarts and wants to drive carts along part of the GWT.

It's clear and windy. Got away before noon. My chaps are comfy riding in the saddle, but I'm sitting tender, babying a bruise on my behind. Saw three cow elk and their calves trot across the road in front of me. Today opens the shotgun season for birds, and muzzle-loaders for elk. Came upon a dead cow elk laying by a water hole—"its ingredients out," as Simone would say—apparently, a slow death from a bow hunter's arrow.

Crossed Niotche Creek and Niotche Pass and down over a bouldery ridge. My thanks to the USFS District Rangers from Niotche Pass. Within the last week, they've marked the trail thoroughly with GWT logos and rock cairns. Without them, I'd have never found my way over the ridge. It's almost as though they readied the trail for me. Must thank them.

Windy all day. Camped at dark by a drift fence next to an empty pasture with tall, beautiful grass. I wondered who the grass was for, and where they were? Puzzling.

While staking the mules, I looked up and, lo and behold, there stood a bunch of elk: six cows, two spikes, one calf, and a big bull, only one hundred and twenty-five yards away.

Ate Val's chokecherry jam on a pancake for supper. Fruity and delicious. Must remember to call and thank him. Nice clear night. Dead tired.

SUNDAY 15 SEPTEMBER 1991

Turns out the fenced pasture wasn't for keeping animals in, but keeping them out. It's a Larkspur area, a poison pasture, toxic to both man and animal. The cattle are fenced out for their safety. Glad I wasn't tempted to break in and let my animals take advantage of the feast. There seems to be a principle here: Sometimes what we might think is good for us, really is not.

Oh, how lovely was the morning! Cattle lowing, grass gently rustling, and sunshine streaking through the quaking aspen leaves. Happy equines; all is calm.

Shortly after I'd heated water for breakfast, two hunters on mountain bikes rode into camp. Austin Baker and his son, from North Ogden, dressed in full camo, arrived in the area late last night, long after dark.

The older man was eager to talk. "After what felt like only a short nap, we began hunting early this morning."

I mixed oatmeal with water and offered them some. "Seen anything?"

"No thanks," Austin said, waving off the oatmeal. "Yeah, ran across a cow, calf and a spike. We got the spike but don't have a way to haul the meat out." Eyeing my mules intently, he offered, "I'll pay you thirty dollars to rent your animals for a couple of hours."

"How far do you need it hauled?" I asked, wondering if Teancum and Teton could do it. I did want Teancum to have meat-packing experience, but worried the smell of blood could spook him.

"Only about three quarters of a mile, maybe a bit longer.

Not too far," he smiled hopefully. "The elk is about a half mile from here."

I agreed, but kept a prayer in my heart that there'd be no rodeo today. I rode Sam with the packsaddles on Teton and Teancum, and followed Austin and son on their bikes up the trail. Gripping Teancum and Teton's halter ropes, I studied them for any sign of fear or possible bolt; the other eye, I kept on Austin and his son as they quartered their elk. Blood pooled in pockets of matted grass, slowly seeping into the ground and leaving dark brown patches where green had been. The combination of the acidic-metallic odors, red knives flashing, and flesh being separated from bone, transported me back to April 14, 1970, on the edge of the shore ice of the Bering Strait outside Wales.

Sally and I taught school in this small Eskimo village on the westernmost tip of Alaska. My whale-hunting crew, a number of villagers, and I had been harvesting a bowhead whale we'd harpooned early that morning. It was a young bowhead, over twenty-six feet in length; its back flukes were about a fathom long (six to seven feet) and the head about sixty-three inches high. The acrid smell of blood mixed with salt hung heavy in the air as we worked. Bloody water surrounded the partially submerged head, the heaviest part of the whale, while pools of red formed near the body and tail, which had been dragged up on the ice edge. The crimson stain around the whale carcass slowly bled into the sparkling crystals of ice, changing white to pink, as we cut meat from body and tail. A few of the Eskimos had knives, but most used an *ulu*, the wooden handle of which is the shape of an egg with an imbedded blade that looks much like a medieval battleaxe. A slice was made with each back and forth see-saw motion and wasted no energy like a knife did.

Anyway, as we carved to remove blubber and meat, the ropes, hooks, and pullies were gradually drawn up, bringing the submerged head closer. As we got closer to the head, we worried the ice would split and break away, as a crack between us and shore inched wider the longer we worked. We kept our eyes on it as we sliced, knowing if we fell in we wouldn't last longer than five or ten minutes in the cold water. In fact, our winter clothes would probably make us sink. The village women kicked snow and ice down into the crack to prevent tripping, as they carried the meat to a place of thicker ice. We worked farther down the whale's back, in an attempt to pull more of the whale's head up onto the ice so knives could do their work.

"You out-Eskimoed the Eskimo," stated Manny with approval and unfamiliar openness. He was a friend whose deeply wrinkled face was set off by black, wide-set, inquisitive eyes hidden under bushy, gray eyebrows. Though stooped with age, Manny's very presence signified respect as the hunters moved to make room for him alongside the carcass. He knelt to help with the carving and division of the maktak–pronounced *muck tuck* (the blubber or fat and the skin of the whale). Swiping the ulu in long, quick motions, he neatly demonstrated how to slice and separate blubber from the meat. The other hunters and I, following his lead, began separating the meat into two piles, one for the whale crew, the other for the helpers. The maktak, in turn, was divided into three parts: one part for me, as striker and owner of the boat, motor, and harpoon gun; one part for the crew; and the last third went to the helpers. The special cuts–flukes, tongue, etc.–could be claimed by those who wanted them. Traditionally, this was how to divide meat.

"You have brought whaling back to my people, when at first we thought you couldn't do it," spoke Manny quietly, as he severed the tail with a final stroke. I sidled up closer to him, watching and learning as he divided the tail meat. "You came to Wales desiring to learn the hunt. But the tradition of hunting is handed down from generation to generation and doesn't allow for the presence of a white man, an outsider. Many of our hunters died, as a result of the epidemic of 1918, taking with them the knowledge of the whale hunt. Since then, until now, we have only hunted seal, walrus and oogrook [a massive bearded seal]. When you came, most villagers had never participated in a whale hunt. You talked to elders of the village, bought books, and invited us to help make your umiak [skin boat]. You invited those who weren't included to join hunting parties, and those who were newcomers to our village to be a part of your crew. You bought a harpoon gun and explosives, and you practiced shooting it behind your house. Yet we watched you with skepticism. You showed us hand-drawn diagrams of where to harpoon for maximum kill: the major artery along the back, or through the eye into the brain, depending on how the whale surfaced. You asked questions, read books, made plans. Meanwhile, we watched you with either disbelief or humor. However, over time you opened our hearts. You have helped restore pride to the Eskimo way of life; a lost tradition is now reclaimed. We honor you as an Eskimo brother."

When he'd finished speaking, Manny gazed intently into my eyes, smiled slightly, and slowly dipped his head in recognition. "Aye," several crew members joined in.

Deeply moved by Manny's sincere words and rarely displayed actions, I swallowed hard and could only nod and reply in kind: "Aye." Then, in silence, we resumed cutting and separating the meat. I remembered the clenched gut I'd had when I initially sensed the skepticism of the natives. It was never blatant or direct, since that was not their way. But more an undercurrent of soft mocking and gentle giggles.

Alas, the whale's head was too heavy to pull completely up on the ice; therefore we salvaged what we could: the tongue (much like a bowed sandpaper surfboard), baleen to be used as fishing line or nets, cheeks, and chin. We had to sink the rest due to our lack of strength and exhaustion. We'd worked all day and into the night, cutting and dividing the whale. My share of meat was to be divided among the widows and those who had no provider. My family didn't care for the meat.

Teancum brought me back to the here and now by snorting nervously at the heavy smell of blood and tugging on the halter rope. But he held still. Austin and his son lifted a quartered portion of the meat up to Teancum's packsaddle, paused, then slowly, laid it on the saddle. I stood spring-loaded, ready for anything. I could tell that Teancum's every muscle was strung tight. His eye's were wide, ears stiff, nostrils quivering, but he held fast. He was a champion.

For his part, Teton didn't bat an eye, just the occasional blink as he grazed. Both animals hauled meat like pros. I could have burst my buttons. I ended up taking twenty dollars and brunch for my efforts. Austin said he'd call Sally and give a favorable report.

The task put me behind schedule, but animals and I moved out late afternoon. Not long on the trail, I met some cowboys who offered me their cabin for the night. I thanked them, but said that, behind schedule, I must keep going. I hope Austin remembers to call Sally. I planned on calling her tomorrow night from Torrey, but won't make it by then. I hope Sally, Anita, and Leland wait a day before worrying. Don't like the sound of a chopper's blades.

Tonight I'm camped between Niotche Pass and Hilgard Mountain.

Chapter 11

Monday 16 September 1991

Camped last night in a little clearing without larkspur, but felt I needed to stake the animals for their own safety. Found Sam this morning wound up around a tree, legs and head scraped up. He looked like a Gladiator.

"Come here, Sparticus," I said as I led him over, under, and through the maze he'd created. He followed like he knew I was offering freedom. Ran my hands over him, checking the scrapes. One, a puncture by his mane, had torn an inch. Will have to keep my eye on that one. Again I wished I had some gas to douse the cut, but made do with Bag Balm and a stern scolding. He looked battle-scarred and a bit gooey with all the Bag Balm. Even so, a Roman crowd would have given him a thumbs up. Looks like he's gonna live.

Got a later start than I'd planned, but had pleasant riding with warm and clear weather. Capitol Reef, off to the east, is gorgeous. Colors, strata erosion, truly a garden spot.

Passed two guys from the Teton County Sheriff's office in Jackson, who work with Leland. Small world.

Learned Mike Logan's "Bronc to Breakfast" poem. Teancum's ears flickered back momentarily when I started; then they rotated to the front, uninterested. It appears I drone on and on when I spout poetry while riding trail. However, I'd like to think of it as BBQ sauce on ribs, honey on a warm biscuit, or berries tucked in a hot pie... I must be hungry.

A nice billboard map had been erected at Hogan's Pass, but there weren't enough markers for the next three miles. Cattle have bared off the feed all along the way. At the unmanned Elkhorn Ranger Station, a layer of nice grass covered the horse pasture, and the campground had grass as well. But the horse pasture was locked and the campground was fenced. Ponies are hungry and getting desperate. I thought seriously about cutting an opening in the campground fence, but rode on. They are hungry most of the time now, which causes me worry.

Rode until dark, when Sam led me to a badly-needed water tank and the ponies found a few short grass nibbles—only a band-aid for a growing problem. The GWT people ought to take the grass and water availability up with the USFS.

Set up camp in a clearing along Meadow Gulch Trail, south of Willies Flat. Good night. Gonna visit a thrift store in St. George for a small quilt to throw over my sleeping bag on chilly nights. Sweats have been at bay, a cause for celebration!

Tuesday 17 September 1991

Once water is found, it's hard to leave it, but we needed to find horsefeed and get on to Torrey for a check-in call.

Along the way, I rode onto a scattered bedroom camp. It was a mess everywhere; looked awful. Then I found a couple of gals cleaning it up. Thank heavens! An outfitter from Torrey had been there with his dudes, camping and riding in the hills. The bulk of the group had just left to return to Torrey, but a few stragglers invited me to stay at the outfitters in town. The animals and I drank our fill from the strong running spring at the camp. Then we rode at the foot of a giant red cliff maze that wound down into Torrey.

Made it to the outfitter's place. It was a veritable Garden of Eden with corrals, hay, water, showers, and washing machines. Ah.

Called Sally to check in, also, Fritz to report on the ride. "Getting any saddlesores?" he asked.

I could sense the grin on his face through the phone. "Naw, pantyhose are working just fine. Can't convert anyone else, but I've tried."

"You're the one going the distance," he said.

I agreed. Fritz is a dear friend and horse brother, one who wears his hat just right.

Talked to Sue Watson to line up a rendezvous in the future. I tried the USFS, but they weren't answering. Too bad. I wanted to thank them for the nice trail work and markings. Called a farrier to shoe Teton and Teancum, as they've worn the shoes right off their hooves. Sam has used me up.

Met a lot of individuals interested in the GWT, the ride, and packing up mules. The Salt Lake City TV interview was even viewed here. Still a star, I guess.

WEDNESDAY 18 SEPTEMBER 1991

The farrier arrived at 9 a.m. this morning. While waiting for him, I visited with some folks who came to take pictures of me. One of them, Donna Lange, showed me collections of arrowheads and Indian artifacts she'd hunted out: bird points with intricate notches carved on them and a thunderbird, too. Like a kid at bedtime, I listened to her stories.

The farrier easily shod Teton, who stood quiet. Teancum stood still on the fronts, but we had to scotch hobble him to get his hinds done. The man knew his trade. A nice, quiet worker, he did a good job, and cost me seventy bucks. My back thanked him more than my wallet did.

Left Torrey at 2 p.m., freshly showered, new shoes on the ponies, water jugs, and bellies full. Donna, the Indian artifacts lady, will mail letters home for me tomorrow. Spent most of the day riding the road. Several people stopped to visit on the way. Nibbled on jerky as I rode. Sam's puncture wound looks good, no infection.

Finally left the road and climbed to the Ponderosa Forest. Wonderful trees, but no feed. No feed! It got too black to see, so I just threw off to the side of the trail, south of Rock

Creek, and bedded down. Mules are holding their weight alright; Teton, however, is clearly losing more than I'd like. Feed is a real problem, one that needs to be addressed with the GWT folks. Like my not purchasing the topographical maps, I wonder how often I'll be writing about no horsefeed.

Warm night. Rode six hours and covered about eighteen to twenty miles today. Will have to kick it up tomorrow to make Escalante by Saturday, the next check-in day.

THURSDAY 19 SEPTEMBER 1991

I staked all the animals last night; didn't want them heading out in search of food. When I found Sam this morning, he looked like he'd competed in a figure-eight race. His rope was wound around stands of small trees, with specialty knots woven between and through clumps of bushes. He was stuck, unable to step left or right. Checked him over for new scrapes; only found old scabs. His puncture is healing nicely.

Teancum's wide eyes darted about as I approached him. It was as if he couldn't look me in the eye. Feeling guilty, I'm sure. His head was immobile, cinched tight with his chin whiskers tickling the top of a bush. He'd worn a semi-circle in the dirt with his hind feet. It looked like one wing of a snow angel. His front feet rotated only enough to complete the wing.

"Teancum," I scolded, rolling my eyes. "How can I boast on mules' superior intelligence when I see you and Sam hog-tied? At least Teton is able to walk the length of his line with a grin on his face." The mule stretched his neck and tried to rub his forehead on my shoulder, but blew his nose in frustration instead. I thought Sam would've learned his lesson. Chalked up Teancum's fix to his being young. I knew Teton was just smart. Nice warm weather as we untangled.

Got away early–a good thing, considering I spent a lot of time getting lost today! Got mixed up twice and went in circles. At Chokecherry Point, it looked like three separate trails. Not knowing which to take, I circled twice along a terrace and had to give it up. Then I decided Fish Lake Trails map was the one to follow in Dixie Forest–a poor choice. After traveling down that trail for a ways, I came to a pile of abandoned trail markers in a heap. Can you imagine? I wanted to yell, so confusing, and there they were in a pile! Went down to the highway, crossed four creeks, passed Bown's Point, and rode southeast about two miles in a cow pasture. Finally, so uneasy because there were no markers, I looked for the Dixie map and found two different Dixie trail areas. Apparently, the two aren't even related! So I went back to Bown's Point and continued to search. The beautiful, deep-red rock wall canyons would have been boogers to get out of, so I rode quite a long way west before I found the right trail.

Came across lots of does and fawns. There must be few mountain lions around here. Met some horsemen who had cattle in the hills, who invited me to stay and camp with them. Beer seemed to be their main energy source. Several wore their hats crooked. I smiled, thanked them, and rode on. Got on past Chris Lake a mile or so and set up camp.

Bull elk were bellowing all night. I regretted packing the pistol at the bottom of one of the Ralide boxes and wondered if I could shinny up a quaky in time to beat a charging bull. Tomorrow I'll pack the gun on top.

FRIDAY 20 SEPTEMBER 1991

OW! This Escalante trail is hard to follow. I can't see any rhyme or reason to its meanderings. Jungly vegetation and spruce thickets are everywhere. Not enough trail logos to be comforting.

Met a young man and his wife–muzzle-loading hunters looking for elk–who walked in on me while I was packing up. I saw lots more deer, again almost all does and fawns. In the evening I rode by three cow elk and two calves. Dozing, they were startled and scattered when I rode by. Also, saw a wild turkey hen with six pullets. Beautiful, she looked as big as a tame turkey.

The whole day was wild and uncertain. Not enjoying it one bit, I was short tempered with my ponies and angry at the Escalante ranger. I thought how difficult it must be for those in tribulation 24/7, all month long. I'm glad to know it will change, hopefully for the better. That knowledge ought to make me less judgmental.

Lost again! Crested a hill and the trail just disappeared. I recovered in thirty minutes and rode hard till dark. It will be hard to make my Escalante rendezvous tomorrow. Commitments cause tension when things don't go as planned.

I threw off in a ponderosa jungle at dark. There is not much feed (surprise). The animals consumed lots of oats. I'll need to carry more oats for when the grass is sparse.

Fixed macaroni noodles in tomato sauce for dinner. It was tasty on the stomach but hurt my blistered lips. My doctor said my skin would be more sensitive; seems it is so.

SATURDAY 21 SEPTEMBER 1991

Lost again! Finally quit the GWT and went down a road in disgust! Signs and better trails are needed if this idea of a GWT is ever going to fly. After four hours of roadriding, I went up an old-time trail, into White Canyon, around Griffin Point and then into the main canyon. At dark I finally made the summit, Escalante, and got back on the trail.

Staked the ponies and headed for town with my thumb out. Some hunters gave me a ride into Escalante. I ate supper at a Phillips 66 gas station, bought ointment for my lips, and called Sally. She told me of a friend's accidental death–was crushed with a tractor. My heart went soft and eyes got leaky. I'll keep his family in my prayers.

Beautiful, clear, warm moonlit night. Feeling not so frustrated and can appreciate my surroundings again. I'm looking forward to church tomorrow.

Sleeping at an RV campground has a different feel than in the mountains.

SUNDAY 22 SEPTEMBER 1991

I got laundered and showered this morning. Felt new. It's interesting how physical and mental cleaning rejuvenates a person.

I walked to church; then got my spiritual bucket refilled. I sat by Lon Mason and his wife, who invited me to their home for dinner. A man from church gave me some grain for the animals, and another one drove me back to where I'd parked them. He got a flat tire for his kindness; I felt sorry, but very appreciative.

Got underway midafternoon. Nice riding. I heard chirping, looked up, and saw eight turkeys strutting up the road ahead of me. Bushwhacked down a canyon to cut off six miles; I found a very old trail, and did beautifully. Camped late at Pine Lake, on John's Valley side. There was only short grass for the animals. I debated on staking or hobbling the ponies and decided to hobble all three. Then, went to bed with fingers crossed.

MONDAY 23 SEPTEMBER 1991

There was much dew and frost this morning. It's 9 a.m. and I'm sitting here in the warm sunlight, drying out and writing. The little grass nearby kept all three animals close to camp. Bell clanked all night, reassuring me. I cooked up a package of oatmeal for breakfast and had a side dish of corn and barley mix left over from last night. Tricked the ponies this morning and mixed it with their grain. They either didn't notice or were too hungry to care. Glad it won't go to waste.

Teancum kept jerking away every time I tried to put the bridle on. Ears were sensitive today, I guess. With the Sabbath break, I was feeling good, as if I could catch a bullet in my teeth, jump a tall building in a single bound. But for the life of me I couldn't take Teancum's orneriness. Time for mule school again. I tied the hobbles on his front feet, laced the halter rope under them, and used the rope to pull his head down. He finally submitted. Tomorrow we'll see if he's learned the lesson.

After resting up from mule school–it's time to get going.

I guessed I could make the twenty miles to Ruby's Inn by tonight, and I did; got in before sunset. First rode to the rodeo grounds in hopes of finding accommodations for my ponies. Frank Alder, who was in charge of the grounds, offered me the rodeo pens, grain and a bale of hay for my animals. Manna from heaven! So many good people everywhere.

While dining at a local restaurant, a gal named Mary stopped by my table. Frank from the rodeo grounds had pointed her my way. She was with the USFS and worked on the GWT with a crew out of Escalante. I invited her to join me for dinner, during which she got an earful, but took it graciously, empathizing and agreeing with me. We shared ideas about how to make the trail north of Escalante better. What a sweet lady. Glad she came by.

Before I left the restaurant, I called Leland. He told me Ivin, a family friend from Utah, had called requesting his son Jonah ride with me for a while. I've watched Jonah grow up–a good kid–but apparently one who'd made some mistakes. A senior in high school, he's been suspended for several weeks. I didn't ask why–it didn't matter–and readily agreed to have Jonah join me at the Grand Canyon. Hope to help.

Threw my bedding down outside my ponies' pen. It's drier here–few water holes. What water there is, is scummy, putrid-looking stuff. Before I leave here, I'll have to make sure we have enough water going south.

Tuesday 24 September 1991

Got up early and talked with Bruce Foster, a horse concessionaire. He reassured me that water could be had all the way to House Rock Valley. He also gave me helpful information about passing through the Grand Canyon, but said most of the riding from these mountains to there is on road. Rats... but I'd expected as much.

Made my phone call to Sally this morning, and also to Craig Kunz to see how my substitute teacher for the gifted kids is doing. I gave out a yell when he told me Bonnie, a fellow teacher who was diagnosed with cancer the same time I was, is clean and doing well. Placed a third call to Kelly, my nephew in St. George. I'm to meet him at noon on Saturday at House Rock on Highway 89. I'll borrow his horse, Sugar, for Jonah, who'll ride with me for a few weeks. He and Leland will meet me on the north side of the Grand Canyon. If I make it early, I'll go to Kanab and visit with Delores, Fritz's sister, and her husband Marlin. Then off to a poetry gathering, where I'll spout the poems I've been reciting to Teancum.

After lunch, when I went to bridle Teancum, I wondered if he'd remember yesterday's mule school. He does have a good memory. And wouldn't you know it, I could have painted his ears, he stood so still. He's learning. Will it stick?

Got away after lunch. There were no trail markings whatsoever, but I can follow USFS roads and trails on the map.

Early evening, Teton began groaning and pulling on his lead rope. He kept trying to walk in the softer areas. I climbed off Teancum to check him. He lifted his legs over and over when I ran my hands down them. Checking his hooves for rocks, when I pressed on each frog, he pulled away, a sure sign of sore legs and feet. The discomfort is adding to his loss of appetite.

Hoping to get a little farther down the trail, we pushed on, Teton groaning and tugging on his rope all the way. Then about half past seven he went down on his knees in the mouth of Crawford Canyon. When I unpacked and unsaddled him, he acted better. A flip-flopping politician? I decided to stay put. Now I'm worried that Teton, not Teancum, will get leg-weary and have to quit. I need to give him rest; will try to take it easy tomorrow.

Philosophy for today: Do I need to break the long-term goals into daily short-term goals? On this trip each day's ride is important for some reason: to reach a destination, to get out of a mess, to get back to the trail, to get to town, to meet people, or to see a particular sight. So that each day is measurable, fulfilling, and satisfying, I'll have to set daily goals. A long way down the road is Nogales. But today... I can achieve today's goal.

Chapter 12

Wednesday 25 September 1991

Today I'll leave the established USFS system and strike out on my own trails using the route I've mapped out. Hopeful, excited, and wondering how I'll do on my own reconnaissance.

I didn't put up the fly last night and woke with lots of dew-turned-frost on my sleeping bag. Bag held, though; dry inside, no sweats. To give Teton extra resting time, I lay in bed until well after sun-up, drying out and writing. The morning warmed quickly, and I had to climb out of my bag and lie on top of it. How peaceful it is to watch the ponies, still lying down, exposing their bellybuttons to the sun. Teton hadn't wandered far from the spot where I'd left him last night. Means he didn't get much food. Hmmm… time to be on our way.

We took a slow, easy ride up to Crawford Pass, then down into Meadow Canyon. Light pink, beautiful cliffs. Rode by a housing development on Old Findlay Ranch. Met a young ranch-hand who was helpful in directing me. No horsefeed anywhere! Teton is placid and just keeps trudging. Rode down Deer Spring Wash. Pretty, but kinda tense, since there was no way out. Kept wondering what was around the corner. I couldn't exit except at the intersection washes. I rode until after dark to make Kitchen Corral Spring. It was pitch black, and we found mud but no water. Aaargh!

I poured the last of my drinking water into my hat; each pony got barely a swallow. The water was gone before it could soak through.

Tied the animals up and fed them grain only. It's been

a disturbing afternoon. Maybe the remaining southbound journey is going to be worse than I imagined.

Thursday 26 September 1991

Desperate for water! Ponies with parched innards. A real low point.

In prayer this morning, I asked for help finding a spring. After saddling up, I heard an engine passing. Seizing the lead rope, I jumped on Teancum and urged him up to the top of a wash, only to see a tractor going up Parks Wash. I rode out of the wash over to the road, where I'd seen the tractor, then scampered left up to where the map showed Kitchen Corral Spring. A partly-buried PVC pipe lead up to an old slab cement catch tank, where, lo and behold, a lone, bright green cottonwood tree rose up against the cliff face. An oasis in the desert. Water!

Needing a drink, the ponies picked up the pace as we made for the tree. No water to be seen; the dirt around the tree was dry. I unpacked the shovel and began digging. Getting past the roots and babying my ribs, it took about thirty minutes before moisture appeared. The hole gradually began to seep and fill with water. The tiny trickle was like gold. I filled my canteen and a gallon jug. Sam and Teancum tried muscling each other out of the way before they discovered they could both drink at the same time.

Teton, meanwhile, just stood and waited his turn. He looks and acts defeated—sure hope it's temporary. He's lost quite a bit of weight and I'm a bit worried about him. He's dragging and walks like he's hurting. After the mules had their fill, I led him over for his drink. When the mules came back for seconds, I shooed them away until I'd made sure Teton had taken his fill. After seconds, they did thirds and fourths.

After six miles of road riding, we crossed Highway 89

from the northeast. It was very hot–melting under the sun.

Next quandary: Whether or not to go down Kaibab Gulch. I'd highlighted it on my map, but it was very deep, very narrow, and six miles long with no way out except backtracking to the beginning. I was worried that if we had to do that, we might be caught in the dark.

The contours of the map showed 250-foot-high walls in some places. There was no trail shown on the map. I prayed for advice, inspiration, or some indication I should not go down it. But in the end I felt alright about taking it. Then I spied on the map the faint lines of a jeep road one mile south, paralleling the deep canyon. So, if we had to come back out before dark, that could be our route. We plunged!

It was beautiful! The high rock walls were colorful–and a bit scary–the ravine very narrow. Often, we saw traces of stock trails, and even two campfire remains. We had to ride down a creek bed part of the time, but made it just fine. Great fun–when it was over and we knew we didn't have to turn around.

Came across a bed of petrified wood along the road in Petrified Hollow. Just before dusk, we crossed from Kane County, Utah, into Coconino County, Arizona. Hey–we're making it! Camped just before dark where the map showed Coyote Spring. Nothing! I tied up the ponies. Once again no foraging, only grain. Opened a can of pork and beans for dinner; ate, then drank all the liquid. I would have rubbed Teton's legs if he'd have let me. But he was in no mood.

The desert heat saps strength. I fell into bed, but shortly after dozing off, was awakened by Teancum's rummaging through the packs. He'd gotten loose and eaten my apples, some candy, and had chewed at the damp bottom of my canteen cover. I retied him, but he had me worried all night. I slept fitfully, waking to check that he wasn't getting into things again. Need to find food and water for ponies!

Friday 27 September 1991

I awoke this morning with warm puffs of breath on my face. Loose again, Teancum loomed intently over me, his nostrils two inches away, waiting patiently for me to rise. Teton and Sam sagged, heads low. Their last drink of water had been yesterday at noon; they were parched. Ferreting out for water was the priority for the day. So much for reassurance of water.

I hiked up onto a ridge to have a look around, nothing but round hills of beautiful pastel, rainbow-like colors. Then I rode up Coyote Wash on the off chance I'd misread the map. Sure enough, a half mile up, there stood buildings and water tanks at Coyote Springs. The signs posted around the water read PRIVATE and were printed in big, black threatening letters. Looked like they meant it. Sure glad they weren't home (ahem). Sorry, but those signs weren't about to hold back the stampeding ponies. Drink now; ask forgiveness later. Ponies revived.

It was about twenty-five miles to House Rock. Hoped to make it by tonight; I thought that if we traveled on the road, we could.

Teancum jerked away twice today. Dang! So we had more mule school. I dunno, maybe I'm just going to have to have a tie-job on him all the time.

I was again on constant lookout for water almost immediately after drinking at the "Private" signs. Didn't want to miss any. In late afternoon, when I'd pull the skin on each pony's neck up into a "tent," it stayed longer than it should have—a sign of dehydration. We needed more water and hadn't seen any since morning. The heat again was sucking us dry. At One Mile Ranch I came upon a trailer, quiet and looking deserted.

"Hello!" I called out, bringing a bent-over, dried-out Arizona grandmother hobbling out.

"I'm Adeline Halvorsen, caretaker of this place," she rasped.

I didn't hear if she said anything else. My eyes just zeroed in on the pistol strapped to her right hip. "I'm looking for water for my horses," I explained. "Can you help me?"

She hesitated. Still, though alone, I'm sure she gathered confidence from her sidearm. I'm afraid my grizzled beard and several days of riding and camping made me look pretty rough. "There's water in the corral and you're welcome to some hay," she said, pointing to the barn.

I led as she followed and gave me directions. As I tended my horses, she stood back, asked where I'd come from and what I was doing in the hills. Reassured that I wasn't on the lam or had thievery in my blood, she warmed up and invited me into her trailer for a glass of grape juice. There at the kitchen table, I savored the smell coming from the glass. My body had missed fruit in my diet and the juice tingled going down.

Despite her hardbitten appearance, Adeline seemed like a fine woman. "I'm planning to hitchhike to Kanab to visit some friends," I told her. "Would you be willing to board my horses?"

"I'm happy to board your animals, but you'll be standing along the road with your thumb out for weeks; then you'll give up 'cuz there's no traffic here. I'm it," she said, smiling and putting the juice bottle back in the ice box. Then I remembered I hadn't seen any other homes for miles around.

"Guess I'll ride, then," I said, trying not to show my disappointment.

She limped to the trailer door and peered out the window. "I just so happen to be driving to Jacob's Lake today and you're welcome to come along," she said.

"I'd appreciate it. Thanks." I set my glass in the sink and turned to follow her out the door.

"Hold it a minute." She reached back with her hand, inches from my chest. I tried to peer past her out the small window but couldn't make out what she was watching. "Tracker's hackles are up and he's agitated," she said, stepping aside so I could see her dog.

"Is there something under the trailer?"

"Tracker's my snake alarm. There's probably a rattler under there." She shuffled back over to the window. "The stoop's clear. We can go; just hurry off the stoop," she said, opening the door. In one practiced, quick step she was off the stoop and facing the trailer. I could never be that nimble, but even so, my feet hardly touched the stoop. From a safe distance, we both stopped to see that, indeed, Tracker, pointing like a birddog, did have a six-foot rattler pinned under the trailer. Before I knew it, Adeline had drawn her pistol and put a bullet through its head–a clean shot. Clearly she'd had lots of practice. Tracker took over then and pounced on the coiled body. Clearly, he too had done this before. I learned this was why she wore the gun. Rattlers come in hordes out of the hills to eat the rats that gather to eat the mule food.

Jacob's Lake lies about fifteen miles over a mountain pass, one I didn't want to maneuver on horseback. Narrow, curvy, and dangerous to pedestrian traffic, I was grateful for the ride offer, as well as for Adeline's pony care. They need a break, especially Teton. I'll also visit nephews in St. George for a few days to help Teton rally.

On the way to Jacob's Lake, Adeline told me a little about herself. She'd broken her pelvis when her horse fell on her up on a bluff. It had taken her three days to crawl to her parked truck and drive herself to the doctor. One tough, tough lady with an undaunted spirit. That's why she's so twisted and hobbling.

After arriving at Jacob's Lake, Adeline took me to a cafe. Turns out when I went to the bathroom to wash up, unbeknownst to me, she stood on a chair in the cafe, gun strapped to her side, and pled my case. "I've got a friend here that needs a ride to Kanab. Who can help me?" she asked. It must have been a little hard to refuse an imposing figure like that. A man who drove a food distribution truck raised his hand. It was then that I came out of the bathroom, and all eyes turned on me. Realizing I'd been the topic of conversation, I grinned and nodded, whereupon Adeline announced, "You've got a ride to Kanab!" I found out later from the truck driver how she'd procured it.

I wondered if the right to bear arms was allowed within the city limits, or if an exception had been made for this beloved lady. She wore the pistol the entire time I was with her. At first glance it would've been easy to group her with Annie Oakley or Calamity Jane. Less refined, her heart was pure gold; she was physically small and twisted, but tall and straight in spirit.

The delivery driver took me right to Marlin and Delores Brown's home. They didn't know I was coming. I knocked, and Delores threw open the door. She reminds me of Fritz, her brother.

"Well, hello, Chuck Christensen. You're shorter and skinnier!"

Humph! My pants are hanging low, tho' I keep hitching them up. She and Marlin had seen my TV coverage and hoped I'd stop by when I got to Kanab. They invited me to eat dinner and stay overnight. Wow, was the meal ever delish! Close friends are like family–rejuvenating. Marlin owns the local newspaper and insisted on interviewing me.

I made it in time for the poetry gathering. Recited some; the cowboys appreciated it more than Teancum had.

I called home and talked to Anita, since Sally was gone to town, and called my nephew, Kelly, in St. George to line up a ride tomorrow. Tonight I'm in heaven: soft bed, hot shower, full tummy. Hope the ponies are feeling as chipper as I.

Saturday 28 September 1991

Ah, so nice to be clean, fed and cared for. Delores fixed fresh tomatoes and scrambled eggs for breakfast. Then she drove me to the feed store to buy hay—at four dollars and seventy-five cents a bale. Gold-plated, I guess! Then, I stopped at the hospital for a blood test. My white count is still low—2.9. Dang! Normal white count is somewhere between 4.3 and 10.8, so I've got a ways to go.

I browsed Delores's, family owned, bookstore and ended up buying three local historical books. I was anxious to learn about this area.

Kelly picked me up at noon and we headed for Adeline's place to feed the ponies. While we were driving, the rain came, heavy and in bursts. So glad I was in the truck and not on the trail. I checked first on Teton, who, under the love and care of Adeline, was doing well.

I drove with Kelly to St. George to spend a couple of nights with him and his family. Also, Teton needs more rest. I called Tawn Mangum, the Grand Canyon rim muleteer. He told me there were seven bridges to cross, that the canyon was steep going in and coming out, and that I'd have to face a long tunnel. Hmmm, we'll see what happens. My mules may dig in their heels, especially on the bridges and traveling by faith in the dark tunnel.

I tried to call Sally, but she still wasn't home. I made sure to leave a message so she'll know where I am and that I'm safe.

Sunday 29 September 1991

On this clear morning, I went to church, and came away renewed. Afterwards I called Fritz, Sally, and Ress.

October 8 is reserved for our Grand Canyon crossing, but

I'll be there six days earlier, by October 2. We'll see what we can do to move that date up.

Tom and Natalie, friends who used to live back home but now reside in St. George, came over to visit. It made me grin when Natalie, who'd been a doubter, is now in "affirmative thought."

Monday 30 September 1991

This morning Kelly and I drove truck and trailer to Beaver to pick up Kelly's mare, Sugar, for Jonah. I'm looking forward to seeing Leland and Jonah on Wednesday evening. At noon we'll return to House Rock and I'll get packed up.

It was fun to see Adeline again. While Kelly reset a shoe on Sugar's hind, I packed and Adeline talked. She's so helpful and eager to share stories, stuff, and labor. Hope she'll know joy for her service. Teton has flourished under her care. His legs and hooves seem better.

Oh, it felt good to be back on the trail–like a fish thrown back in the pond. The ponies were eager, too. Teton was rejuvenated. We seemed to fairly skip along the first couple of miles.

Got away at 6:30 p.m. and rode until nearly dark. Totaling about four or five miles, the last three were along a USFS fence in House Rock Valley. Grrr. No gate, and the fence appeared to go on forever. My entrance up onto Kiabab is indefinite, since I can't get past the fence. I've seen several alternatives, but each is on the other side of the fence.

Just had to throw off at the side of the fence tonight. Now I know how a caged wild animal must feel, all its energy spent trying to breach its enclosure.

There is not much feed here, I staked both horses and hobbled the mules; I didn't want to have to go off searching for them. Warm, tucked in my bag trying to identify constellations, I only got a few before my eyes drooped and closed for good.

Tuesday 1 October 1991

The fence was interminable! My chances of finding a way through seemed as likely as "the Snake" getting through the pearly gates. Finally, I gave up on finding a gate and used Leland's special gate-makers. He told me wirecutters would come in handy, and sure enough they did. I felt a bit guilty, but was in a bind and made sure to rewire the hole closed as best I could.

Bushwhacked west up over gradual, rocky, prickly-pear slopes toward a jeep road. Sam and Teton did well following Teancum's lead. Sugar, though, brought up the rear and didn't follow as well. We tried to dodge the prickly pears but were not successful. We had to stop periodically and pull out spines from all their forelegs. Sugar, fresher than the other animals, hopped about as I worked on her. She got to the point that, when she saw the pliers coming, she began to dance. I finished up with my ponies and was almost done with Sugar, when one of her knees, caught me square in the forehead over my right eye. Saw black for a couple of seconds, then fell back on my butt, put my head between my knees, and sat there until my vision could come back in focus. A goose egg pulsed above my clenched eye. Fluid leaked over my closed lid. After tenderly patting my forehead, I was relieved to discover that it was sweat, not blood. It must have beaded up when the goose egg appeared. I sat there for about ten minutes before I felt I could stand. Glad she didn't knock me flat.

Found the road and watered at Three Lakes corral tank. I bathed my goose bump with a cold wet compress and rode with a headache. Quit the road later to bushwhack a short-cut—steep and rocky with oak thickets and ponderosa. I found a blue backpack sitting on a rock. By its bleached-out appearance I could tell it had been there awhile, but I left it where it was. Then found the road I was looking for right after.

Came to a beautiful ponderosa forest on the plateau, a place sprinkled with loads of deer, cattle and loggers. Just before dark, we rode into Little Pleasant Valley by the side of the highway. It was exactly what I was hoping for and we camped by the roadside.

I'm more than halfway on this flat stretch to the North Rim of the Grand Canyon. It was a long day, sun-up to sun-down. Tired, but high spirits, despite the egg. I had cold canned chili for dinner; it was too much effort to fire up the Coleman. My head pounds when I lie down, sure hope I can sleep.

Wednesday 2 October 1991

I may have slept in a state of total unconsciousness. Lots of dew this morning; it actually froze to my sleeping bag and cracked off in small shards as I shook the bag.

After breakfast, a fellow from northern Georgia stopped by to talk as I was packing up. His accent was so thick that, at first, I wondered if it was English he was speaking. As a youngster, he'd worked mules in Mississippi, and, seeing mine, had stopped to admire them. (Ahem, maybe "admiring" was only in my mind.) But he obviously loved mules. I looked up with a smile to engage in the conversation, but had only spoken a word or two when he sucked in a big breath and broke in with, "Are you alright, sir?" A look of concern creased his forehead as, squinting with concern, he studied my injury.

"Peachy, how are you?" I stood and extended my hand.

"I'm fine; your eye, is it ok?" He reached up to touch his own eye socket and absent-mindedly shook my hand.

Seeing the man's pained expression, I realized it must look pretty bad. "Oh, this. I haven't seen it. Bad, huh?" Tender to the touch, I knew my eye was swollen because I could see the inside of my eyelid. I tried to raise my lid to show it wasn't as bad as it looked, but the muscle movement hurt so I just let it droop in a half-wink. I twisted my head slightly and centered my good eye on him.

"You've got quite the black eye," he said, craning his neck closer. "Almost looks like a bullseye with different colors for each ring, and the lump on your forehead looks like a boulder."

Felt like a Neanderthal. Who needs a mirror, huh? I changed the subject with, "So, you like mules?"

He enthusiastically gave evidence that indeed he did. He even told me about the "mule column" in his hometown newspaper. I had to listen carefully so as to understand him. After he left, I was able to wrap my small brain around the column idea and realized it was a very good one. Then this Neanderthal finished packing up his bone tools, crude shelter, fire-starting stones, and hunting weapon.

On my way to the North Rim of the Grand Canyon, I passed beautiful meadows and stands of ponderosa. Teancum's easy, rocking gait was lulling me to sleep when a truck pulled up from behind and a cheery voice called out, "Howdy, stranger!"

Pulling alongside and hanging out the driver's window, Leland chuckled and asked, "Hey, Dad! How does the other guy look? Or should I ask, is the mule still alive?"

I grinned back smugly and stopped my procession. "The mules stood like milk cows; it was Sugar who gave me grief." Why does everyone assume the mule first?

At the entrance of the Grand Canyon, Jonah kicked at the dust as he waited for us to arrive. I climbed from Teancum and gave him a hug. His short black hair—as I'd remembered it—now rested several inches below his shoulders and he'd grown a few inches since I'd seen him last. He hugged me softly as I reassured him I was glad he was here. He nodded, but couldn't look me in the eye.

We met Park Ranger Ralph Hopkins, who proved to be helpful almost to the point of our salvation. First, he pointed out where we should camp. Then, all on his after-hours time, he set up our horse camp, provided potable water, filled the horse tank, and arranged with the head ranger for us to get a "tomorrow" permit to hike and camp in the canyon. Such permits are unheard of in administrative park circles! Remember, we were nearly a week ahead of schedule. Permits are usually reserved from four months to a year ahead of time. He steered us around and even offered me his personal shower. I hope I can repay him sometime for all his help and generosity. Thanks again, dear family, for your prayers.

Our camp tonight is by Tawn Mangum's mule corrals. His mules are the beautiful china-doll variety, on the small side. All uniform, they look like they came from the same jack and mare. They keep calling to my mules with their distinctive mule bray, a combination of the horse whinny at the beginning and the "e-aw" of the donkey at the end. My mules bray back. Sounds like an orchestra to me. Tawn rents out his mules to folks so they can ride down into the canyon. I hope mine do alright. They're not as seasoned as his.

My right eye has swollen to a slit. I can only partially see out of it, but I'm glad I've still got one good eye. With my limited vision, I'm a little worried about descending a narrow, unfamiliar trail on donks who've never traveled it before.

Before dinner, Leland stretched his leg muscles and took a few laps around his vehicle. Jonah, watching from the open tailgate, asked, "Are you ready for the Grand Canyon? Have you been training or anything?"

"You saw me; I just did," Leland said, straightfaced. "This isn't my first rodeo."

Jonah hesitated, then snickered. His right hand angled at Leland as if he were a spotter at an auction. With each snicker he punctuated the sale. The faster the snicker, the faster the hand movement.

I'd barely hobbled both horses when all our ponies took off at a fast hop, headed for a dark, forested area. It was as though the same deceptively charming sirens, who'd called to Jason and his Argonauts, were summoning my ponies. They wouldn't turn back. We forgot about dinner and ran after them, with Leland heading the animals just before they entered the eerie forest. Close call. Very odd.

Ah, fruit again. My good eye zeroed in on the quart of orange juice with the two giant pizzas Leland brought from the truck. I'll pick up some more juice later.

Sitting around after dinner, letting our food digest, we gave Jonah some pointers on riding, mainly how to read his mount by watching the animal's ears, eyes, mouth, and breathing. He listened with a false sense of confidence, all the while nodding as if it were something he already knew. I knew better; he hadn't a clue.

"Don't flap your arms; it makes animals nervous," I instructed.

"They'll think you're trying to take off, so they will too," Leland added.

"They can tell if you're frightened," I continued. "And don't kick 'em in the flank."

"Unless you want a rodeo," interrupted Leland.

I cleared my throat to cut Leland off. "Keep half your weight on your feet in the stirrups and half your weight on your butt in the saddle." Handing him some pantyhose, I said, "You'll need these." I explained why. The concept didn't seem strange to him in the least–after all, I was the expert. I handed him my knife so he could cut off the feet. I could have suggested using them to strain bugs from dinner. Seemed plausible.

Leland, revealing a set of straight, perfect teeth like Jube's, couldn't help but add, "You'll be ready for church at a moments notice, too," bringing a nervous laugh from Jonah.

"Laugh if you want. You'll see," I told him, nodding my head in the affirmative.

After our food settled, we waddled out to Bright Angel Point on the north rim of the Grand Canyon. What a spectacle! Pillars, chasms, colors, sheer drops, depths almost to the bowels of the earth. Magnificent, majestic. A constructed walkway takes visitors out to a vista they'd otherwise be unable to experience. The sun was just beginning to set as we got there, and we watched the darkness begin to fill the canyon. Each twist took on the fading hues of sunlight and deepened the color of its walls. Finally all we could see were stars and the faint outlines of points and spires. I had the feeling that it was like gazing into eternity. I imagined this was similar to when the earth was created; or had time carved it out since?

Philosophy for today: To see the big picture, or gain true perspective, one must distance himself from the close view or the immediate experience.

Chuck with Teancum, 1992. (*Courtesy of Dawn Fullmer*)

Chuck visits his dedicatory plaque at Teton Canyon Transfer Camp in Teton Canyon, fall 1992.

Dedicatory plaque at Teton Canyon Transfer Camp in Teton Canyon on the Teton Basin Ranger District of the Caribou-Targhee National Forest.

North of Hurricane Pass in the Tetons, Chuck teaches Teancum to tail as they prepare for the ride to Mexico, 1991. (*Courtesy of Rudy Puzey*)

Attempting to toughen up Teton too, 1991. (*Courtesy of Rudy Puzey*)

Jube pauses for a photo before he goes for a ride, 2012.

Jube waiting his turn to target shoot, family reunion, 2012.

Fritz Kaufman honors
Chuck with an original
poem at dedication of
Teton Canyon Transfer
Camp, fall 1990. *(Courtesy
of Teton Valley News,
Driggs, Idaho.)*

Ty McCowin with his
matching blacks, 1991.

10 lb. cloth bags made by Jube, Laurel and Chuck, 1991.

Chuck received $20.00 and lunch as payment for packing out a hunter's elk, 1991.

Chuck, in white, harvesting a young bowhead whale, Wales, Alaska, 1970.

Unknown man prepares Chuck for TV interview, Parley's Summit, near Salt Lake City, 1991.

Chuck and Adeline Halvorson, House Rock Valley, Arizona 1991.

Chuck recovering from black eye after being kneed by the horse, Grand Canyon, 1991.

Leland hiking, Chuck on Teancum, unknown woman, north rim of the Grand Canyon, 1991.

Leland pointing to his grandfather's name, Morris Christensen, at the bottom of the ice caves, Darby Canyon, Wyoming, 1986.

Teancum crossing bridge in Grand Canyon, 1991.

Chuck, Teancum and Teton, Anderson Mesa, Arizona, 1991.

Rock house on Montana mountain, Tonto National Forest, Arizona, 1991.

Makeshift bed in rock house, 1991.

Chuck's typical campsite on his way to Mexico, 1991.

Chuck braiding the end of Sadie's (Sam in this book) lash rope, 1991. (Sadie, not Sam, is the actual mule who made the trip to Mexico with Chuck, Teancum and Teton. After returning home, an accident ended her life. Sam traveled part of the way to Canada and was known to the author, Sadie was not, so Sam was substituted, in this work, for Sadie.)

After grazing, ponies come back into camp for oats, 1991.

Chuck, Teancum, Sadie (Sam), and Teton prepare to ride into Mexico, 1991.

Finally, after 105 days, Chuck crosses over into Mexico, 1991.

Skinny horses at the Mexican border. Chuck and Lewis Freeman with horses ready to load in the horse trailer before starting back to Phoenix, 1991.

Chuck and Sharon Skenandore on the last leg of the Canada trip, Hale Trout Farm, 1995.

Chuck makes his final ride April 12, 2005. Blue and Thinker, Chuck's mules, pull the wagon he rests on while grandson Hunter leads a beloved, saddled, riderless Teancum. Grandson, Jed, brings up the rear. Friends, Clyde Waddell and Ryan Jeppson drive the team. (*Courtesy of Becky Rich*)

Chapter 13

Thursday 3 October 1991

I awoke aware that my right eye's range of sight had increased. The swelling was going down. Anxiety over my injury subsided. Thank you, family, for your prayers.

We were excited as we rolled from our bags. After showing Jonah how to saddle Sugar, Leland and I started packing the Ralide boxes. My eyebrows raised when Jonah brought his backpack over, indicating it was all he'd brought. His own raised when he took in the dozen or so boxes of Anita's diaper wipes I'd packed. "Without modern conveniences, those'll come in handy," he said, then began pantomiming, mostly with his hands: face and hand washing, cooking clean-up, and wound care. He didn't demonstrate the obvious one.

Leland brought quite a few MREs (Military Meals Ready to Eat). What a treat those will be! Since I was traveling with my limited provisions to reduce weight, there was plenty of room on the packsaddles for everything.

Got packed up before eight, earlier than Tawn's dudes. "Mount on Sugar's left side," I directed Jonah. With her reins uneven and loose, Sugar began circling as Jonah tried to put his right foot in the stirrup.

"Tighten up your reins and use your left foot," I said, willing to take time for him to practice. Leland, impatient, hovered close by to show Jonah how to hold the reins and climb on.

Properly mounted up, Jonah bounced and jostled from one side of his saddle to the other as we headed down the trail. I led, followed by Sam and Teton, then Jonah on Sugar; Leland served as caboose, walking.

Most people who come to the Canyon visit the South Rim, so it'll be nice to have less of a crowd as we break in the mules. The first half of the trail, fourteen miles to Bright Angel Campground and a five and a half hour ride, was cut right out of the canyon wall. Nice, but a tight fit if two horses with packs have to pass each other. The first section had lotsa zig-zags, but we felt secure because brush on the rim obscured our view. But soon enough, above Roaring Springs, we came to spots on the trail where there was nothing between us and the edge except space and the opposite wall of the canyon. Literally breathtaking, even to the point of hyperventilating! I couldn't look at my outside stirrup; there was only air, way too much air. My stomach churned. Maybe hiking, being closer to the ground on foot, would've eliminated my feelings of being precariously suspended over a chasm.

My mind instantly returned to June 1985, a time and place of wide blue skies and open air. But I had a parachute on then. Trying to control my breathing, I crawled to the plane's open door with the assurance that thousands had jumped before me, and *their* parachutes had opened. Intermittently I wondered, "What was it that made me want to go skydiving?" Still, I reached out, grabbed the strut, arched my back, and, with trailing feet, let go. I dropped rapidly, disoriented for a moment. The wind buffeted at my face, and then the chute opened. As I looked back on that day, I knew why I'd wanted to skydive: freedom, view, triumph over fear, a small victory over self. I also knew that, with an open chute, my descent would be slow and I'd land safely.

Today, however, coming down the trail on Teancum's back, I had no chute on and no safety net below.

I also thought back to the summer of 1977 when I climbed the Grand Teton with a few family members. Crawling up a rock face with a sizeable overhang above and only valley floor far below, our climbing guide gave some expert advice: "Don't look down." It had worked then; it would work now.

I kept my eyes focused on the trail and admired the texture, layers, and red color of the rock wall so close to my uphill ear. I scrutinized plants and water pods, anything but the canyon floor. The trail that I could see lay between Teancum's erect ears. During a portion of the descent, I fixated on his ears and thought them to be smaller than donkey ears but larger than horses' ears. I noticed he needed his ragged mane trimmed; I studied his neck hair and thought of oiling his bridle–willing myself to keep my mind off the wide open space below. I pictured each small, narrow, well-placed hoof of my mount, reminding myself that the park had no record of a mule going over the edge. Of course, the park's mules are experienced and calm ones, who make this trip daily. But I took comfort knowing that mules in general are known for their surefootedness, and believed Teton and Sugar would mirror the calm demeanor of Teancum and Sam.

"Keep your outside foot out of the stirrup, just in case you need to bail," I cautioned Jonah. I didn't want to scare him, just help him stay alert.

I was noticing how Teancum's hair grows in a swirl by his left ear, when hikers, toting imposing backpacks that towered above their heads, suddenly rounded a bend towards us. I pulled Teancum to a stop.

"Hullo, hikers," I called. "Would you please stand real still while we pass?" The lead hiker waved in response and the party of three halted and hugged the canyon wall. With a prayer in my heart that the hikers wouldn't twitch and spook the horses, we started forward. Teancum, ears straining ahead and head down, had been intently focusing on the trail. As we approached, he timidly lifted his head a little higher with each step, crooking his neck to eye the hikers and their scary-looking backpacks. His head was turned enough for me to see his wide eye. I hoped he had lizard eyes, able to move independently of each other, with one focused on the hikers, the other on the trail. He must have. The bronzed hikers hunkered like statues as close to the wall as possible. That left us the outside edge. Oh, what seemed narrow before now shrunk to the width of masking tape. Nervous! My foot that hung out over the canyon was out of the stirrup, just in case. Jonah exercised remarkable restraint, his nervous hands motionless but white as he gripped the saddlehorn and leaned at a 45-degree angle uphill, away from the edge. As we passed each hiker Teancum blew and snorted, but continued without flinching.

Inhaling deeply and in need of both air and water (I couldn't have produced enough spit to sizzle on a griddle), I croaked a weak but sincere, "Thanks," as I passed the last hiker. Sam, Teton, and Sugar followed Teancum's lead and calmly passed by. I felt like jumping off and throwing my arms around Teancum, the million-dollar mule, but couldn't pry my fingers from around the saddlehorn. It would have to wait.

Afterwards, Leland called from behind, "You ok, Dad? Jonah?"

"Yup," I called back. I noticed Jonah just nod, but the color was returning to his hands. I repeated my "please stand still" request each time hikers approached. Ponies continued to do well, but Jonah's and my reaction was the same with every group. White-knuckle time!

We stopped to rest and have lunch at Roaring Springs. Jonah offered to walk while Leland rode, but he declined.

It was a piece of cake from there on down, but we still had several miles in the hot corridor called The Box before reaching Bright Angel Campground. Sugar threw a front shoe and wore her hoof down to a nub.

After arriving at the canyon floor, I looked up to admire the red rock we'd traversed. Slowly pivoting, I took in the breathtaking view. All the synonyms for *beautiful* would still be lacking descriptive power. It was magnificent!

I was struck by the contrast between our peaceful experience last night at Bright Angel Point–our look into eternity–and this morning's study in close-up fears. Exact opposites. Seeing the big picture and the close-up detail are both necessary. Neither far nor near is complete in and of itself.

Bright Angel Campground is shaded by giant cottonwood trees, but is still very hot! So hot, we almost didn't have to cook the food, just let the sun do it. The squirrels are bold. We felt surrounded. One hopped on the picnic bench and sat next to me. I could have shared each bite, had I wanted to. He failed to strike up a conversation, though, just watched me like a wolf watches sheep. Thought I could have put him in a hypnotic trance by swinging food back and forth in my hand. I wonder if any squirrel bites had been reported to Canyon authorities? Leland chased squirrels away while Jonah coaxed them back. Fun to have their company.

There are many tame deer and spotted skunks in the area. After dinner, we covered food items so as not to attract foxes and squirrels during the night. We enjoy all the conveniences of home: toilets, phones, water, and tables. Nice.

Phantom Ranch is about a half mile from Bright Angel Campground. It's a commercial reservation operation for guests who rent South Rim mules, with cabins and dormitories for the tourists. I wandered over to visit with the mule wrangler. Congenial.

Warm evening. We'd come from pleasant forest land, filled with pines and greenery, to the scorching desert. It was over 100 degrees in the bottom of the canyon; it felt like the stove dial was turned on broil. What a pleasure to lie down on top of my sleeping bag, remove my rib belt, and stretch out my tense, aching spine. I'd been leaning uphill the entire ride down, but not to the degree Jonah did.

I'm lying in bed thinking of the walk we took to the edge of the spectacular Colorado River. Its light-green, semi-clear water winds through the bottom of the Canyon like a milky, emerald-colored band. As I watched its meandering current, it gave me a feeling of eternal movement, and I wondered: "Am I where I'm supposed to be in life, or am I swimming against the current? Am I moving on the waves and riffles, or rolling in a back current? Am I lodged against an obstruction, which I or others made, or water-logged and submerged in the river bottom, awaiting petrification? What is progress? Might all these experiences be part of life's progression, regardless of how we see them at the time?" Just reflecting, taking inventory again.

FRIDAY 4 OCTOBER 1991

We got up early to ride out with the mule wrangler and his tourists. We didn't want to meet a packer head-on coming down South Kiabab Trail. A trail with an open edge is not the place for unacquainted mules to get acquainted.

But first we had to shoe Sugar's front hoof. She wouldn't hold her leg up for us, so we tied it up with a rope. I held her still while Leland did the shoeing, working fast, hammering between Sugar's struggling fits. She continued to fight until the other front shoe came off. Leland muttered something I didn't hear, but could have guessed.

Jonah, looking on, cleared his throat. "I'm not used to that kind of language," he smirked.

Leland, playing along, dropped Sugar's hoof, straightened, and squinched up his face as if in deep thought. "How about biblical words then? Hell? Damn? How about ass?" With that, he arched his brows and shot Jonah an innocent stare. Jonah cracked first. His lips turned up, then he chuckled and waved his hand in the air as if he were shooing a fly. "Oh, ya!" he sputtered, and turned to pack the rest of his bag.

By then, the wrangler had left with his group. He was already over the bridge and up the south side of the canyon wall before we finished shoeing Sugar. Leland deposited a cloth bag in a Ralide box. "Dad, did you see the bridge we need to cross? Do you think it'll be a problem?"

"It might be. I'm worried the mules will balk. If you have any ideas, I'm all ears." I threw the tarp over Teton's pack and tied it down. Jonah saddled Sugar, then led her over for me to check the cinch. "The saddle needs to come forward on the withers," I said, pointing to where it should be. "As we climb out of the canyon it might end up that far back, but you don't want to start with it there."

Leland held the saddle blanket as Jonah slid the saddle forward, then climbed on.

As I mounted Teancum, Leland offered, "How about if I walk first and you keep Teancum's head right up in my back, and we'll see if that helps him so he won't panic."

"Let's try it," I said. Leland handed me Sam's halter rope and stepped out in lead, Teancum and me right on his tail. Sam and Teton stayed close, with Jonah and Sugar bringing up the rear.

The bridge appeared wide enough to accommodate one horse with a packsaddle. The railing, however, was sufficiently low so that a mule could easily peer over the edge and see how far down the river runs, then gauge his jump—not a good thing. I hoped Sam wouldn't put his jumping skill to use. Right off the end of the bridge is a dark tunnel. I told myself not to worry, the ponies had done well so far.

Without hesitating, Leland strode onto the bridge. "Come on, boy; you can do it," he cooed. Ready for a rodeo, I held my breath as Teancum placed one hoof on the bridge. Leland kept talking; I nudged Teancum so close to Leland's back that his nose looked to be in Leland's hind pocket, seemingly coaxed by a sugar cube. After several yards, I realized

I was the one holding my breath, while Teancum's breathing hadn't changed in the least. He clopped along, ears flopping, no sweat! Could have been yawning. Even when we came to the tunnel, he sauntered through the dark air, comfortable as a mole. And I had doubted him. Shame! The other horses followed behind without a hitch. As he came out the other end, Leland sidestepped and filed in behind Jonah. Slick!

South Kiabab Trail has some beautiful sights. Steep, though. It felt like we were traveling straight up hill for seven long miles!

"Leland, grab on to Sugar's tail and let her pull you," I called back when we stopped to give the ponies a breather.

"I'm fine, thanks." Using a kerchief, he swabbed a coating of dusty red sweat from his face, then downed a long drink of water. However, the red didn't wipe off. The sun was making a furnace of the rocks, and baking us all, including the ponies, all in a lather.

I stopped about halfway up and dismounted next to Leland, who'd begun to lag behind. "Leland, it's time you rode."

"He can ride Sugar; I'll walk for a while," Jonah chimed in, reining Sugar to a halt. He'd begun to relax in the saddle, as his confidence with Sugar grew.

"No, I need to stretch, and walking will feel good," I said, handing Leland Teancum's reins. His shirt was sweat-soaked from shoulder to shoulder, and down the centers of both back and belly, with odd dry panels under his arms to the hemline.

"Alright. Even Superman spends some time as Clark Kent," he wheezed, and climbed onto Teancum, took Sam's rope, and started off. I fell in behind Sugar and grabbed ahold of her tail.

"How ya doing, Jonah?" I asked, my walking muscles loosening up.

He paused before answering. "Fine, but my butt is dying."

"Walking will help with that."

"I will in a few minutes," he replied. "Look, no hands." He flashed me his palms over his shoulders, fingers spread wide.

Only a few minutes had passed when Jonah stood in his stirrups, reached into his front jeans pocket, and retrieved a piece of gum. Plopping it in his mouth, he chewed and blew a bubble that echoed when it popped. Sugar, startled by the new sound, had Jonah grabbing for the saddlehorn again. White-faced, Jonah half-whispered, "I'd like to walk now."

"Riding out of the Grand Canyon isn't the time or place to teach your mount something new," I scolded. "Are you all right?"

Nodding, he dismounted.

"I'll take Sugar for a bit," I said, gathering the reins out of his tight fist.

He and I had walked for about twenty minutes when Leland was ready to join us, saying he'd rather be on foot, too. After his ride in sweat-soaked shorts, maybe he wished he had some hose on, too. Jonah and I climbed back into our saddles, and, this time, Leland took hold of Sugar's tail to make the going easier.

It seemed that every few minutes I was crying out, "Please stand still until we pass." Sometimes the clusters of backpackers were so close together that the trailing hikers would obey my request given to the first group, stopping and backing into the canyon wall before we even reached them. The steady stream of humanity descending the canyon made me think of a colony of ants fleeing an anthill. We didn't teeter as much on the masking-tape edge riding up out of the canyon as we did riding down. Only four or five smaller places on the south trail are like that one on the north, above Roaring Springs. My nerves weren't in constant fray, but I did find additional distraction with all the hikers. Chatting. Lots of chatting.

We came across folks from Peru, China, Germany, and India. I was beginning to relax somewhat when we approached two female Peruvian hikers resting against the wall. We happened to be in one of the wide-open places. I called out my request, they both nodded, and we quietly passed the first woman, whose only movements were the smile tugging at her lips and a set of eyes darting back and forth between Teancum and Sugar. Teancum's head had just come even with the second woman, when her arm suddenly snaked out, her hand seizing Teancum's bridle, and with a slight accent squealed, "May I take a picture?" With that, she waved her camera in front of her face with her free hand.

I almost tossed my breakfast! My chest muscles tightened as if in a garlic press. The way Teancum surely would lurch about while in the grip of this woman, I instantly thought, "Here I go; this is it! The first man and mule to go over the edge." The mind moves at an amazing speed when one is in danger. In a millisecond, in a veritable flash, I thought of my sweet family, was reassured they'd be fine, and knew my affairs were in order. I wondered which family members and friends I'd see first on the other side. Gratitude swept through my body; I'd had a good life. Then I prepared mentally for one last glimpse at the awe-inspiring canyon as I fell, determined to enjoy my last seconds on earth. The blood returned to my face when I noticed Teancum hadn't flinched a bit. He could have been a doodler in chemistry class, for all the interest he showed.

I gathered my wits and offered a feeble smile. "Sure. Does it have a flash?" I asked, still feeling plenty lightheaded.

"No," she said, clicking several shots while still clutching Teancum's bridle. After the photo session, my heart beat like a bass drum against my ribs each time we skirted hikers. To my delight, the rest of the way to the top, Teancum kept passing hikers like a vegan passes roast beef.

The ride out took about four and a half hours. We ran out of drinking water and felt as wrinkled as raisins by the time we reached the rim. I wanted to kneel and kiss the level ground. My ribs were more than sore, maybe from leaning uphill, maybe from alternately deep then shallow, irregular breathing. And I think I may have popped a rib during the photo shoot. My sternum is tender. I stopped to straighten my spine and tighten my rib belt for support, and prayed the rib soon would straighten or pop back in place.

After reaching the top of the Canyon, Leland lay down to rest for a few minutes before we followed the South Rim wrangler to his mule barns. We hoped we could board our animals there, but his boss said no go. A park ranger mapped us a horse camp location. Even following its guidelines, we set up camp too close to the entry, and the ranger made us decamp and move a quarter-mile farther south.

The store on this side of the Canyon offered much-needed vegetables and fruit. Had to keep wiping the slobber off my chin as I wandered the aisles. I bought as much as I thought we could eat before it would spoil. With fresh fruit, veggies, and Leland's army rations, we'll eat like kings.

Three nights in a row with restrooms and running water, we've been spoiled. It seems drier on this side of the canyon, and finding water might become more of a problem.

We met Stuart Tait, a horse power in northern Arizona. He gave us hay and I invited him to come to the Tetons next summer. Nice guy. Leland worried about my rib, then showed Jonah how to help saddle the packhorses. To ease the pain, I've tightened my rib belt as far as it'll go. It should help, if I can keep breathing. I'll just have to wait it out.

It was hard to say goodbye to Leland–for both Jonah and me. What a treat to have had him here. Kelly arrived to take him back to his truck. He asked about my multi-colored eye; very surprised that Sugar was the one responsible. I insisted that Leland take the Python .357 magnum home with him. I'm not sure the ponies will notice the reduced weight, not with the added load placed on my heart when Leland and Kelly drove away.

Remembered my chemo pills and started them today.

LELAND'S JOURNAL ENTRY, OCT. 4, 1991

Up early, we'd planned to follow the mule wrangler up out of the canyon. But he got away without us because, first, I had to recite a few choice biblical curses and nail a new pair of shoes on Sugar. I was anxious to start climbing. After all, I'd made it down into the canyon, and all I had to do was hike the shorter route back out. I was well prepared with three bottles of water and plenty of high-energy snacks in my backpack. I warmed up my legs doing the boxer shuffle, took a few uppercuts to loosen my biceps, and did some jumping jacks to get the cardio going.

"Slow down, son. You're gunna take off if you're not careful," Dad chuckled, making a spiral motion toward the sky with his fore-finger. I planned to follow behind the horses, like yesterday, while Dad and Jonah rode, but instead I led across the bridge and through the tunnel. All the while, Teancum's head was nudging my back. Then I fell in line behind Sugar and kept pace with the horses for the first hour. I knew I could keep up.

After a couple more hours I began to melt. Hades kept adding fuel to his fire. I could've broken an egg against my stomach and immediately enjoyed it sunny-side up. Sweat gathered at the base of my neck and ran in a constant stream down my back and belly, funneling right into my shorts. I didn't care to see where it ran after that, but I could feel it. I wondered, "Can big boys get diaper rash?" The salt stream stung my eyes despite the handkerchief sweatband tied around my forehead. The red dirt streaked across my face must have made me look like an Apache on the warpath. I wondered how people could survive living here.

About the time I felt my wet shorts were going to rub off every layer of skin between my thighs, Dad said that it was my turn to ride. Okay, riding could save that first or second layer of skin, right? So I jumped on. Not so! I only rode about half an hour before I had to get off again. The skin on my raw butt felt like it had been peeled back a little further with each gentle rock in the saddle. I would've proudly pranced around in pantyhose just to avoid the pain.

With about an hour left of hiking, I felt like a man in Death Valley crawling towards an oasis. The boxer shuffle had turned into an old-man shuffle, feet sliding and toes gripping to keep slippers on. This morning's loosened biceps were now elongated, saggy muscles with no elasticity to prevent my limbs from flopping uncontrollably with each shuffle. And the cardio was in climb mode, threatening to launch my heart from my chest. The sun had sucked every bit of moisture from inside my wrinkled body and spit it out on my outside, a glistening prune with legs. My swollen tongue restricted my airway and reduced my breath to a shallow wheeze. My water bottles were empty and the high-energy snacks a fraud. The trail's fine red powder was kicked up by the horses; it floated and hovered at the level of my nose, forming a dark paste that collected in rings around each nostril. I must have looked like a crazed bull.

When Dad stopped so a lady could take a few pictures of him and Teancum, I collapsed, spread-eagle on the ground. My glazed eyes stared skyward, watching for circling buzzards, wondering when they'd land on me and begin feasting.

"Leland, are you sure you don't want to ride?" Jonah asked as he swivelled around and patted his saddle.

"Do I look like I need to ride?" I asked, pulling myself to a sitting position and trying to control my breathing.

"Only if you want to live," he said, smirking.

"I'm good. Thanks, though." No way was I getting back on that horse. My thighs thanked me.

Jonah laughed as I flopped my loose elbow joints into a pathetic muscle pose, one I was only able to hold for a few seconds. "Get rid of the cryptonite in your back pocket. It seems to be sapping your strength."

I stood, swaying and gazing up at the sky, when Dad started off again. Still no buzzards, no bones, either, and I'm still alive, so I shuffled after Sugar. The photographers were approaching, so I forced a smile, which cracked my lips and turned my expression into a grimace. When I licked my teeth in an attempt to rid them of the red film, it only succeeded in smearing it. I tried to pick up my feet, just in case they wanted a picture of this fine specimen. They didn't.

A half-melted puddle of quivering jello, but I made it to the top! My muscles had given way. I attempted to make it look planned as I collapsed like an accordion.

"How ya doing?" Dad asked, looking down from Teancum's back.

"Fine. Just resting," I replied with closed eyes. "Why do you ask?" I cracked an eye half open, squinted up at him, and offered a pained grin. He nodded knowingly and said something to Jonah about horses needing a break. I don't remember much after that, only Jonah asking for a spoon to scrape up the jello.

After a nap, I am able to write about the climb out. On top of the rim, rested and watered, my head has cleared and I can write on a more serious note.

When I wasn't gulping for air, I trudged behind Sugar and watched Dad sit hunched in the saddle. I was so proud to be his son. At first, I'd thought I was too busy to come with him on this part of his ride. I almost let this experience pass by. After seeing him living out his dream, I realized I was only limiting myself. If I really wanted to do something, if I was determined enough, I could do it.

I thought back to a time that perhaps revealed where Dad had gotten his adventurer's spirit. I stood at a low point in the ice caves located in Darby Canyon, Wyoming, reading the name of my grandfather, Morris Christensen, among others, inscribed on the rock wall below the date 1936. The ice caves consist of one climb and *seven different ice rappels, the longest being about 50 feet. Tight tunnels only wide enough to let one man pass at a time inflict a claustrophobic feeling. Only in 1980, six years before my own climb, had spelunkers entered these ice caves and found an exit through an adjoining cave. Morris' signature was scratched out at a point in the cave where he either could no longer proceed or considered it too unsafe to go on. Morris, going where few had ever gone, seeking adventure, had made his descent into the cave while he was ill. He sounds like Dad—not letting his condition ever stop him.*

There have been so many doubters, including myself. Dad has faced doubters all his life, and, one by one, proved them wrong. One such person was Sherman Roberts.

Dad joined the National Guard in his early twenties. He wanted to become an officer. Sherman, an executive officer in Dad's unit, claimed Dad wasn't smart or tough enough to go to Officer Candidate School (OCS). Tired of people telling him he couldn't, and determined to prove Sherman wrong, Dad took the test, sent in the applications, and was accepted. He struggled with math, though. He'd gone through grade school and middle school thinking he couldn't do math and flunked Algebra in high school. He almost flunked out of OCS, too, but by sheer grit (and by taking a math correspondence course), he became a Redbird and graduated as a second lieutenant. Later, he even considered teaching math, as he found that indeed he did have an affinity for it. He also became a captain in the Utah National Guard.

Others may not have known they were part of the reason for his success. I and my fellow doubters pushed him to greater heights. With every can't, he'd only smile, but his heart would be saying, "Just watch me." Dad, we are all watching.

Be safe.

Chapter 14

Jonah and I were lazy getting up and lazy eating breakfast. It tasted alright, and I at least kept it down. At last my rib seems to have popped back in place. Still sore, but should feel better soon. We decided to visit the Grand Canyon Visitor Center this morning, then ride to Tusayan.

Last night I called Ty McCowin, friend and doctor who made my clam-shell brace. When I asked him how he was doing, there came a pause. Then: "I've been diagnosed with Lou Gehrig's Disease." He couldn't hide the chill in his voice, and I couldn't hide my shock. Felt like I'd been hit in the chest with a crowbar. I knew this was a disease that caused muscle to become weak, atrophy, then shut down, all while the mind stayed alert.

When the line went silent, I held the phone away from my mouth, hoping my sob would go unnoticed. In only a few moments I'd lived Ty's diagnosis, the hopelessness and despair, as I had experienced them in my own life. "Come ride with me," I managed to croak.

"I'd like that. I'll come soon, before it gets too difficult."

He'll join us at Strawberry, Arizona.

Jonah and I tied up the ponies and headed to the Visitor Center, featuring history of the area, the early pioneers, and river runners. Last year four million tourists came to visit this fragile environment. How careful its stewards need to be. Preservation for the future, and enjoyment for now, must be judiciously balanced. It only takes six footprints in the same spot to reduce the groundcover to pulverized dust, preventing vegetation from regenerating. We came away grateful for the chance to visit the Canyon.

I ate a beef sandwich and it set alright on my stomach. As Jonah and I exited the deli, we were met by a panting, red-faced ranger who was clearly in a hurry to find us. "Are you the ones who camped over there with animals?" His voice was tight; his tone hard. He pointed in the direction of our camp, then pointed again for emphasis.

"Yes. Is there a problem?" I asked. The answer was obvious. Out of the corner of my eye I saw two other rangers, slim and fit, approaching on the run. Before the first ranger had time to answer, we were surrounded by all three.

"You've got a horse at the rangers' office. You must *never, ever* leave your horses unattended!" The perspiring ranger then added "*Ever!*" a bit louder, just in case we were deaf. Teton had gotten loose and wandered, of all places, to the rangers' office, where office personnel had tied him up and sent the men on the manhunt. We felt like criminals. After they read us the riot act and spelled out the regulations, the rangers' demeanor suddenly changed. Apparently they thought we could help them with their cause. They solicited our help in their efforts to keep the horse facility open. Some park resource sections were trying to close it.

We were then escorted to the office to retrieve Teton, who was surrounded by a ring of tourists, petting and crooning over him. A half-dozen rangers stood on the porch, watching over the offender; they craned their necks to witness the guilty as we approached. The tourists, sensing the tension, stopped petting Teton and parted as if we were being led to the gallows. Jonah stayed close, eyes round, guilty by association. I apologized to the rangers. Then, as I began untying Teton's rope, I noticed a small woman on the backside of him, who, unfazed by the friction, had continued to pet him. She peppered me with questions. Had we ridden the canyon? Where from? Where were we going? The nearby tourists turned their attention to the woman and me as I answered her questions, creating a buffer from the steely stares on the porch. Jonah and I left the rangers' office to clean up horse biscuits and break up camp. I felt like a condemned man turned hero.

Through ignorance, we had broken some rules. We'd turned some of our horses loose to scavenge and left ponies unattended, had not packed enough feed, nor given advance notice that we were coming. But we'll write to the park managers and encourage them to keep the horse facility open, don't want to ruin it for other riders.

Packed up and got away at 2 p.m. Decided to follow the highway to Tusayan so we could access water. Then went southeast towards Mogui Stage Stop. Along the road, Todd Morgan, who helps organize wagon trains in Cove Creek, offered us pasture and water for the night at his camp. The ponies loved the freedom to gambol. We slept on cots in a tent–comfy, cool, nice. Todd checked often on our comforts.

Jonah has saddlesores despite the pantyhose. He drew a visual in the air as to where they were. I offered him the Bag Balm. It helped Sam; it should help him. He's trying hard to learn all about the horses and is doing well. But I had to gently get after him for wrapping Sugar's lead rope around his hand, explaining that he always needed to be able to drop the rope so he wouldn't get dragged. He's a good student.

Have enjoyed the vegetables and fruit. The heat wilts them, but they're still tasty.

Sunday 6 October 1991

Teton has developed sores on his back–hard, marble-like welts under his skin. Luckily, they're behind the saddle, so it doesn't irritate them. Todd and I cleaned the area and examined the bumps. Looked like cattle grubs. I put a saltwater scrub on them–and *how* Teton winced! A little squeeze and the larvae popped out like ripe pimples. Then I applied peroxide and Furacin using one of Todd's wash cloths. The wagon-train camp was surely an oasis of water and friendship. Grateful for people like Todd.

Got away mid-morning. We'd been riding about thirty minutes when I drew from my vast store of knowledge and experience and explained to Jonah that no elk venture out on the flat desert and stay only in the trees. He's traveled the globe but never seen an elk. Not three minutes later, a cow elk lumbered across the road. Chagrined. Then as we rode over a ridge, there stood a spike, a cow, and her calf, grazing out in the open brush. So much for my knowledge! I tried to convince him they were cattle, but he didn't swallow it. Before they saw us, we skirted around them until we got within one hundred and fifty yards. Fat, beautiful beasts.

Rode the wrong road for five miles before we discovered I was reading a misprinted USFS map. While studying the map, I must've seemed confused, because an avid outdoorsman from Phoenix stopped to offer help. He carried water in tubs in his truck and shared it with my ponies, while helping me with map inspection. We set a new course and returned to the right road.

Before dark we met a government mule shoer, Slim Rivers, and his wife, Shelly, on the road by Curley Fletcher's tank. He gave us a good map and invited us to pasture our ponies and stay with him in Flagstaff. There surely are scads of wonderful folks in the world.

Todd Morgan said it was seventy-six miles from his Cove Creek chuck wagon camp to Flagstaff. Whew! Rode until dark and got two miles east of Curley Fletcher's tank, west of Mogui Stage Stop. Couldn't find the flashlight, so we ate army rations and oranges in the dark. Stomach still holding.

Comfy temperatures and good horse grass make for a good night.

Monday 7 October 1991

While sitting propped up in my bag this morning, enjoying the spectacular desert scenery, I spied a bull elk cross the road two hundred yards west. He seemed hell-bent on showing that my vast knowledge is pucky! Spent a leisurely morning listening to birds, relishing the peace and quiet, and letting ponies fill up on sweet grass.

Got away at noon. Jonah is learning a lot about ponies and how to pack them. He's a great help, but is walking sore and bowlegged. I offered him more pantyhose, suggesting he could double up. Surprisingly, he took me up on it.

Rode all day. Watered the horses at Harbison and New Automobile. Passed a cattle outfit, they weren't so friendly or informative. Finally, we made it to Mogui Stage Stop. Passed Kaibab Forest boundary, watered ponies, then at dark, camped two miles southeast of the Lockwood water tank in Lockwood Canyon.

Jonah tied Sugar to a tree. I hobbled the mules and tied the bell on Teton's neck, intending to hobble him after I laid out camp and bedding. The night air was cool. Coyotes yapped as we ate army MREs. I soon discovered we'd run out of drinking water; I'm so upset with myself for allowing it to happen. Made do with pear juice. Tired, flopped into bed.

Around midnight, I jerked awake to what sounded like a gunshot. Realizing it was just a car backfiring, I rolled over and closed my eyes. It was so quiet. Too quiet, actually. The cowbell was gone. I'd forgotten to hobble Teton! Greenhorn! I rolled from my bag and dressed as I ran. Sugar strained at her rope, her head turned in the direction, I assumed, the ponies had gone. I untied Sugar, then remembered my rib belt. Went back, fumbled around in the dark, and found it. Carefully, I climbed on Sugar's bare back, let her have her head, and we galloped off into the blackness. Afraid of being left behind, she soon had us within bell range. By the rapid clanking, I could tell Teton was traveling fast.

After about one and a half miles, Sugar and I caught up with the runaways. Teancum and Sam hopped behind Teton, their hobbles doing little good. The herd was on a headlong run, like homing pigeons set free. So much for my being weary. Back at camp, I hobbled front and hind feet of all three animals. Boy, were they miffed!

TUESDAY 8 OCTOBER 1991

Teancum's ankles are raw from the skinny rope hobbles I put on him last night. Damn, I should've wrapped 'em! Ponies, staying pretty much where we'd secured them, didn't get much grazing done.

Packed up ponies and got away early. Needed to get water for Jonah and me. Shouldn't be a problem, but still chastising myself for running dry.

Today we rode by a couple of abandoned hogans and met three Navajo men building a new one. Turns out we'd camped on the west arm of their reservation. They warned us about a herd of wild horses in this neighborhood. We were lucky the mustangs hadn't enfolded our runaways last night and left us afoot, bringing the ride to a screeching halt.

Traveled out of Lockwood Canyon onto the flats, where we found horse water at O'Dell's tank. The cattle surely look tough. No feed! The range is absolutely barren! It's easy to see why the environmentalists are campaigning for the area to be cattle-free by 1993. The mountain forest land, where only wildlife is found, is beautiful. The area is still dry, but grassy and plant-covered with signs of elk.

Finally got through the fences to Tub Ranch. The place was vacant. I assumed they were rounding up cattle. Helped ourselves by pumping drinking water from the cattle tank, then rode south across the flats to Cedar and east over a ridge to camp south of Missouri Bill Hill, north of San Francisco Peak.

We set up camp at dark. There are a lot of cactus around–makes one careful! I learned the hard way all about goat heads, goat beards, or goat something, flat-lying weeds that conceal round seedpods about the size of double aught buckshot. The pod has one-fourth inch thorns that not only stick you bad enough to make you cuss, but also inject a toxin that makes you swollen and sore for a day. Demonic little vipers! First time I've really thought about Father Adam's being told that, due to his transgression, the earth would bring forth thorns and thistles.

Ate the last of our MREs last night, so had to make do tonight with a can of peaches and Ramen. Soft on the stomach, but I still felt a bit queasy. Too tired to light up the Coleman, we just ate the Ramen dry and saved the flavor packet for another time. Ramen's not bad dry; tastes sorta like a cracker. Just requires a lot of water afterwards, so it's a good thing we had some. Water or any liquid is not to be wasted. We've learned we need to guard it jealously.

The ponies are tired. Maybe last night's mad dash did 'em in.

JONAH'S JOURNAL ENTRY, OCT. 8, 1991

There are too many spiders, centipedes, crickets, and lizards in Arizona. I step very carefully here–seems like hairy-legged, round-bodied tarantulas are everywhere.

We had black beans and corn for breakfast. I opened the can of corn and, before dumping it into the Dutch oven, drained the water onto the ground. I heard Chuck clear his throat as the dirt soaked it up. The sound was enough. I should have remembered Boy Scouts 101–drink all liquid. I hope his patience holds.

The pantyhose Chuck gave me help a little. But I think my butt bones have punctured my skin, despite my wearing two pair of hose. In an effort to redistribute my weight to avoid worsening the sores, I continually change positions in the saddle.

WEDNESDAY 9 OCTOBER 1991

We're almost out of groceries, so we got up early and broke camp by 8 a.m. We'll stock up when we get to Flagstaff.

The beautiful ride to the San Francisco Mountains lifted my spirits. I sang "Amazing Grace" and taught Jonah the words. We talked about the song, "The Little Drummer Boy," the lad who gave the best he had at Jesus' birth. It makes me wonder if I'm offering *my* best. Then either whistled or sang almost every other song I could think of.

Got confused with the map and rode a two-mile circle inside a fence before I found the correct route. Our happy spirits crashed! We did find precious water, though, so there was a silver lining. Decided I'd better shelve the music man and pay more attention to where we were going. From then on, I was continually checking my map, the sun, and my watch to help orient and guide us.

Riding west of the San Francisco peaks was jaw-dropping—some of the prettiest country on earth. Dodged traffic as we rode along the dirt road and admired the yellow leaves set against the green pines. Seemed everyone was out for one last glimpse of fall. The giant quaking aspens were dropping golden leaves. The late sun and horizon mist cast everything in the same golden hue: my hands, horses, plants, rocks… everything. It's easy to see why the Greeks told of Midas. My favorite part of the Midas story isn't the golden touch, but rather his donkey ears. Midas sided against the God Apollo in a music contest, so Apollo gave Midas donkey ears to help him hear better. Wonder if donks wish they had dormouse ears when I sing?

Lo and behold, while we were taking in the leaves, a guy pulled up in his truck and asked, "You the guy from Wyoming?" It was Tony Pittman, an Arizona trail man who I'd wanted to confer with about the GWT organization and the route south. We visited. He gave us a map and reassured us about the trail. Tony and I will meet at Anderson Mesa this weekend.

Before reaching Fort Valley I noticed fresh claw marks on a tree. The height of the scratches indicated one big bear. I became more attentive. Sure enough, I spotted pie-plate-size bear tracks and fresh bear scat at several spots. So I brought back the music man: sang more songs, quoted some poetry, and whistled the same songs again for the hour and a half it took us to get to town. Each new bear marking or dropping made me sing louder. I was croaking like a frog by the time we arrived outside Fort Valley. Vocal cords were shot.

"You sing great," Jonah said as we approached the outskirts of town. "And you sang for so long!"

I cleared my throat to quiet the frog. "I was making sure the bear heard us and was hoping he'd stay away," I said, watching his eyes grow large.

"Oh, I'll join in next time," was all he could say.

By the time we got to Fort Valley I suddenly started feeling sick with a bad headcold. I'll have to pill-it-to-death with my antibiotics. A severe cold, in light of my weakened immune system, could spell trouble.

Rode by some homeless folks; I gave my last sack of jerky to the "starving" (at least they said they were starving). Boarded horses with a little daylight left and found a KOA and restaurant still open. The chicken and pasta was good; the shower was better.

Forgot to take my chemo pill this morning; too worried

about getting out of the canyon. So took it this evening. Done with chemo for another month.

By bedtime, my head felt ready to pop. Jonah crawled into his sleeping bag; I crawled into mine. Beads of sweat began to form on my forehead. My body shook and teeth chattered as I alternated between hot and cold, cold and hot. I shut my eyes, trying to ignore the fine layer of dust that hung in the air. After a coughing-sneezing fit, I crawled from my bag to find my rib belt and strap it on to protect my ribs.

Again I lay down. My eyes watered and my nose dripped. I used tissue after tissue and wondered how my sinuses could feel so pressured and plugged, yet drip incessantly? Miserable!

I tried to stifle my coughs and blow my nose quietly so as not to bother Jonah. He lay quiet for some time before I heard gentle snores. I finally ended up on my back, staring into the dark sky, the pressure in my head building.

Will try to sleep. Plan to make Flagstaff tomorrow.

Nope. Couldn't sleep, what with my pounding noggin threatening to explode. The pressure is worse lying down and the dust aggravates my headcold. So I think I'll write some more.

I had an interesting conversation with Jonah tonight while setting up camp. He's very worried about my cold and cough turning into pneumonia. He urged me to see a doctor. I tried to reassure him by taking another antibiotic pill. "This is what he gave me," I said, swallowing, hoping the pill would soon make a difference.

"Should we hole up here until you feel better?" His brow wrinkled as he looked me in the eye, hair tucked behind each ear.

"No, let's keep riding. We'll give the pills a few days to kick in." I tried not to cough, but couldn't hold it in. My arms hugged my rib belt as the coughing fit shook my body.

"What if you just get sicker? What if we're out in the

middle of nowhere and you need a doctor or a hospital?"
Camp set-up complete, he fidgeted, flexing his hands as he
looked at me across the picnic table.

"I'll be alright. The medicine's going to work." My finger-
tips massaged at my pulsing temples.

His voice was quiet. "What if it doesn't? What will I do if
something happens to you?"

"If I die?"

"Yes," he whispered, wiping the corners of his eyes with
the back of his hands. He sat hunched, head down, his hair
partially covering his face. "What will I do?"

"Jonah, I'd be on this ride even if you weren't here. If I
were alone and something happened, I'd be at the mercy of
the Lord and His elements. My family and I, with excep-
tions, accepted this. Everyone understands the risks. One risk
is that I might not return from the mountains. I'm not saying
it would be easy, but just leave me."

With unaccustomed seriousness his head snapped up,
eyes flashing. "Leave you? Ride out and not look back?"

"I'm glad for your company, but you're not obligated."

"Obligated?" His eyes narrowed. "Obligated? You're trying to help me by taking me on this ride. *I'd* certainly try to
help you. No, I'll not leave you. I *care* about you and want to
do right not only by you, but also by your family. Can you
imagine how guilty I'd feel if I left your body in the mountains? Regardless of everyone's understanding." His open,
empty palms mirrored his frustration as they punched in the
air to emphasize each word.

I thought I was too sick to do battle, but apparently not.
"You're not responsible for me," I said defensively, feeling
backed into a corner. "If my family can accept the risks, so
can you."

I realized my error as soon as the words left my mouth.
He sat there in stunned silence. In an attempt not to

inconvenience or burden, I'd allowed my pride to offend and hurt him. "I'm sorry," I said, exhaling.

It was then I remembered the rest of his words–words of care for me and my family, of doing the right thing, and his feelings of sorrow. Gratitude swept over me. The sick feeling in my heart dwarfed my physical illness. I'd hurt a friend. "I didn't mean to hurt your feelings. I'm sorry. I'm sure I'd feel the same way." Tears ran down my cheeks, this time from my heart, not the headcold. He, too, melted–a puddle of tears. We gripped hands across the tabletop and leaned close. He was worried about losing a friend, I was worried about hurting one.

After drying our tears, we talked openly and honestly about what he might do if I should become incapacitated. Leaving my body until he could return with help was scratched due to hot sun, wild animals, and guilt. Burial wasn't considered either, due to hardship of digging, marking the spot, then trying to find it again. The only option that pacified Jonah was to find a way to bring my body out. We agreed he could do anything he put his heart and mind to, and that this task, if he felt he had to do it, was not impossible. I showed him some knots he'd find useful. I suggested he tie my body to Teancum, or between the pack boxes on Sam. This solution helped calm his anxiety.

After re-reading the preceding few paragraphs, I realize how heartless and insensitive I've been to Jonah. Friends and family literally pulled me back from despair when I learned I had cancer. I need to remember I'm not alone. We move forward by helping each other. I'm proud of him for thinking ahead and trying to be prepared. I'm truly blessed to be on the receiving end of such a friendship. I'll try to convey that to him tomorrow.

Jonah's Journal Entry, Oct. 9, 1991

Tonight Chuck taught me some knots I hope to never have to use. I feel better, but will ride with a continual prayer in my heart. Our traumatic conversation, about his possible death in the mountains, has turned my heart to my loved ones—I realize its not just about me.

I'm laying in my bag, worrying about my friend. He's extremely sick. He looks so frail, even in his jacket wrapped in several blankets. He wants to keep riding, though. So we will.

Earlier this evening I took my first shower in eight days! Goose bumps rose on my skin as the warm water ran over it and rinsed through my dirty, matted hair. The brown water left a layer of dirt in the corners of the shower.

I ached all over, but finally my muscles relaxed. I gradually turned up the water temperature until I could just barely stand the heat. Steam turned the bathroom into a sauna. I had to scrub hard to remove all the dead skin. The shampoo refused to lather as I massaged my oily scalp. More shampoo was needed.

After forty minutes, I turned off the water. Drying my backside, I noticed red streaks on the towel. Wiping the steam film from the floor-length mirror, I stood with my back to it and looked over my shoulder to check my saddlesores. They had opened and were bleeding. I gently patted them dry and thought, "Where's the Bag Balm?"

Thursday 10 October 1991

I feel like crap! Suffered fever and chills through the night and woke with a sore throat from drainage. Shortly after breakfast, my stomach began swirling. Salivary glands started producing extra, and I lost breakfast. I assume it's residual chemo. Took more antibiotics, and kept riding. Had a hard time distinguishing my actual heartbeat from the throbbing I felt in my head and stomach. I pulsed everywhere. Teancum's rocking gait added another movement of discomfort. Jonah was patient with my frequent upset-stomach stops. I sense a change in him since our talk last night–more introspection.

On the outskirts of Flagstaff, I called Slim Rivers, the government mule shoer I'd met on the road west of Moqui. He and his wife, Shelly, had invited us to their home when we got to Flagstaff. But it's on the opposite side of town, too far away. So they drove over to visit with us and brought supplies to shoe Sam. Glad I hired him to do the job, because just the thought of bending over brought added pressure to my head and sour stomach.

Sam had thrown a shoe and his other three were thin as onion skin. Slim used foot ropes to tie Sam's hinds to the ground. He also used an iron bosal (hackamore) with a jerk rope. When Sam started fighting, I offered to pay Slim more for the job. But he loosened the ropes and stepped away. "I can't shoe him. I haven't the equipment to do it safely and can't take a chance on getting hurt." He continued, "What Sam needs is a week or two where you pick up each foot, quietly tap on the hoof, stroke and pat him to reassure him, then repeat the process."

I agreed. But what do we do *now*? Made some quick calls to find another farrier. Found one willing to come right away. He came with plenty of rope, ready to tie Sam in knots.

Slim and Shelly returned to Flagstaff, where they called the newspaper and told them of our ride. Soon a guy and gal came out to interview me. They kept it short, after I sneezed and coughed on 'em.

After the shoeing and interview, the ponies found a place along the road filled with green, leafy, succulent alfalfa. They went wild! They grazed for about thirty minutes within ten feet of whizzing cars. An old rancher stopped to visit and share some cookies and grapes with us.

The trail passes right through the center of Flagstaff. Can you imagine? What were the "feasability people" thinking? I asked a policeman where we could camp. "You didn't hear it from me," he replied. "But try the city park. Plenty of room there."

We packed up, watered the animals, and rode along the highway, heading for Flagstaff City Park, where we unloaded. *Thought* we'd picked a quiet, out-of-the-way spot, but after we set up camp, we realized we hadn't. Apparently we were camped on a well-used shortcut. Stayed put, though, and hunkered down. Jonah hoofed it over to a nearby grocery store to shop and drop our letters in a mailbox.

I'm lying in bed, listening to the rich variety of sounds. The trains chug and whistle constantly. I wonder if they'll carry on through the night.

Felt lousy today. Sore stomach muscles from coughing, but I'm glad it wasn't my ribs. There's always something to be grateful for. Only rode ten miles, but it was a long day.

Jonah's Journal Entry, Oct.10, 1991

Today I went grocery shopping. As I stepped into the store, I was overwhelmed by the food choices: bananas, fresh fish, salad bar, and gallons of orange juice. I grabbed two cans of pie filling, two cans of peaches and some yellow cake mixes for cobblers. As I filled my cart, I realized I was selecting the same kinds of food we'd been eating all along: pancake mix, oatmeal, jerky, dried fruit, nuts, canned meat, canned fruit, noodles, potatoes, and onions. So I picked up some M&M trail mix and a box of six deli-muffins. Shopping is hard when limited by weight, short cooking time and no refrigeration. Our best, most well-rounded meals were the MREs.

Chuck sized up my choice of groceries. Lifting the pie filling, he said, "Good choice, Jonah. Hopefully dessert will help keep my pants up." He smiled weakly to show his approval, even though I knew no food looked good to him. We've stopped several times so he could empty his stomach behind a bush. I can't believe he keeps going. He's tough as nails, persistent as a salesman, and as focused on his goal as the squirrels who tried to steal our food in the Grand Canyon.

"Look what else I got. These will help with your pants, too." I pointed to the muffins. "We'll eat them when you feel better." His pants hang lose and are gathered at the waist with a rope. He and Teton are a skinny pair. His exaggerated nod was for my benefit. I'm worried.

Though Chuck is sick, he puts on a happy-to-talk-to-you face. We've had people who stopped to chat, then left feeling important and cheered up, never knowing he was ill. When I asked him how he did it, he answered, "Focusing on only one aspect of the journey is likely to warp our value judgement and sour our day's evaluation. There's more to life than feeling sick. I don't want to miss the chance to meet good people. They lift me up."

Friday 11 October 1991

Hallelujah! Antibiotics kicked in. Starting to feel better. Still coughing, and have a burning sore throat, but believe my cold is on its way out.

Nice park in Flagstaff, despite the all-night trains. Lotsa room, ponderosa, water, playing fields–and joggers, many of whom stopped to visit with us. (So much for out-of-the-way.) Indian kids cut through the park on their way to school. All morning a steady stream of students traipsed up to our camp's edge, then skirted around us. Most were reserved, but two gals stopped to chat and admire our animals. They missed their own horses. Three boys also lagged behind, looking for an excuse to play hooky from school. The adventurer in me wanted them to stay and hear about our ride; the school teacher in me wanted to hurry them on their way. In the end, they heard a condensed version of the ride and raced off to school, late.

We packed Sam with the canned goods, Teton with the dry items to lighten his load. His steady downward spiral worries me.

Riding through the west suburbs of town was nice. Got across the railroad tracks onto Highway 66, then rode south to Walmart and crossed under Interstate 40. Took Lake Mary Road and traveled the roadside until we found a trail going east. It actually veered too far east, so we circled back to the road.

Even roadriding offers rich variety of sights and sounds. A light blue pickup pulled over and a man handed me the newspaper article about my ride. Well written, despite the short interview and flying germs.

I felt Teancum slow his stride as we approached what looked like a walking trash pile. Clorox bottles, heavy and full, swung from multiple strings tied to a worn Army backpack. Camp paraphernalia hung from other strings; two skinny legs propelled the tall pile forward; a clanking mess kit dangled from the bottom of the pack. As we approached the "pile," Teancum tensed, his eyes locked on the odd, walking contraption. I prodded him forward as I called ahead, "Hullo up there." A man in a floppy hat with a red bandana tied to the back of the hat brim, stopped and turned to reveal a gap-toothed smile. He waved and waited for us to catch up.

The quieted mess kit twirled slowly. Teancum stepped gingerly as I cooed to urge him forward, whereupon the man opened his arms as if Teancum were a long lost friend. "Oh, how beautiful," he gushed when Teancum reached his finger-tips, stopped, and stood stiff with flared nostrils. He quivered as the fingers reached out to stroke his velvet nose. The man explained that he was walking from the Flagstaff city water tank back to his camp in the woods. He lived in Los Angeles in the winter and Flagstaff in the summer. Settling in for a long visit, he removed his backpack. I listened, only adding an occasional "Really" or "Oh," as the fellow made his way around me to gently pat Teancum up and down. Teton and Sam found grass along the roadside, and Sugar, with Jonah astride, had wandered off to graze.

"Would you like a bite?" the man asked, pulling a half-eaten apple from his pocket. "I found it and it's still good."

"No, but thank you," I replied. I noticed the twinkle leave his eye and his smile droop. "On second thought, I'm kinda hungry," I said quickly, which restored his grin. As I munched on what remained of the apple, the street man rummaged in his backpack, carefully retrieved a ball of newspaper and gently unrolled it. Inside lay a dead pine squirrel. "How about some squirrel?" he asked hopefully. The road-kill was partially flattened like a tortilla, but other parts seemed edible. "I've got more at camp." He grinned again, holding it up for me to see. Declining, I thanked him and explained that Jonah and I needed to get going.

Before we shoved off, the smiling man handed each of us a tiny rolled-up strip of paper. Mine read, "Jesus is Lord." Jonah's, "Love God. Pray always." He explained that every day he took these types of rolled-up messages to town and left them in public places, such as a phone booth or the park. It was his way to spread his love of the Lord. To keep it safe, I put the paper in my shirt pocket, right by Hunter's kiss. After reading his message several times, Jonah put his message in his pocket. What a good, kind man, willing to share all he had. How rich our lives can be when we stop to listen and recognize the goodness of others.

At dark we camped near the road along Upper Lake Mary.

I cooked spaghetti for supper, while Jonah wrote a letter to his family. Glad to have him along. He's becoming proficient with horses, camping, and packing. And he's beginning to be at peace with himself. We're hoping Ty still feels up to joining us on the 19th.

Some folks stopped by our camp. They make a living buying at garage sales and then re-selling the items at flea markets. Interesting, friendly people. They offered to mail Jonah's letter.

Jonah spent some time reflecting, wandering amongst the horses as they grazed. By the time he got back, my stomach felt good and I was ready to devour the muffins. Waited for him with the muffin box on my lap. Indeed, the antibiotics seem to be doing their job, and my headcold is down to a mere drippy nose. Why does it take being sick to appreciate being well? Jonah walked over, sat beside me, and smiled. We silently devoured muffin after muffin until the box was empty. Jonah licked his fingers. I wiped the crumbs from my mouth and sighed.

Chapter 15

Saturday 12 October 1991

Ate our leftover spaghetti for breakfast. It's not so good the next day.

We left the roadside camp by Lake Mary and got back up on the trail heading for Pine Camp at Lake Ashurst. Hit Forest Service Road 82. Planned to meet Tony Pittman to discuss his suggested southern-trail routes. Passed some beautiful pronghorn antelope along the way.

Horses are not allowed in Pine Campground, so we camped nearby on a rocky hillside. There was a stream, but no flat area to sleep, so we collected flat rocks, laid them side by side on the ground, and spread the horse blankets and sleeping bags on top. Not the best for sleeping, but a good spot for horses.

After setting up camp we walked to the lake and waited for Tony. It's hard to believe there are so many man-made lakes atop these hills. Birds everywhere, good fishing, too. I had time to write a letter to Ress and sent her the Flagstaff newspaper article. Asked her to copy it and forward it to Sally. I'll have Tony mail my letter.

Tony arrived along with James Durrant, a USFS Recreation Officer. In 1985, James hiked all the proposed Arizona trail routes which might be included in the GWT, and knew each and every section. He brought six maps and drew routes like crazy. So now I'm mapped all the way to Patagonia, or Coronado. Nice! I'd asked Tony to bring grain for the ponies. He did.

On my way home in November, James, Tony and I plan to meet up in Flagstaff to review my Arizona ride experience.

Tony is adamant that the Arizona Trail *not* be related to the GWT in any way, shape, or form, him being against any motor vehicle traveling on the Arizona Trail.

Jonah and I walked the camp perimeter in search of a ride to church tomorrow. No go. Got back to camp, climbed in bed, and listened to an elk bugle from across the lake. It must've been a spike, surely warbled and trilled.

JONAH'S JOURNAL ENTRY, OCT. 12, 1991

Spam for dinner with canned sweet potatoes and the juice for dessert. Chuck requested these food items when I went shopping. No wonder I'm getting skinny.

SUNDAY 13 OCTOBER 1991

Got up early; watered horses. On the way back, a man offered us a ride to town. We quickly tied the horses and just left stuff scattered about, as the folks were late for work and were leaving right then. For fifteen miles we rode sitting in the back of the pickup, with the wind whipping us.

A beautiful church building. Got there early enough to clean up in the restroom. We sang "How Great Thou Art" in Sunday School. Knew all the words. Wonderful! Jonah and I sat by Edward Frey, who invited us to dinner. His sweet wife, Alice, insisted that we come—and I didn't need any prodding. Got to call Sally and Fritz. The Freys know someone who goes to the same oncologist that I do. After a delish dinner and warm visiting, Edward hauled us back to camp.

Upon our return, we discovered that some stray cattle had eaten all but about ten pounds of our grain. They'd also made themselves at home within the perimeter of our camp, leaving dozens of "pies" for us to enjoy. Grateful they missed decorating our sleeping bags.

We saddled up and got away midafternoon. Lost the trail a mile out and rambled through fields of rocks. It was terrible on the horses' feet and legs. Finally got on what we thought was Forest Service Road 82. Then, camped in a meadow just inside a fence, a few miles from the road. We loose-hobbled all four ponies so they could forage but not roam too far. Fed the last of the grain to the horses. Surely hope they don't lose too much flesh. Blasted cattle!

MONDAY 14 OCTOBER 1991

Wonderful camp. The horses grazed all night and stayed close. Plenty of water, and the elk bugled off and on all night. Heavenly.

Got away by nine. Nice riding. Then we lost the trail and made a seven-mile elbow. Yuck! While circling, we jumped fifteen cows, several calves, and one bull elk. Came across two electric fences, knee high. I wondered if these were game management tools. We finally bushwhacked to Kinnikinnick Lake and got straightened out again. Then rode Forest Service Road 82 southeast past Jay Cox Mountain into Soldier Annex Lake and camped there. Several fishing parties looked like they'd been at the lake quite a while because they had clothes lines hung and chairs and tables set out under awnings. Plenty of mobile campers, too.

Even after circling for those seven extra miles, we made eighteen to twenty miles today. Surely peaceful out on the mesa; makes it easy to reflect. The environment, though harsh, is in balance, and what we feel in it is of our own making, not the environment's doing. No matter our circumstances, we can choose to be happy and filled with hope, or to be bitter and angry. Which do I choose? Can I mature and learn to apply the better choice in my every day?

On Wednesday we should cross Mogollon Rim, then head southwest to the town of Pine. A little anxious about crossing Mogollon, which should be a mini deja vu of the Grand Canyon. (After that last paragraph, I'd better *choose* courage!)

TUESDAY 15 OCTOBER 1991

This morning the lake edge was beautiful but chilly. Got on our way early. Jonah packed Sam by himself. He's getting it.

Road-riding most of the day. Met a USFS man who gave us good directions to Blue Ridge, Rock Crossing, and down over the Rim. We then missed the trail at Blue Ridge and had to bushwhack; likewise at Rock Crossing. Either the USFS man wasn't so good with directions or we were in la-la land. I'm sure the latter. We finally found our way by circling.

Coming around one bend, there parked on the trail, stood a bull elk. The ponies didn't falter. They're ho-humming wild-life now—no more tense, ready-to-run muscles. Cool moist air above the Blue Ridge Reservoir. Had to bushwhack to Road 123, then rode through an idyllic Ponderosa forest. Threw off at dark when we found the "plunge" off Mogollon Rim into Clear Creek.

Courage, man, courage! A warm evening—or is it just me, due to my rising blood pressure?

WEDNESDAY 16 OCTOBER 1991

This is General Crook country. Quite the history. Picked up a book about the General from Delores Brown when I stopped in Kanab, Utah. Will dig in.

After breakfast, I swallowed hard and went looking for Tunnel Trail, an old, abandoned railroad track cut into the cliff ledge. Very steep, but the donks took to it like a cow to cud. Could have split my shirt seams.

Back on the trail, we stopped about halfway down from Mogollon Rim, at a spring running along the bottom of a wash. Lunched, soaked feet, and washed socks. Now our socks are lighter gray and not so stiff. Before, you'd take them off and they'd looked like they had feet still in them. Turns out the trail wasn't steep the entire way, just in spots, and it was a short ride. Those steep spots were scary, but I needn't have worked myself into a tizzy. Now that it's over, I'm sounding courageous and wise; looking back is always easier.

Got down onto Highway 31 and rode west for Pine. Pushed hard. *No* feed anywhere after we descended the Rim. Is this indicative of the trail farther south?

Rode, rode, rode. At last, one and a half hours into the moonlight, we got to Pine. Jonah stayed with the animals while I knocked on doors to find where I could board them. Some doors only opened a crack, quite skeptical. Don't blame 'em, as I look a might scrappy.

Finally gave up asking for a place for animals and started to ask where the local chapel of The Church of Jesus Christ of Latter-day Saints (LDS) was. After riding through scattered timber, we finally got to the church building just as people were leaving. I met Joe Lawrence from Jackson, Wyoming, who was excited to see folks from home. He's visiting Pine but works construction in Roosevelt, Arizona. He encouraged me to look him up there when I passed through. Also met Don and Mella Smith, who run Strawberry Mountain Stables in Strawberry, north of Pine. So we rode four more miles up the highway to where the ponies finally got hay and water.

Sleeping out by the stables; dead tired.

Jonah's Journal Entry, Oct. 17, 1991

Yesterday we rode for fifteen hours. My buns were hamburger, almost literally. We started out at 8 a.m. and crawled off our animals about 11 p.m.

After we stabled our horses last night, I walked straight to my sleeping bag. It could've been crawling with snakes and I wouldn't have noticed. I crawled in and flattened my spine against the ground. My vertebrae felt like a jack-hammer had been at them. Tired to the point of hallucination, I lay immobile, body numb, backside raw, spine compressed, waiting for sleep's relief.

Off in the distance I'd heard the lid of a sardine can being rolled back. All was fading... "Jonah, here's your dinner, sardines." My mind and lips couldn't coordinate a reply. "Jonah?"

At that point, I couldn't have moved my body even if I'd wanted to. Sardines were hardly a reason to try. Didn't remember anything after that. I feel better this morning.

Thursday 17 October 1991

Stable sounds woke us early. I followed Mella while she fed her animal borders. We ended up by her Lipizzaners. The famous Lipizzaners of Vienna, Austria, are born black and get lighter each year. Usually around seven years old they're turned completely white. Mella's Lipizzaners were all pure white. The breed owes its salvation to General George S. Patton. During WWII the breeding stock was seized by the Nazis, then fell to the Soviets. Fearing the horses would be used for food, captured German officers asked the Americans to help save the breed. Patton went behind Soviet lines and rescued the noble animals. I've seen them perform and have marveled at the dancing white stallions and their fancy air jumps. A handsome breed!

Mella charged twenty-five bucks to keep our four horses for two days. Jonah and I will hitchhike to Eager, Arizona, about a two-hour drive. I want to see my daughter, Catherine, and Teton badly needs a rest.

We caught a ride with Mella to Payson and had breakfast at the local diner's buffet. Wowie! A smorgasbord of *real* food! I believe Jonah and I partook in some of everything. With bowed back I slowly walked to the cash register, pulled out my checkbook, and looked around for a pen.

The woman behind the counter stopped me. "I need to check with my manager to see if we accept checks," she said, disappearing through the swinging doors behind her. She was gone longer than seemed necessary, but finally came back with the manager in tow. He looked like we felt: shirt buttons stretched tight, ready to burst.

"May I help you?" he asked, looking us up and down. I explained that we had no cash and needed to write a check. He tried to couch his reply with words of "sorry" and "policy," but we heard loud and clear: "Hell no! *You* can't write a check!" They held Jonah hostage while I slunk off to the bank and returned with cash. My last look at Jonah before leaving showed him wearing an "I got this" grin. I hoped it wasn't a flashback of jail time. We must look a terrible sight. Thought they wouldn't get their money, I guess. Hmmph.

After mailing three letters at the Post Office, we returned to the road to hitchhike to Eager. It was tough. Got a ride for about fifteen miles, then sat on the road for hours–nothing! Said a silent prayer. Then about half past one a guy drove by, stopped, backed up, stuck his head out the window, smiled, and said, "Need a ride? I'm going to Eager." Exactly where we wanted to go!

Davey Burns, from southern Arizona, was headed for

Montrose, Colorado, to work as an outfitter in a hunting camp. He builds wildlife trick water tanks. Such tanks surround a spring, the water piped into troughs a hundred feet or more away, thus keeping wildlife out of the spring. Davey had planned to go through Flagstaff, but decided on the spur of the moment to take the Payson/Eager route. How's that for prayer being answered!

Davey dropped us off in Springerville, about a mile from Eager. We started to walk the mile when suddenly we heard from behind, "Hi, Dad!" Catherine jumped from the car and swallowed me in an embrace. My leaky faucet opened. She had come looking for us. Wonderful to see her! She'd arranged supper for us at Glen Sherman's. Jonah and I will stay with them. Had a delish supper of very hot tamales and wonderful salsa. Two great meals in one day–almost overwhelming.

The hot shower was therapeutic. Laundered clothes and called home. Sally wasn't in, so I dialed up Anita and the kids. She told me Leland and his search-and-rescue team were out looking for a crashed plane around Dubois, Wyoming. My heart hurts for the family of the lost pilot. Also phoned Ty McCowin. He'll meet us in two days at Strawberry to ride with us. Anxious to see him!

Friday 18 October 1991

Up early. Our host, Glen, invited us to go cowboying with him. Catherine had meetings all day, so we accepted.

Perfect fall weather to work with horses and cattle. We caught the horses, gave each a nose bag with grain, then chased down the cattle so we could doctor 'em. Jonah and I pig-tailed in the pickup with supplies, water, and lunch. Met up with Seth Sherman, Glen's brother, a retired teacher of thirty years, and his friend, Abe. Abe and Seth are both divorced and single, but neither has given up on finding a good woman.

After the roundup, we all sat down around a crackling fire for a meal. Abe tugged at his thin jowls. "Nah, I'm too old and wrinkly," he muttered.

"We're all old," chuckled Seth. "Marriage quality at our age rests on good cookin', sense of humor, and a good heart; I've got all three. So why haven't I been snatched up?"

The banter went back and forth as others joined in on the matchmaking. It was fun to hear old men turn into high school freshmen again, talking about girls and fixing one another up. "Old" is a tired, worn-out heart, not an age. The cliche "young at heart" fits here. Enjoying the outdoors, while snarfing down tinfoil dinners with good company, took me back to the hunting camps in Wyoming. Some sweet memories.

Wrote letters to friends and family, then had dinner with Catherine at Elk Land. Tried a burrito and another tamale. Oh, I must learn how to make tamales when I get home.

Jonah and I returned to Sherman's. A friend of Catherine's will transport us back to Strawberry early tomorrow. My farewell to Catherine was like my other ones, tearful and heart-melting. There's no substitute for family.

Chapter 16

Saturday 19 October 1991

We jumped into the truck with Mr. Sakmann, a plump, bearded Englishman, and enjoyed the early-morning ride back to our ponies. His free spirit and humor kept us chuckling, and made the drive-time fly. Surely appreciate helpful people.

There was time to lounge while we waited for Ty, so I helped Mella around the stables, then shod Sam's front hooves. The first shoe was a long fight, even though I tied him in a ball. The two-day rest had given him extra energy. But by the second foot he was exhausted and stood like a flamingo with the leg I needed to work on nicely tucked up

Teton's demeanor was improved. His head was up and he expressed interest when we entered the stables. Mella said he'd been eating nonstop. Was I glad to hear that! Surely hope a two-day vacation is enough to start gaining back his lost weight.

I'd just finished oiling a packsaddle breeching when a smiling Ty pulled up in the late afternoon. He looked good. I went to shake his hand, but wrapped my arms around him instead. Couldn't hug him tight, but I could hug him long. "Chuck," was all he could say. I could tell by the catch in his voice that his smile had faded. My vision blurred; I choked out, "Ty." How precious to have him here.

We unloaded his beautifully-matched, sleek black Tennessee Walkers–both geldings, named Bow and Arrow. He shared news from home; I shared news from the trail and expressed gratitude for the plastic brace he'd made for me. It had bolstered both my confidence and my comfort, and made it possible for me to ride. Ty has since given up his medical practice to spend time with loved ones. I hope he gets to do all he wants to do.

After Bow and Arrow joined my ponies in the boarding stall, Jonah, Ty, and I went to a cafe for BBQ ribs. The last few days of good food is spoiling us. I won't relish my sardines quite as much now.

After talking with Don and Mella, I'm a little worried about the trail south. They said it was rugged and may be dry. We talked of going by E Verde River, but still need to check the trails for the GWT. At last, we decided to chance the E Verde River route.

Ty will ride with us as far as Roosevelt Dam; then, he'll head home. We hope to make it by Friday. Broke Ty in right away as we flopped down for one more night sleeping by the stables.

SUNDAY 20 OCTOBER 1991

Up early and went back to the church in Pine where we'd met Mella and Don. Enjoyed lovely music, friendly people, and the sweet Spirit. Joe Lawrence was especially friendly offering to help with anything we needed. He'll get Ty's truck and trailer transported to Roosevelt Dam by Thursday.

Snacked for lunch as we hurried to pack up. Got away a little after three, easily finding the trail out of Strawberry. Then rode two to three miles up onto Hardscrabble Mesa. Ty rode Bow, behind Sugar and Jonah, with Arrow serving as packhorse. About an hour into our ride I noticed Ty had wrapped Arrow's lead rope around the saddlehorn, and cautioned him about the dangers of being tied to a packhorse. Getting caught in the middle of two spooked horses, one could get hurt. A rider always needs to be able to drop the lead rope. Later, I glanced back again and saw that he'd re-tied Arrow's lead rope around his saddlehorn. This time I let him do for himself.

We came to a ground-level cattle tank, its water about three feet deep. Teancum stopped at the edge, his body tight, breath fast and shallow, his ears on guard as if expecting a shark attack.

"Keep the animals at the edge," I called over my shoulder to Jonah and Ty. Each of my horses drank his fill and moved away from the tank. Bow drank, then wandered right into the middle of the cattle tank. Ty must have not heard my caution. Though the water looked shallow and harmless, Bow immediately began to sink in the oozy bottom—a deja vu of Teancum's mud bog battle. Bow lunged instinctively, yanking Arrow with him into the sucking mud. I'd seen that domino effect before. Scared, Arrow threw his head back, tightening his lead rope, which was fastened to Ty's saddle. Ty lost his balance momentarily, but managed to right himself in the saddle and grab for the horn. Suddenly Bow foundered, lost his footing completely, and was swallowed in thick brown water; Ty disappeared with him.

I looked on in horror at what, only seconds before, had been a peaceful scene. Ty, submerged, groped frantically to free his foot from the stirrup. Arrow, still upright, hopped, threatening to trample both Ty and Bow. I jumped from Teancum and scurried over, fumbling for my pocket knife. I knew I had to cut Arrow's lead rope to get him away from Ty, and needed to cut the stirrup off to free Ty's boot. Luckily, only a two-inch strap held stirrup to saddle.

Bow surfaced and scrambled; Ty, gasping for breath, clung tightly to the horn with one hand, and with the other worked frantically on his caught boot. Bow, off-balance due to Arrow's pulling, went under yet again. By the time I'd waded out to Ty, he'd managed to free his boot, but had gone under and surfaced yet again, choking, still vainly trying to untie Arrow's wet, jerked-tight lead rope. The slimy water and

Bow's frantic tugging made it hard to grip the horn.

"Just leave it!" I yelled as I grabbed his arm. We both clambered away from the horses and churning water. Visibly shaken, Ty stood at the edge of the water tank and watched as both animals engaged in a life-and-death tug of war. By fits and bits, Bow and Arrow eventually made their way to dry land, where both stood with heaving sides and low heads.

"I retied the rope. I'm sorry," Ty said quietly, reaching to gather Bow's reins. Thick mud dripped from his hair into his eyes. He fumbled to loosen the knot around the saddlehorn, but gave up, took his knife, and, in disgust, cut the rope.

"It's a lesson to learn. Important thing is, you're safe," I said. I plunked myself down to drain the muddy water from my boots, so grateful we were all safe that I couldn't be upset. Jonah had gathered Teancum, Teton and Sam and led them to me. We discussed staying there to dry out, but grass was sparse. Ty insisted he was alright, so we rode for a half hour until we found horsefeed. By the time we stopped, Ty's lips were turning blue, he was shaking violently, and his speech was beginning to slur–signs of hypothermia. I chastised myself for not keeping a closer eye on him. Jonah and I wrapped him in our coats and I hurried to unpack the ponies to get my sleeping bag and the camp stove set up. I lit the stove and put water, along with a Ramen flavor packet, on the heat, while Jonah used Anita's diaper wipes to clean Ty's face. Then, stripping him to his underwear, he crawled into the sleeping bag. We watched him closely, sensing his apathy, and encouraged him to take more broth, Jonah holding the cup to his lips. I massaged his limbs to encourage circulation, and eventually he began to respond. Stopped shivering; calmed down and his mind perked up. Close call! What would I have done had something happened to him? I understood a little better Jonah and Jube's earlier concern over me.

We were grateful for the warm evening. Jonah and I set up

Ty's tent, a Taj Mahal, and hung his sopping, mud-streaked clothes around camp. After an hour or so on his back, he joined in helping us set up camp. He'd brought only one pair of pants, but luckily he fit into my extra pair. After we were settled, Jonah used more wipes to clean mud from the faces and nostrils of the blacks. Have to admit those wipes are quite handy.

As I lie in my bag and reflect on today, I'm so thankful we're all safe. The night is beautiful, with the moon and stars lighting the heavens. The Lord is closer than we think. My only concern is our dry camp. No water!

MONDAY 21 OCTOBER 1991

This morning I checked the horses' legs and feet; found both of Teancum's front shoes split at the toe. Had only one extra shoe, a worn one; Teancum stood quietly as I tacked it on. I wrapped his other hoof in duct tape as a temporary "boot."

Got underway half past nine. Very rocky, even on the trail off Hardscrabble and along Whiterock Mesa. Ty is fully recovered and doing everything I suggest to exactness. I hope I lead him right.

Sweltering hot today, and no water along the way. After a dry camp last night, my concern is for the animals. I pinched the skin on Teancum's withers; again, it stays too long in a tent shape.

Rode off into E Verde River Canyon and came to Polk Spring. Out in the middle of nowhere, we found an oasis in the desert. Believe it or not, it had a running stream, apple trees with leaves, and shade. Met Maryann Pratt, a ranch owner, who told us the history of her place. An old mining claim founded in 1846, it's now a cattle ranch within the Mazatzal Wilderness. Maryann showed us rose cuttings that had come from England, dating back to the 1700s. She also gave us a bottle of prickly pear jelly. Whooee, nice! Then she filled us with prickly pears–crab-apple size, dark purple, sweet, and seedy. Fun to try something new. Said she knew Tony Pittman and gave me a horseshoe. Will tack it on tonight to replace the duct tape.

The water revived the ponies and the prickly pears revived us. Said our goodbyes and rode up an extremely brushy trail out of Bullfrog Canyon, camping above the first rimrock. Ate fried taters 'n onions and peach cobbler for supper. Mmmmm. After dinner, Jonah and I taught Ty all the words to "Amazing Grace." The man's got some lungs in him; boomed out the chorus.

Another beautiful, clear evening; stars twinkle peacefully. Glad I'm not in the tent castle, as I wouldn't be able to see the sky. I encouraged Ty to join us under the open sky. He did.

Another dry camp. Will finding water be each day's priority from here on out?

Tuesday 22 October 1991

The stars lost their twinkle during the night. This morning, while waiting for the sun to dry out our soggy beds, I thought I'd write a little.

When we crawled into our sleeping bags last night, it looked so clear we could've counted every star and planet. Thought I didn't need to pitch the fly. Only after we were sound asleep did the rainclouds move in and dump on us like a giant faucet alternately being turned on and off. Between showers, we spread the fly over everything. Slept as best we could, though with the fly laying directly on our wet bags it caused us to sweat like pigs in a blanket.

This morning the bags and blankets should dry quickly. Looks sunny and clear (but that's what I thought last night). I'm thinking I'll have to do some fast talking before Ty will sleep under the open sky again. With the way things have gone so far, I'm sure he will filter my suggestions from now on.

It's hard to believe I've been out seventy-eight days now. Despite my worries over advancing cancer, water shortage, tender ribs, bushwhacking, saddlesores, and missing my family, the trip so far has been therapeutic. I'm content, and there's still much joy to be experienced.

Jonah is boiling water for our oatmeal and raisin breakfast. He's been good company–seems happier. He can now pack up camp, saddle up horses and load them like a pro. He enjoys Sugar; smothers her with coos and pats, and gives her carrots and apples.

Ty is checking on his blacks. I'm worried about him. He goes through spurts where leg muscles jerk spontaneously, making it easy to stumble. His hand muscles are weak. Frustration in doing simple things often causes him to give up trying. Glad he's here, though. I hope this ride gives him what it is giving me: a feeling of triumph.

Well, the bags and saddle blankets are dry, so we'll start packing up.

The day turned out just like it started, sunny and clear. Unsure of the trail, we took a couple of short bushwhacks. Found a trail, but it ended about three miles short of where we needed to be. Kept riding 'til we found water at Chillson Spring. What a relief! We were getting desperate. What an irony–soaked last night but still frantic for water. Visited with a hiker who was camped at the spring. He'd been out five days; appeared ragged but serene.

Mazatzal Peak was breathtaking. The spectacular, rugged, high red-rock steeple was banded with white and looked like Indian Ghost Mountain. We hugged the Continental Divide, rode a long time, and looked for water in every direction. Towards dark we found some rainwater pooled in rock pans, but not much grass. Decided to camp nearby, north of

Mazatzal Peak, on a bench that over-looks deep, jagged cliffs. Will scout for horsefeed and water tomorrow. The landscape's beauty won't matter a bit, if we can't find water.

This is our third night camping with little to drink, for us or the horses. The GWT folks need to consider the lack of water on their trails. They might need to reroute.

Exhausted tonight, but still put up the fly, despite the twinkling stars. With a chuckle and shake of his head, Ty shelved my invitation to sleep outside, opting to put up his tent.

Gotta find water, and not in the form of a cloudburst!

WEDNESDAY 23 OCTOBER 1991

This morning we spent a couple of hours pulling prickly pear spines out of Ty's face. He'd stepped out in the night for a little privacy, and stumbled face-first into a prickly pear bush. Ouch! Instead of awaking us, he'd crawled back into bed without a sound and waited for light. By this morning his face was red, tight and swollen. Checked my first aid kit–nothing. We thought about applying duct tape over the spines, then gently peeling it back to remove the barbs, but chose to go with the tweezers folded inside my Swiss Army knife. Ty sat without complaint as I gently extracted the tiny, fine-barbed spines. Due to the puffiness, they were hard to see and stubborn to remove. Soon Jonah took over pulling out spines as his eyesight was better than mine. He frequently pulled whiskers, thinking they were barbs. Ty sat stoic, never made a peep, while occasionally Jonah would step back and draw a picture in the air, or point to his own face to show Ty where he'd pull from next.

Found water today at Thicket Spring; ponies were sponges. It brought me relief. As we rode through a brush-patch at Thicket Spring, Sam's pack snagged a long, spiny-branch. Poor Ty, riding behind Sam, tried to deflect it, but it snapped back and whipped him in the face, leaving a nasty gash across his cheek. By the time we got to a clearing, blood had run down his neck and soaked the front of his collar. Again I opened my saddlebag's first aid kit to see what we could use: bandages, iodine, fish hook and line, scissors, tape, antiseptic towelettes, one rescue blanket, and a stick of gum. The kit's wrapper read, "This kit could save your life." Hmmm, would hate to put it to the test. If there are no fish to catch, gum isn't a very big meal.

Ty held a gauze bandage against his cheek to stop the bleeding; I applied Bag Balm, then taped a clean gauze patch over the wound. His jaw clenched when I pressed the tape against his already puffy skin. No doubt Jonah and I had missed some prickly pear spines, but not a murmur came from Ty. He looked a sight, but didn't complain. With Anita's handy-dandy wipes, Jonah cleaned what remained of the blood trail from Ty's cheek and neck.

While looking for #88 Sheep Creek Trail, we ended up losing the faint path we were on. Everywhere seemed bouldery, brushy and steep. The tall, thorny mesquite-bushes were thick, always reaching out to tear at our clothes and packs. Darkness had overtaken us, but we rode on by moonlight, desperately trying to find a place to camp. Finally we just stopped and threw off in a dry, narrow creek-bed in MacFarlane Canyon. Unrolled our sleeping bags in prospect holes that had been dug out by old-time miners. Worried about the possibility of a flash flood. Rainwater can turn into a raging torrent in no time.

Tied the horses for the night; no feed.

THURSDAY 24 OCTOBER 1991

It sprinkled during the night. Didn't sleep well with the pitter-patter on the tarp.

Escaped our rocky, funnel-like camp spot as early as

possible; didn't even dry out the gear. Too busy packing up camp, we failed even to notice Sam was gone–probably meandered in search of food. While tracking him, purely by accident we stumbled onto the trail we were looking for last night. Thanks, Sam! The trailhead was about a fourth mile from where we'd camped, a full mile farther than the posted sign indicated. In some places, the trail apparently forks into a creek bed and there seems to be no exit. It needs better markings!

Smooth riding on a well-cared-for trail. Met two elderly hikers at an uncertain cutoff. Seeing Ty's condition, they offered their help and first aid kit, a large American Red Cross version.

"It looks worse than it is," Ty smiled, grimacing with the effort, which caused his cheek bandage to rise and force his eye closed. He thanked them, but insisted he needed no more doctoring. Then they struck off on one trail, and we took the other.

It turned out that ours was the right one, but we soon were lost again. Finding ourselves on private property, we came to a fence with a padlocked gate. I climbed off Teancum to see if I could jigger it; no need, as the lock was already open. Fortunate! Rode through the gate and over to the Circle Bar corrals, where a cowboy was clearing the area of debris. He explained that the property had been sold to a developer. Everywhere we looked we saw the sad evidence: No Trespass signs, fences and locks. The cowboy explained how we could get under the highway and up to Sycamore Creek and the main trail leading to Roosevelt, Arizona.

Water today was sparse; only a few small ponds in a creek bed. No feed anywhere. The surrounding countryside seems to supply either water or feed, but not both. Camped on a windy ridge by Sycamore Creek so we could dry out after last night's rain. I pitched the fly in spite of the clear sky.

After dinner, I again removed Ty's bandage. It was an ugly gash, but at least didn't look infected. His face, however, is covered with oozing, pinprick-size pustules from the embedded barbs we'd missed. There wasn't much we could do, but I pulled out my tweezers again and handed them to Jonah, who would point his finger at a spot on Ty's face and raise his eyebrows, whereupon Ty'd respond with a "pluck away!" thumbs up gesture and a clenched jaw. I completed Ty's doctoring by applying a long strip of white tape that, meeting up with the bandage, reached from hairline to hairline across his nose and gave him the look of a pirate with a slipped eye patch.

Sugar is sick this evening. As soon as Jonah let her go, she lay down and didn't scavenge all evening. Arrow is sick, too. Did they eat the same thing? What was it?

There's been *nothing* for the horses to eat. I fed them the last of the grain two days ago. Teton looks awfully rough. I'm having doubts; wondering about cashing out of the trip. With Sugar ill, Teton struggling, little or no water and grass, maybe it's time to go home. I could ride back with Ty.

FRIDAY 25 OCTOBER 1991

This morning Sugar was right where Jonah had left her last night. But Arrow is feeling better and was out scavenging with the other ponies. Today, Teton plodded and shuffled; Sugar jerked and jolted. Hmmm. Her stiff, halting step seems to be caused by sore feet and legs.

Good riding. Rough trail but easy to follow. The cowboy's directions were excellent. Looking out on Roosevelt Lake from the Continental Divide showed we could ride cross-country to get to the dam quicker, but we stayed on the trail road. Saw two of Davey Burns's trick tanks. Efficient systems, but these were not maintained; ramshackled, with no water. So we watered at Pigeon Spring. What a relief, for us and the ponies!

Considered my two alternatives all day. Go or stay? Stay the course and finish the ride, or prematurely end my dream?

Camped right in the middle of the trail at the trailhead at Lone Pine Pass, north of Four Peaks. Peaceful night. Pitched the fly for shelter from wind.

Every evening we try to think what might be needed to minimize our discomfort during the night. If it looks like rain, the fly goes up. If it looks like horses may take off, we tie instead of hobble them. If we're camping on a ridge and are subject to wind, we build a windbreak with the Ralide boxes. Right now, we're preparing for scorpions. Nocturnal, the scorpion hunts and feeds while we sleep, so our preparation includes closing anything that's open.

Last night I slowly and methodically removed my comfy, custom-made boots and made a brave display of leaving them standing Twin Towers tall at the foot of my bed. Tried to show that I wasn't overly concerned, and that Jonah needn't be either. "You know, Jonah, if you get stung, you'll only have a little pain, numbness, and swelling. Right? The scorpions that kill humans live in North Africa."

This morning, though, I saw that Ty shook and clapped together his boots upside down before putting them on. Indeed, a scorpion popped out and scurried away. I climbed from my bag and picked up my proud boots, still standing at attention at the end of my bag, subtly turned them upside down and gently gave them a shake–then shook them a bit more vigorously, just to make sure. Out of the corner of my eye I noticed Jonah sitting on his bag, grinning like the Cheshire Cat.

Saturday 26 October 1991

Ty's blacks got loose twice last night, due to slippery halter rope made from military surplus nylon. The first time, about midnight, a car scared 'em back and Ty retied them.

We were all asleep the next time they escaped. Ty woke to check on them and found they'd jumped ship. Thinking the moonlight would be enough, he went out looking for them without a flashlight. I woke and found him gone. Wished he'd awakened us so we could've helped! I worried and fumed that he might not make it back; he did, but without his blacks. He worried and fussed all night, so none of us got much sleep. At daylight he and I saddled both mules and went in pursuit. Lo' and behold, a mile up the road and a quarter mile down by a spring, there they were. Couldn't be upset with them. Water is as scarce as ducks' teeth.

Checked Ty's face, which looks a bit better. The pustules have opened, leaving a red rash.

Sure that by midafternoon we'd arrive at the dam and a store, we ate the last of our canned goods this morning. I'm anxious to replace the horse grain. Don't like them going without.

Nice trail east of Four Peaks–high, narrow, scenic, it seemed like a miniature Grand Canyon. Then we rode onto an uncleaned trail with thickets. Thorns of five different kinds. Saw our first cholla and saguaro. The saguaro is a beast! Seems like all plants in Arizona are prickly. Lost the trail three times and had to bushwhack up a steep slope out of a wash.

Ran out of drinking water. I'm disgusted with myself that I hadn't budgeted better. My tongue feels stiff as a chicken's. I now empathize with the ponies.

Pushing, we rode on in the dark, trying to make the highway. Sugar kept pace, but is in obvious pain. Finally, Teancum just stopped and started to forage for what seemed like imaginary food. Couldn't blame 'em; the ponies are hungry. We gave up and camped northwest of Roosevelt Dam. No water, no horsefeed, no dinner. Exhausted, we just passed out in heaps. Found out later we were only a half mile from the highway.

Sunday 27 October 1991

Woke at 3:30 a.m., dreaming of donks with tongues like dried jerky. Ty was packing up, anxious to get to his truck and trailer, parked at the dam. He left camp at 4 a.m. He's had a rough week. Hope he's not sorry he came. I realize my ride might not do for others what it's doing for me, even amid the hardship.

Following Ty's example, Jonah and I struck camp early. But while checking Teton, I found two batches of cholla impaled in his shoulder. These cholla balls, while looking friendly and fuzzy, are deceptively painful. The fuzzy part is actually made up of dense spines so toxic that they can cause numbness to the traumatized area. They have backward-facing barbs that, after puncturing the skin, grip like a fish hook. First I thought of using my horse comb to remove each cholla ball, but I realized it may cause the demon barbs to merely embed in a new place.

My hair comb seemed the perfect extraction tool. I could place the teeth under the cholla ball and pry it off Teton's shoulder, being careful not to catapult it into myself. Using leather gloves, I gently placed the comb under a ball. If there was any numbness, it quickly dissipated as I began prying. Teton came alive! Wide-eyed and blowing air hard out his nostrils, he squealed and wiggled. I'll have to watch that he doesn't stagger into any more cholla.

Jonah and I packed up and got away by 8 a.m., riding the last four miles along the highway to Roosevelt Dam. Not much traffic. Thankful for that. The dam bridge has a spectacular blue arch support. An amazing structure.

A light rain began before we arrived. We found Ty's truck parked near the horse pens, with him asleep inside. Met a sheriff's deputy outside a little store and asked him where we could buy hay. He said to try Duff Drummond's ranch eight miles east. We woke Ty and the three of us bought breakfast at the store.

Duff Drummond, very gracious, gave us grain and two bales of slightly moldy hay. Back at the horse pens, oblivious to the cold rain that had gathered momentum, the ponies went after the feed like wolves after a kill. After finishing off the hay, Ty loaded Bow and Arrow and raised his eyebrows as if to inquire if I'd be loading my ponies. He knew I'd been wrestling with the idea of quitting. I was leaning toward going with him, but when I saw the open trailer gate I shook my head, muttering, "Naw, I'm staying." I knew I'd be disappointed in myself and didn't want to go through my remaining days wondering "What if…"

"I thought you'd stay." He nodded; his smile lifted the curled corners of the bandaged patch away from his cheek. He reached out and placed a hand on my shoulder. "You'll make it, Chuck. I know you will." The strength in his voice contradicted the weak squeeze of his hand.

"I will," I said, drawing strength from his confidence. I laid my hand on his and wondered how a beet-red, bandaged, rashy face could look so beautiful. I'm not sure why I feel so driven. Maybe it's the concept of giving up that has me scared; that by giving up on the ride, I'd somehow be giving up on life. I worry that by acknowledging and accepting I *can't*, the track of *can do* would be blocked forever, like a boarded up train tunnel, never to be traveled again. I worry I'd be returning home to wait for the inevitable.

The muddy roads and dismal gray mist that came with the rain helped Jonah and me decide to leave the horses at the dam and ride to Mesa with Ty. Called a cousin, Lynn Waddell, and we'll stay the night with him. Sugar and Teton badly need to rest anyway.

In front of Lynn's house, Jonah hung back as Ty and

I climbed from the truck and prepared to say goodbye. Ty stepped forward. It was too much. As we embraced, I broke down and cried.

"It was good to ride with you, friend," croaked Ty. "Thanks so much for helping me." Tears flooded faster when I tried to return the sentiments. I finished by mumbling into his collar, "That's what friends do; they help each other."

As Ty drove away, I felt alone. He was the kind of company I liked.

Lynn and his family, though, really made us feel welcome. After a shave and a luxurious, hot bath, I wondered, Who is that man in the mirror? When did I become old? So much loose skin!

Got laundered, fed, and pampered. What a rich blessing for a traveler to visit loving relatives. Revived!

Phoned Sally to check in and feel her love. Made three other phone calls: Tony Pittman to report on trail conditions, the forest service to volunteer to clear the Buckhorn Trail (lots of bureaucracy!), and Joe Lawrence to tell him where I am. Learned that he's on a construction site close to the dam. Asked him to check on my ponies.

Almost midnight and I'm close to passing out.

Chapter 17

Monday 28 October 1991

Being with Lynn's loving family makes Jonah and me miss our own. Jonah has decided it's time to go home and mend bridges. His dad will come and get him later today.

After lunch, I prepared to leave, but first a farewell to Jonah. His arms gently encircled me as he whispered in my ear, "Thank you so much for inviting me to come, and for being so patient. You taught me many things: How to saddle and pack horses. How to cook over a fire. To ration liquids when water's scarce. And that a comb can be a multi-purpose tool. But, I learned most of all that I am cherished and important. You accepted me, warts and all…" A sob escaped his lips and he couldn't finish. I must've exhaled right then, because my loose pants begin to slip. Saved 'em with a mad grab. I'd lost a fair amount of weight, even before the ride, and am still getting skinnier. I'm guessing I'm down to about 120 pounds. Pre-cancer, I was about 170.

The mad-grab effort to save my modesty lightened the atmosphere, however, and we both let out a hearty laugh. I returned Jonah's hug; he felt thinner, too. I'll miss him. I stepped back and cinched my belt as tight as I dared. Jonah finished his sentence as his hands spoke for him, folded into an attitude of prayer. Then he pointed both index fingers at me, and placed both hands over his heart. I understood, and mirrored the gesture.

Later, Lynn took me shopping. Picked up two shirts, one pair of levis, groceries, grain, horseshoes and one hundred and thirty dollars cash. Whew! Ran myself ragged. As he drove me back to my ponies, I enjoyed the desert scenery with all its trappings. It's a lot different seen from a car window than from a mule's back. Another lesson in perspective: both views, distant and close, are sweet and valuable.

Ponies rested and fed, having gobbled up the remainder of their grain and hay. Joe Lawrence had watered them, too. Teton was responsive. I just wish his improvement would last longer than a day. Sugar is still stiff and jerky. She needs the vet.

Visitors at the dam ogled over my ponies. Teancum was polite as I replaced his two worn shoes and then packed up. Joe Lawrence invited me to a spaghetti supper. We visited and I slept in his construction trailer parked near Roosevelt Dam.

Tuesday 29 October 1991

Up early and packed; rode out before eight, stopped often, grazing the ponies by the roadside. South of Roosevelt the impressive cactus are in abundance–saguaro, ocotillo, cholla, prickly pear, and barrel. Saguaro, the cactus that we recognize from old western movies, are monstrously tall; some are two hundred years old. Ocotillo are the ones that have "arms" like jellyfish tentacles reaching to the sky. Cholla come in several varieties, including ground creepers, trees, and shrubs. In this dry climate one might think the barrel cactus is full of water. A myth. In fact, it's filled with a dangerous liquid that, if swallowed, can cause the body to lose water and its temperature to drop, and may even cause hypothermia. And barrel cactus spines are so dangerous they can put down a horse. We always make sure to sweep wide when we pass a barrel. Prickly pear reminds me of Ty's injured face–or, on a happier note, of Maryann's delicious jam.

Teton seemed to have learned his lesson, staying far away from cactus today. I regularly check ponies for impaled spines.

Wild-looking country. Superstition is a good name for it. The USFS hasn't cleared Cottonwood Creek trail for a long time. It was jungly, but there was beautiful waving grass at the trailhead, which the ponies appreciated very much.

Got nearly to Reevis Ranch, south of Boulder, when dark caught us. Threw off and ate. Sky was clear. Gambled on weather and lost. Began raining before midnight. I just unfolded the fly over my bed and put saddle pads between it and me. It worked! Not so wet and steamy as before. Of course, some things got wet anyway. I'm wondering why I didn't bring my overshoes! So wet. Rained off and on all night.

WEDNESDAY 30 OCTOBER 1991

I lay in bed until 8:30 a.m. and waited for the sun to burn off the fog. It didn't. So breakfasted, then packed the animals in the fog and wind. Cold. Got underway by mid-morning and found that I'd camped just northeast of Reevis Ranch, where there was a good roof on an old house–(Hey, could have saved me from getting wet last night). The house and nice old barn and sheds looked like someone's labor of love. An apple orchard was nearby, but no apples. Saw a gray-white doe drinking from the creek that ran alongside the buildings.

I took a southwest route up the canyon. Tall grass often enticed me to stop and let the animals graze. Had a nice ride into Rogers Canyon and then up to Montana Mountain. Took a switchback road instead of Tony Pittman's suggested shortcut trail, which was muddy from the rain.

Glad I took the switchback road, on which I found and slept in an old, empty rock house about eight miles north of Superior. Apparently it'd been used by the law as a waystation for prisoners headed for the Yuma jail. Bars on the window and locks on the door, it was built solid. Next to the rock house was a nice side building and a good horse pen. Cowboys must stay here during roundups.

Worried that some creature residents might join me in my sleeping bag, I drew the string tight around my face. There would be no extra space for visitors. I actually never saw any mice, just droppings, but knew they'd be out and about at dark. I understand that they were here first, that I'm the visitor, so I'll respect their right to live and occupy. Nice night on the squeaky old bed springs, out of the wind.

Will have a short ride into Superior tomorrow.

THURSDAY 31 OCTOBER 1991

The cattle range is *bare*. Ponies won't get to eat until we get to town. We were road-riding until we got to an arboretum outside Superior, where the counter lady helped me locate Rita Sabin. Tony Pittman had given me Rita's name as a helpful contact in this area. She met me on the highway and found a place for my horses to stay, hay to feed them, and a trailer to take Sugar to the vet in Globe. So kind and hospitable to wandering horse folk.

It turns out Sugar has tendinitis in both front legs, a sore knee, a fever, and loss of appetite. Me, I had a fifty-seven dollar vet bill. Vet said Sugar will not get better on the trip. So, it looks like I'll pen and retire her with Rita until L.J. Dewitt, a friend in Mesa, will pick her up–said he'd board her until I stop and get her on the way home.

After the vet diagnosis, Rita drove me to her home in Superior. Then cousin Lynn Waddell came to take me to his home in Mesa again. Will hole up there for several days so Teton can rest and hopefully put some meat back on his bones.

Surely are some rich, wonderful people in the world. Hmmm... how to repay?

FRIDAY 1 NOVEMBER 1991

Bought grain and horseshoes, then jumped in L.J. Dewitt's truck and helped him gather up some horses for a sale tomorrow. He invited me to come along to the sale, too, which should be fun. All day long I felt like a kid on Christmas Eve.

A round-up is all it's cracked up to be. Then on the way home we stopped at Art Freeman's, a friend of L.J.'s, who shared some luscious dried fruit with me.

I called Ken Cooper, a friend from Alta, Wyoming, who now lives in Bowie, Arizona. We'll meet outside Tucson. Had a tasty supper and restful evening, a much-needed departure from riding the trail.

Just laid around relaxing after dinner. Read about Geronimo and General Crook from one of the books I bought at Delores Brown's bookstore in Kanab, Utah. Lounging—it's therapeutic. Hope the ponies think so, too.

SATURDAY 2 NOVEMBER 1991

Up early and visited with Lynn and his wife, Janet. Then L.J. and I headed an hour north on I-17 for the mule show and horse sale, which started at 9 a.m. There were two arenas going at once, lots of booths, and food! Wished I had Teancum's lizard eyes, one for each arena. Met Hugh Hudson, a packer, trainer, rider, and driver, who told me about building U.S. military pack-saddles for mules carrying weaponry into the mountains of Afghanistan. Gave lots of neat training ideas. I invited him to visit us in Wyoming. Hope he comes.

I also met Max Harsha from New Mexico, who authored *Mule Skinner's Bible.* He's got a video and another book in the works, which will be ready by mid-December. I'll track down copies when I get home. Max mentioned a restraint that is quicker and simpler than tying an animal's feet to the ground. The rope contraption raises a hind foot and tucks the nose down, immobilizing the animal. Then it's easy to clip, shoe, bridle, and so on. It starts out like a Scotch hobble. Then the rope is threaded through the side of the halter, followed by a nose band loop, which is tied to the foot rope. Finally, the rope end is threaded back through the neck loop, so that when you pull on it, the nose is tucked around sideways and the foot is off the ground.

During lunch I recited for L.J. and Tony Pittman, who'd come from Flagstaff to buy some mules for his retirement "trail patrol," the cowboy poems "Shoeing" and "60 Day Run." Then at the auction I had to sit on my hands so I wouldn't be tempted to bid. Sally might be upset if I came home with extra mules. One of the mules, a good one, sold for $725, though most went for $400 or so. Some more expensive mules didn't even sell. The owner was asking too much: $2,600 to $2,900. Ouch! There were some Tennessee mules from Tucson who were young but well-trained. The trainer even laid them all down and crawled over their legs.

Got back to Lynn's home around 10 p.m. Tired. Wonderful bed. Ah, a day at the candy shop!

Sunday 3 November 1991

On the way to church Lynn warned me about the "Pharisee Dress Code." I wore what I had–my riding clothes. After all, they were clean and my heart was good.

On entering the building, I was approached by two men who asked, "May we help you?" I had to smooth my hackles. After I explained about my ride, they welcomed me. Grumbled to myself for a few minutes, but then saw their side and my error. So much for "my heart was good." I let it go. Luckily, my pride circle ran small. I wasted little time before I could enjoy the sweet Spirit. Lots of friendly folks came up and visited with me.

Lynn and Janet invited me to do some poetry after dinner. Then later that evening L.J. called to remind me of the interview he'd set up for me with *Arizona Cowboy*, a program that's aired nationally on satellite via the agribusiness channel. I called Rita Sabin in Superior and primed her for the filming. She'll ride with us tomorrow and reported that Sugar is doing better. She surely has been thoughtful and considerate to doctor and feed that mare so faithfully. Nice lady.

Surely grateful for many wonderful blessings: health, family support, friends, relatives along the route, beautiful world, companionship of animals, church, and the Lord.

Monday 4 November 1991

L.J. Dewitt and Art Freeman hauled their mules to Superior to ride with me. They brought a mule for Lynn, too. We went early and nailed shoes on Sam's hind hooves. He fought, so I tied him in knots. Disgusted, he gave up quickly.

Rita Sabin and a friend came shortly after I'd shod Sam. The film crew for *Arizona Cowboy* also came and shot some footage while L.J. narrated. It'll be interesting to see what comes of it. Rita's friend showcased and roughed up her buckskin colt for the camera. Yuck!

On the trail again. Windy but nice. Feels like heading back into light! Being atop a mule, on a rugged trail, somehow must have eternal qualities about it. Teton benefitted greatly from the four-day rest. He's still thin but attentive. Sam and Teancum are plain spunky.

Lynn, L.J., Art, Rita, and "Showcaser" rode with me for several hours, then turned back after Rita gave me directions to a trail out of Telegraph and into Box Canyon. L.J. reassured me he'd pick up Sugar and take her to Mesa.

At dark Teancum threw a shoe as I rode into Box Canyon, a stunning canyon with high, sheer, red cliffs pinched right into the edge of a sandy creek bed. Just a car's width. *Wow!* Too dark to photograph.

Camped north of Gila River.

Tuesday 5 November 1991

Got up early, had oatmeal and dried fruit for breakfast, then replaced the missing hind shoe on Teancum.

The creek-bed trail had thick, jungly borders and was a

little puddly. The bed itself was empty because the water was shut down upriver at San Carlos, but there were lots of ponds leading down Box Canyon to Gila River. I crossed the Gila at Ashurst-Hayden Diversion Dam and rode back up-river to Box O Wash. Rode the wide sandy wash for twelve to fifteen miles, southeast back toward Barkerville.

Rode over to visit with a beekeeper who was checking her hives that sat alongside the road. She showed me a rattler crossing the road not far from where I'd been. I and Teancum had missed it completely! Dismounting, with Teancum's reins and Teton's halter rope in hand, I stepped carefully toward the snake for a closer look. So well camouflaged, I could've stepped on him before I even knew he was there. He seemed very businesslike, so I backed away carefully.

Right then, one end of my vest, which was tied to the saddle, came loose, flapping as it hung low over Teancum's withers. Snorting, he shied sideways. The unexpected jerk on my arm flicked the end of Teton's lead rope into my chest, a blow that felt like that of a bull whip. I grunted, then gulped for air as the crack of the whip coincided with the crack of a lower rib. Wide-eyed with fear, Teancum bucked in an attempt to rid himself of the "cougar" on his back. His reins jerked my arm one more time before I dropped them and doubled over to cradle my left side.

My eyes registered only black. In time I began to see gray, then color as I forced shallow breaths in and out of my lungs. The bee woman came to my aid, but I slowly straightened and reassured her that I was okay. Adjusting my rib belt for optimal support, I tucked my elbow firmly against my rib and started off after Teancum.

It again was time for mule school. Craning his neck, Teancum eyed the hanging vest like it was about to eat him. As Sam and Teton foraged, I gently rubbed the vest over Teancum's back and down his legs, neck and face, using my right arm; the left was tucked snugly against my rib cage. After "school," I retied the vest and allowed it to flap as I walked Teancum around. This time, the "cougar" turned "gnat" didn't warrant a backward glance.

Rode hunched in the saddle until I could camp. Held both reins and lead rope in my right hand, my left arm still giving support to my rib belt. Got to Hayden Ranch, a lambing camp, watered the ponies, and visited with a Mexican family camped in the wash. Then I gingerly set up camp north of the lambing shed.

It seems Teton somehow staggered into more cholla. Several balls were embedded in his hip. Despite my precautions at my last cholla removal, a few barbs had worked their way into my forefinger, and I'd picked at them for days. This time I double-gloved. These balls could have inspired the all-purpose Velcro, though I think it was a seed found in the Alps that Velcro was patterned after. The idea is the same, though: tiny, hooked barbs that stick in most everything.

I slid my comb under a ball and gently began prying. Two things worried me: applying enough torque to extract the ball without hurting my rib and launching the ball into myself or onto a different spot on Teton. He flinched, then exhibited more energy than I'd seen in him in quite a while. Nearly went down from pain before I'd removed the last ball. Is he not paying attention, or is he too tired and numb? He doesn't look like the same horse who left Alta, Wyoming, in August.

I can see the glow of lights from Phoenix and Tucson in the night sky. A housing development is planned and staked, even way out here—aaargh!

WEDNESDAY 6 NOVEMBER 1991

Burned breakfast! Amazing how small, insignificant things, when stacked up against other undesirable events, seem like an unsurmountable mountain. Threw the mess away and went without.

Packed camp and gathered horses. When I caught Teancum I found his lips stitched shut on one side with a cholla ball. So much for my thinking the mules were smart enough to avoid cactus. The majority of the ball was embedded inside his mouth, partly in his lower gum and partly in the cheek. Pulled out my handy comb again; I'm using it more on the animals than on me. Double-gloved and tied Teancum up short, then gently pulled his lips back as far as I could, instantly setting him fighting, snorting and thrashing. His hind legs slid under him and he sat on his haunches.

I stood back, let him settle down, then tried again. My fears that I might roll the cholla ball onto his tongue or the roof of his mouth, now outweighed my worry of stuck fingers. Gripping and tugging with the comb, the ball was like a giant rat's nest that refused to comb out. Teancum danced, squealed, and thrashed. Worried about getting hurt, I decide to give Max Harsha's restraint a try. After threading and knotting, the rope lifted Teancum's hind leg and drew his nose down, tucking it neatly against his foreleg. It worked wonderfully, keeping him immobile enough for me to peel back his lips and place the comb under the ball against his gums.

Extricating the gum-side of the ball was only half the problem; the cheek-side would still be embedded. Thinking it best to remove the ball from both places simultaneously, I gripped the ball with thumb and forefinger, then yanked while prying with the comb. Teancum squealed in pain, and after a valiant battle on his part, it was over. I'd won.

As soon as the ball was out of his mouth, he began licking his lips. My glove was curled in a fist around the cholla ball. The barbs hadn't penetrated the second pair, so I was able to remove my hand without punctures.

Teancum's head restraint and cholla extraction from tender tissue, reminded me of another operation I'd performed.

It was in Alaska, July, 1966. The family had motored upriver in the plywood boat I'd made to picnic and fish. Leland, age seven, and LeAnn, age six, were perched on the side of the river fishing for salmon, as Sally and I sat on a blanket, playing with our toddler, Mathew. Janelle, age four, was playing nearby on a homemade log teetertotter. I'd just glanced over to check on the older children, when I saw Janelle suddenly jerked from her seat. Her sharp, piercing cry sent me racing to her side. She lay curled in a ball, screaming, with both hands covering her left eye. Sally gently pulled Janelle's hands back to reveal a large, wicked-looking fish hook dangling from the crease of her eyelid. Luckily, it had missed her eyeball and hooked just the skin fold; its barb lay hidden behind the lid.

In our small village there was no doctor. I was it. I pulled out my pocketknife to cut the line and sent Leland for the wirecutters that I kept in the boat's toolbox. Then, holding her close, I explained to Janelle what needed to be done. She whimpered, then nodded bravely. Sally spread a blanket on the ground, on which I laid Janelle. Then kneeling, I locked her head between my knees. Sally helped hold her still, acting as an anchor from above.

Examining the entry point, I knew I'd do even more damage if I pulled it out the way it had gone in. I needed to push it the rest of the way through. With a nod from Sally, she applied all her weight to hold Janelle still while I pulled the loose skin away from the eyeball and drew the hook through the skin and from behind the eyelid. Leland curiously watched the procedure. For her part, LeAnn, pale and close to tears, stood with fishing pole still in hand, the severed line gently wafting in the breeze. I carefully snipped off the hook end with the wirecutters, then pulled the rest of it out.

The hard part over, I dared to breathe. God's watchful care and some thoughtful, clear action, had saved the day. I felt the same way today after Teancum's cholla removal as I had with Janelle's long-ago fishhook episode. I hope not to have to do anything like that ever again!

Afterwards, I filled my cloth bags, stripped the saddles to their lightest weight, and began walking the pack-saddle up Sam's side, alternating each end. About halfway up, I paused to breathe and give my clenched chest muscles a rest, leaning against the pack-saddle, which was pinned between Sam and me, and hoping he'd stand still. Wouldn't you know it, he side-stepped away from me. Caught off guard and off balance, I dropped the saddle and barely managed to stay on my feet. Disgusted, I bent too quickly to retrieve the saddle from the dirt, exhaled with a grunt, and saw black again. I crumpled.

After what seemed like minutes–but was probably only seconds–I struggled to my feet. I realized that I needed to pick up the saddle using my legs, not my back muscles. Now, squatting with a straight back is hard; but standing up again, with a straight back, saddle in hand, is even harder. My legs quivered like they did that day in the barnyard, when I got on the bucket and first tried to mount Teancum. This time as I walked the saddle up Sam's side, I was prepared if he moved. Success. My muscles cramped around the sore rib as I finished saddling Sam and Teancum. With head low, Teton stood planted as I saddled him. Now I understood more fully the old adage about adding straw to the camel's back.

Rode up onto Barkerville Road and headed south to Oracle. The area I planned to ride is all fenced. I came upon a cowboy who explained, "This is cattle range and private property, *but*, if you're just passing through, it's okay to ride on the road only." Then he added, "And the gates are all locked."

Did I look like a cattle thief, or was this just a case of "it's mine and you're not welcome"? Humph! So, I rode the road all day long. The cowboy's cattle are a big, tough, wild-looking Brahma cross. It seems the breed is excellent for these parts in that they have more sweat glands and are better equipped than other types of cattle to withstand heat.

Saw another rattler crawling in a cholla heap. Began to wonder how many snakes I've passed unaware. Vowed to keep my eyes open. A snakebite, I'm afraid, would put us all down.

Camped in a swale off a gasline road on Warm Spring Ranch. After a dinner of Spam, I used my tweezers and spent the evening pulling the cholla barbs from my leather gloves.

THURSDAY 7 NOVEMBER 1991

So tired of the sweats. Rain or shine, my sleeping bag is wet almost every night. I delayed my start time this morning so my bag could dry.

Ate Vienna sausages and fried spuds for breakfast, then headed out. Tried to get to Oracle on a gasline road, but it was fenced solid. Bushwhacked along the south fence to a blind spot and used Leland's "gatemakers," patching the cut wire with the end of a lash rope. Also had to cut an E-W fence and patched that one with Sam's halter rope. Will the fences never end? Do I have enough rope?

It was late in the day when I finally got to the highway gate. It, being unlocked, unlike what the cowboy had said, saved me a lead rope. Turns out I could've ridden the road all the way; would have been quicker.

Rode the six miles into town, watered the horses, bought grain and groceries, and headed out once more. Turns out my map was mislabeled. Got lost! Took me four times circling to get out onto the Oracle Ridge Trail. Camped a half-mile above Oracle.

Not much feed for animals. They're scavenging.

FRIDAY 8 NOVEMBER 1991

Awoke flat on my back in the same position as when I lay down. My sore rib wakes me if I move, so I've learned to sleep stone-like. I crawled from my bag, turned it inside out to dry, and saw my wet silhouette stamped on the interior. The dark shape gave me an eerie feeling, the sense that a part of me still occupied the bag.

I strung a line and hung it up. Then as I looked for the pan to boil water for oatmeal, out of the corner of my eye, I caught sight of the image of a man who seemed to be hanging from the line. The disturbing outline gently swayed in the breeze. I walked back to the line and flipped the bag over. No dark shadow would watch me eat.

Spooning in my oatmeal, I noticed Teancum and Sam were chewing on cow chips. I immediately lost my appetite, and from then on just watched soft donk muzzles push the chips around, nibble the edges, then break them open and eat. My heart sank. Is this what we'd been reduced to? Would my animals get worms? I felt like a father who couldn't provide for his children. Teton stood hunched, his head low. He'd given up on scavenging, and cow chips weren't even an option. The grain is not enough; he's getting too thin.

I gathered up Teton to shoe his hinds. We're going through shoes like they were paper. Tried, with gritted teeth, to lift Teton's foot. He doesn't fight like Sam, but still had to tie his foot up with a Scotch hobble.

Hurting, I didn't fully appreciate the beautiful ridge ride. Lots of ups and downs to the trail, and it was brushy with manzanita and mesquite trees. Finally got on an old-time trail to Mount Lemmon. The planned three-hour ride took much longer. My thoughts returned to the disturbing image of starving ponies. Wondered again if I needed to quit, even though I'm so close to the finish line. At last I came to the conclusion that when cow chips are broken open they smell like grass, and the donks know what they need, which helped me relax a bit. But Teton?

Stopped at a ski resort store, ate a burrito, and inquired about the trail. Everyone I spoke to gave the same hazy answer: "Yeah, the trail's pretty well marked." They either don't hike the hills much or don't pay attention to the lack of signs. No one even knew for sure where the trailhead was. For that matter, there simply was no trail to be found.

Wondered if I could continue on. Climbed a rocky point and, using map and visual reconnaissance, guessed where, in theory, the trail might be and planned my direction of travel. Fortunately, my map, my visual, and my guess coincided! My predicted trail locations in Marshall Saddle and Aomero Pass were correct. After I looped around a mountain and finally found "the trail" on the west side of Mount Lemmon, it was dark, so I set up camp. I could hear vehicles traveling the Arizona Summerhaven highway not far away.

Teton is slipping fast, despite the rest and care he'd received a few days ago. Shortly before camping, he caught me unprepared, planting his feet and jerking my lead-rope arm back, causing me to pop a rib. Thankfully, it wasn't the cracked rib, but higher up. Sore, sore chest!

What's wrong with Sam? He isn't feeling well; it's his stomach. Since the morning pies, he's eaten only a little. He ate a fair amount of barley this morning; maybe that's the problem. Is this the straw that finally will break the camel's back? Very dismal horsefeed prospects, but no water at all. When water is plentiful it's easy to overlook its importance, but when water is scarce, life gets serious.

I fluffed my sleeping bag; my dark silhouette is dried and gone. Lying here stone-like, so tired and hurting, but can't sleep. Worried about Sam. I guess I'll write a little more.

I watch Sam and hear his groans. I can empathize with him. I'm reminded of several times when I had severe abdominal pain and tried to doctor myself. Before my cancer diagnosis, my gassy stomach sometimes felt like it would burst. Belching didn't help. I'd doctored bloated calves with a hose down their throat, which released the gas, so I had Sally buy a piece of surgical hose—much to her horror. Figured what's good for the calf is good for the old cowboy. But I couldn't get it down my throat; it didn't work.

Another time I thought I had worms, so I took a leftover horse dewormer pill. What was I thinking? Sally ended up calling poison control. Again, embarrassed, she explained to them what I'd done. Their advice was to drink a glass of water with a little dish soap in it. That worked; I purged. Wish it were that simple for Sam!

CROSSROADS

Chapter 18

SATURDAY 9 NOVEMBER 1991

I repeat: I write tonight not knowing if I should continue or abort my ride. I feel broken and beaten. For the first time since beginning this ride to Mexico, I have no hope. Do I try to keep going? Is it time to go home? What should I do?

Dripping wet, I awoke this morning flat on my back, protectively cradling my cracked rib. Sweat beads rolled down my temples as I crawled from my soggy sleeping bag. The outside of my bag was wet to the touch, despite its "moisture releasing" shell, clear skies, and dry air. My underwear was twisted and stuck to my body in damp bunches from the nightly sweats that continually plague me.

It wasn't the sweats last night or the continual buzzing of cars that travel the Arizona Summerhaven highway, or even the cracked rib that disturbed my sleep, it was the anxiety over, Sam, and my frequent need to get up to check on him. What if Sam doesn't make it? I fear my friend is dying, and I worry that tomorrow will prove me right. My guess is he has a twisted gut or suffers from severe colic. The colic could be from parasites he's picked up along the way, possibly from the cow chips he's been eating, or it could be the painful buildup of stomach acid, since there's been no food to digest.

Teton, now shows his sharp hipbones and ribs I can count. He stumbles frequently from fatigue. I'm worried about him going down and not getting back up. While the mules eat cowpies in the mountains and aren't so picky, Teton just doesn't eat.

I rode hunched in my saddle most of the day, attempting without success to shield my rib. I'm jolted by each of Teancum's steps; the rib belt seems to do little good. A day of continually clenched teeth and knotted muscles has left me exhausted.

Today while traversing the trail, with my frequent backward glances at Sam, it was hard to appreciate the strikingly beautiful rock country with its gigantic, rounded boulders stacked one atop the other. I had packed him as light as I could, tying several cloth bags onto Teancum's saddle to lighten Sam's load. I didn't dare load any extra on Teton.

I occasionally walked and led Sam slowly up the trail, allowing him to stop as he wished. He plodded along close to my shoulder. Teancum followed behind Sam, with Teton bringing up the rear. Descending west from Mount Lemmon, Sam stumbled along the steep and rocky path as I held my breath. Evidently it hadn't been cleared for horses in quite a while, but Sam managed to stay upright. He lay down often; luckily, it wasn't on the steepest part of the trail. He'd groan, drop to his knees, and attempt to roll onto his back, an action prevented by the pack boxes. Teancum would pause and patiently wait for Sam to get back up. Teton, with head hung low, glad for the rest, would pull up behind Teancum. I'd cluck encouraging words to Sam, "You can do it boy," or "Hang in there; you're okay," but I had a hard time believing myself.

The going was slow as we made our way past sheer rock walls and giant rocks that partially covered the trail. The spectacular view to Romero Pass went mostly unnoticed. Sights that would have brought such joy days ago, now looked cold and hard. Slumped in the saddle, with my left arm wrapped around my rib cage, I descended Sabino Canyon. Then it was again up to Camp Canyon, to Sycamore Canyon, and finally to Molino campground, where camp set-up was tedious and lengthy.

Molino campground bustles with campers and hunters. A lanky, loose-jointed cowboy, with a waxed handlebar mustache and quick smile, just left my campsite. He'd approached me with a smile and pleasantly asked, "Howdy, where you comin' from?" As he extended his hand, I set down my plate of spaghetti and stood up.

"Hi there. I've ridden down from Wyoming, headed to Mexico."

"You've come all the way from Wyoming?"

"Yup."

"Whew," he whistled. "That's quite a ride."

I nodded, gesturing for him to sit if he'd like. Shaking his head, he said, "No thanks. I just wanted to offer you some water for your animals. I know it's hard to come by around here. We packed in plenty for our stock; you're welcome to it, if you'd like."

I smiled gratefully, and my spirits rose. "Thank you. I'll take you up on the offer; there hasn't been much water up in the mountains."

"Is there anything else you need?" he asked, taking my hand and shaking it gently.

"I've gone through several sets of horseshoes and am low on nails. Do you happen to have any extra?"

"You bet. Just a minute." He returned shortly with a handful of nails.

"You sure you wouldn't like some spaghetti?"

Wagging his head, he declined. "Are you alright? Looks like you've hurt yourself."

"Think I cracked a rib. I'll be okay," I replied, straightening up to prove myself fit.

"Holler if you need anything; good luck with your ride."

I finished my meal alone, half-heartedly pondering what

to do. Now, I'm trying to put to paper my thoughts and feelings.

The animals are tied for the night. I worry about Sam as he continues to groan, lying down flat, only to stand, then lay down again and roll repeatedly back and forth, while keeping his feet in the air, trying to relieve the pain in his belly. Then he repeats the cycle. He hasn't eaten or drunk anything today, and I've fretted over it all day long. Poor Sam! I led him in circles this evening in hopes that if the problem is a twisted gut, the kink would straighten, but no luck. No doubt the shortage of water added to his problem. But now when we have water, he isn't interested.

Please Lord watch over Sam. Help me know what to do.

SUNDAY 10 NOVEMBER 1991

Sam's alive! My prayer has been answered. I awoke to find him still lying down, but his head was up. He eventually made his way up the canyon to graze. As I looked on, tears rolled down my cheeks. Thank you, Lord, for extending his life.

Sam is back in shape, his gut straightened out, just like my battered hat after I push my fist into the dome. Again I ask, do we keep going or quit? Sam is alive! Hope is alive! I'm alive! Black clouds are turning gray; light rays are shining through. We go on!

Using the lanky cowboy's nails, I shod Teancum's remaining hind. We had to have another half-hour session of mule school before he'd let me put the bridle over his ears. I didn't even mind.

The same kind cowboy gave us water again today, so Teton and Sam hung their heads in his camper window to see what else there was to eat. He was generous with some hay.

Traveled the new USFS trail to West Spring, which is on the Dellotta Ranch. Then *rain*! Torrents of rain! I thought I could tough it out and ride, but the downpour drenched me.

I need my overshoes! Cold and miserable for the rest of the day. The wind pierced every piece of my clothing and gave me goose bumps all over.

After dark I arrived at Redington Land and Cattle Company just east of Tucson. Called Ken Cooper, who encouraged me to bail out for a few days, stable my ponies there, and stay with him for a stretch. I agreed. Ponies and I need some down time. He'll pick me up tomorrow. Then came another downpour! But now ponies and I have food and shelter. The stabler, hosting a big group of young travelers from New Zealand, Australia, and West Germany, invited me to a steak supper. Happy taste buds!

Slept in the bunkhouse. Oh, it's nice to dry out and be warm. Still babying my cracked rib, but my sternum feels better. Ponies loved the leafy, green alfalfa.

Chapter 19

MONDAY 11 NOVEMBER 1991

While waiting for Ken to come get me, I shod Teton's hind hoof. Was able to do it without a tie-up this time. I met Nate Jackson, a Redington employee, and R&B Mule peddler on the side. He's a cocky Tennessean who owns some well-trained, two-year-old Tennessee-walker mules. Nate was extremely hospitable. He'll feed and care for my ponies until I get back from Ken's.

I'm green with envy, though! Those Tennessee-walkers are beautiful animals. They remind me of my bay mare at home, also a "walker." They're known for their inherited "running walk," a smooth gait that literally feels like a rocking chair, one that makes traveling at six to twelve miles per hour easy.

Ken Cooper came and hauled me to his ranch. It was good to see his twinkling eyes and lopsided smile that showed teeth behind his gray beard. Had a nice one and a half hour drive east along I-10 to Bowie, Arizona. Along the way, Ken shared with me some fascinating soldier/Indian lore.

It seems Ken's place is literally in the shadow of Bowie Mountain, which was used by U.S. soldiers as a heliograph picket during the Apache wars. Just outside his front door sits Apache Pass, site of Old Fort Bowie, which was used by the army during these wars. Ken and his wife, Anne, own a treasure-house of relics, events, books, and memorabilia. Theirs was the first home built after Fort Bowie was abandoned.

I soaked in a Jacuzzi hot-tub. My muscles relaxed, even around my cracked rib. Climbed from the hot-tub and felt like a wobbly cooked noodle, soft to the core. My gray clouds had receded allowing light and sunshine to enter. I needed this rest as much as the ponies. Then Anne fixed huevos rancheros (egg and pepper burrito with cheese and beans) for lunch. Mmmm. I got the recipe for her homemade salsa.

Ken turned me loose in his wonderful library of local history books and contemporary serious works. Devoured a book about Fort Bowie, then finished the evening with a wonderful supper of pasta and sauce, plus an apple crisp.

Leland called. Great fun to visit with him.

TUESDAY 12 NOVEMBER 1991

Called Lynn Waddell to check on Mexico housing possibilities. I'd like to visit Mexico for a few days before I head home. He'll call back.

Ken and I went to Fort Bowie Monument. Neat building remnants. Ken's books gave interesting information on General George Crook, considered by the Army to be the greatest Indian fighter. President Ulysses S. Grant placed Crook in charge of the Arizona Territory to fight the Apaches, led by Geronimo. Despite his reputation as an enemy of the Indians, General Crook spent his last years of life speaking out against their ill-treatment.

After the Monument, we drove into Safford to shop. Rain overshoes cost thirty dollars, so I didn't get them, figuring next time it rains I'll hole up to keep my feet dry.

Anne prepared a beef roast in a Dutch oven. Gracious hosts. The Coopers make a visitor feel as if his visit in itself is the greatest gift he could have brought them.

Ken and Anne have done vast amounts of restorative work on their house and grounds. It's truly been a creative leap of love back in time for them. Much effort and dreaming is evident in their Bowie "Coyote Creek Ranch." Precious to bask in the aura of their place.

Babied my rib today. Sore. The bed last night was too soft, I will try the floor tonight.

WEDNESDAY 13 NOVEMBER 1991

Up early, feeling good. The floor helped my rib. I breakfasted and got away to the stable by 6:15 a.m. Spouted a little poetry for Ken and Anne before I left. They were appreciative. They packed a "Bowie Special" for me, which included pistachios, Bowie apples, ginger candy, plus a package of their special hamburger meat with spices. Those thoughtful types of gifts make for fond memories. Can't hardly wait to dive into the goodies later this evening.

Surely nice to get back to the ponies. Believe they're anxious to go, too. Sam has joined Teancum again with the "puff belly" game, and I was glad to see it this morning. The rest has done Teton good. His head is up. He should be able to make it to the border. The poor fellow started the ride around eight hundred pounds, and I would guess he's lost close to two hundred, first fat, then flesh. I'll rest him good when we get home.

Nate was very helpful and had taken good care of the ponies. I invited him and his wife to visit the Tetons sometime and go on a pack trip with me. Packed up. The Tucson TV crew hadn't shown for the scheduled interview, so we headed out.

Got away around ten. Met a thin, blond park volunteer, who helped me onto the Saguaro Monument Trail. She rode halfway to the first turning point, sharing her knowledge of the area. She was an excellent public relations person for the trail. She tempered her eagerness to share Saguaro Monument information with an interest in my ride. Nice company. Good ride over the top of Cow's Head and down to Medrone Ranger Station. Rib got more tender as I rode, so I adjusted my rib-belt a little differently to see if that would help.

Threw off at dark one mile below the park on some private property. Oops! I didn't know it yet, but my world was about to come loose. It turns out I'd camped in the middle of a Homeowners' Association nest.

After unloading the packhorses and setting up camp, I began to rummage through the food pack for a can of Pork 'n Beans. All I needed was a quick meal and a warm bed; I was cold, hungry, and my rib was hurting.

Then all at once a shiny, black Ford pickup truck pulled up and skidded to a stop. Out of the driver's side stepped a tall man carrying a hefty air of self-importance. Dressed in slacks and a starched button-down collar shirt, he looked all business, ready to go two-stepping in his polished black cowboy boots. In fact, they were a little too shiny–all boot and no cow. Likewise, his hat was tipped too far back, was too small, and set ridged on the crown of his head. I wanted to tell him, "You shouldn't wear your hat like that," but I refrained.

Strutting over, he began spitting questions at me as if he were firing a pistol: "What's your name? What are you doing here? Are you aware this is private property?" His cologne hit me as I straightened up from my can of unopened beans. Though I extended my hand and began answering his questions, he ignored the gesture, stopped, hands on hips, feet spread, a sour expression on his face, and looked at me down his nose. I was trying to explain that I was moving through on my way to Mexico, when his eyes narrowed and looked at me like I milked geese.

Yet another man stepped from the truck, he, too, looking as if he'd caught scent of a rancid skunk. Short and stocky, and wearing a T-shirt that emphasized his muscle-bound physique, he wore no hat on his bald, polished dome. Less explosive than his partner, this guy stayed next to the truck–stiff and silent. He kept his arms folded, his only movement being a subconscious caress of his biceps. At least I hoped it wasn't conscious; if so, it'd land him squarely in the middle-school crowd. Maybe he'd been brought along in case I offered some resistance. Humph…

They identified themselves as homeowner association officers of this "private" development, the residents of which had requested I leave immediately. Apparently the grapevine is alive and well here. From the moment I'd arrived the phones had been ringing to make everyone aware that an outsider had invaded the property, an attitude I really don't undertand. Just because you're on the high-horse doesn't mean you need to trample others.

Though I was hurting, cold, and hungry, I said I'd move on and started packing. In a show of clemency, the big-talker made a great show of relenting as long as I was gone *before* daylight! He spoke this demand slowly, enunciating each syllable as if he were talking to a slow-witted jury. A fresh cowpie couldn't have been slicker. I guess if I'm gone before anyone sees me, these two can save face with their constituents and still appear to me to be compassionate. True politicians; a charitable bunch.

I've crawled into bed to fret and stew. I'll be up before first light and be on my way.

Thursday 14 November 1991

Slept fitfully. Woke up to what I thought was 2:45 a.m., packed up camp and saddled my ponies in the dark. Didn't want to run into the homeowner police again. My cracked rib is giving me grief. I can hardly hoist the cloth bags to put them over the edge of the Ralide boxes. My left arm and entire left side of my chest is almost immobile. Any movement at all sends sharp pains throughout my chest cavity. I guess the rib belt doesn't keep the ribs stationary enough.

I finally was ready to leave, and still it was not getting light. Checked my watch again, and found that I'd gotten up at 9:15 p.m.! Aaargh! So I rode out anyway. I'm sure the association fellows were relieved I was gone when they returned this morning.

Rode six to seven miles before light came; slept riding in the saddle. When daylight finally arrived, ate cold spam and raisins. The few minutes of sleep I'd gotten just wasn't enough. When I got to the road, there was no gate, only a cattleguard, which added to my discouragement. I was met, however, by a stream of onlookers and local residents watching for me. Felt like a guppy surrounded by piranha. Apparently the wind carried the word that a squatter was traveling the countryside. One friendly face, Hal Wall, showed interest in my ride and offered several different ways he could help with food, hay, and directions. His generous offer and positive attitude lifted my spirits. Finally I sneaked away from the crowds and cattleguard, found a quiet place, and used the gatemakers again. Then I headed up the pike. Glad to leave the area.

I watered at a wash-puddle trapped in an asphalt pothole. Came to a ranch, where I planned to bushwhack for six miles. The ranch owner, a round stocky man, stepped out from behind his barn as I rode past, which caused both ponies and me to jump. After I explained what I was doing and where I was going, he offered me a can of lemonade from several cases stacked in his barn. "It's warm, but it's wet," he said, smiling.

I thanked him. His kindness warmed my soul and helped renew my faith in mankind. I hope I'm his kind of person, not the "You're not welcome" kind.

After I'd explained my galactic out-and-back zig-zag, he chuckled and pointed off west. "Go over that pass, south to Black Bridge, and you'll be in Cienega Creek Wash." It was so simple compared to my wild bushwhacking plans. Thanking him again, I climbed the hill right above his barn and was confronted by six javelina–pretty, little wild pigs. They held their ground, eyeing us as if they were kings and we were serfs. They have a strong odor about them. The horses snorted and shied as we tip-toed carefully past, the javelinas' beady eyes following us until we were out of sight.

As I rode, I enjoyed the lemonade, even though some splashed on me when Teancum, startled by two whitetail does and a buck bolting from the brush, took me for a little rodeo. The tangy taste continued to warm me even after it was gone. It's amazing how a small gesture can lift others. I'll remember that.

Got into Cienega Creek Wash without a hitch and watered there. I exited the wash too soon, but with some careful map study, I could see the way was quite a bit shorter than I'd originally thought. So here I am, camped early in a narrow wash in some brush to break the wind, across the road from Andrada Ranch. My animals can rest and graze. Figure we'll get to Patagonia on the 19th. No sweat, if I do or don't.

So what did I learn from my private property tangle?

1. There are all kinds of people wherever you go. Some will kick you out in the middle of the night; some will welcome you in. Which kind will I be?

2. Worry and fuss do no good, just cause festering. Let it go.

3. Enter after dark. Heh, heh…

FRIDAY 15 NOVEMBER 1991

It rained off and on all night. Since I was flat in the wash, I woke several times worried that a wall of water might rage down the wash. It didn't. Flash flood–that wouldn't have been good. Gray overcast morning. Felt like long-john weather, so I pulled them out and put them on over the pantyhose. Much warmer.

Packed using just my right hand today, tucking my left arm close to my body, under my ribs for support. It's been eleven days with this cracked rib, and my left side is still limited. Teancum seems to know the drill: I lead him to a rock, log, or hillside, and he holds still while I clamber ungracefully onto him. Sam and Teton wait patiently. They're all such good ponies.

Road-riding all day. Before noon, the rain became serious, soaking my feet. Funny how my glorious resolve evaporates into whimpering self-pity when my feet are cold. All of a sudden thirty dollars for some rain boots doesn't seem too much.

Ate lunch with a biker under a roadside table roof. He's en route from San Diego to Florida. He doesn't think much of Arizonians, since several have tried to run him off the road. I thought about asking him if one was a black Ford truck with a chrome-dome musclebound man leaning out the window, but thought better of it.

Windy and cold all day and into the evening. Walked partway, leading Teancum, to keep the blood circulating in my feet. When I got to the turnoff to the Santa Rita Mountains, the mountain was blanketed by a black storm cloud. Sopping wet and so cold, I opted to ride to Patagonia along the roadside. Should make it there by tomorrow night. Felt guilty leaving the trail. Do I need to feel guilty? When should I accede peacefully and when should I hang tough? The answer to both questions is when the end or means is affected negatively. How do I tell the negative effect from my stubborn pride? After pondering, I felt much relieved by my decision to take the road, even if the mountain weather clears during the night and the morning is gloriously sunny. Tomorrow I ride with my gut and not my pride.

Six miles north of Sonoita, I pulled into a little valley not far from the road and pitched my fly under a big tree. Being out of the wind helped warm my limbs and toes. Macaroni and tomatoes for supper, yummy. Slept soundly flat on my back.

Saturday 16 November 1991

The Santa Ritas were snowy this morning. Sure am glad

I chose the valley road instead of the mountains! This morning felt like a meat locker, frost everywhere. The wind carried my steamy breath quickly away, but I remain warm in my heart. My rib even feels better. Beautiful fall day. The biker I lunched with yesterday passed me again. He'd camped in front of me, but I rode out earlier than he did.

When I pulled into Sonoita, a cheery voice called from an open truck window, "Would those animals like a little hay?" Walt, a local cowboy, offered part of a bale of nice alfalfa. Wow! Ponies fell on it like locusts.

A while later I crossed the road to an eatery, a dim-lit bar where three-quarter-pounder BBQ hamburgers sold for nine dollars and twenty-five cents. Worth every dollar! Got back out to the ponies, where Denise Bryers, a Western artist's wife, had brought her husband, Duane, to photograph and fuss over me. Seemed I had gone from TV star to artist's model. Will look for one of his painting books when I get home.

Rode to Patagonia and arrived at dark. Asked a couple of boys, who were playing tennis, if they knew of any place to board my animals. They suggested a horseman named Jake Hopper and gave me directions to his home. Turns out Jake and his wife, Abby, being the gracious, welcoming kind of folk, invited me to stay and stable my ponies. We talked cattle, rodeo, butchering and so forth over Abby's scrumptious supper. Jake raises steers, the team-roping kind. Sells them all over the Western states. The ideal of a long, lean, understatement of a cowboy, he leads an active life, nonchalantly travels great distances, and is on speaking terms with people all over southern Arizona and northern Mexico. I enjoyed our visit very much.

Lots of cowboy gear and rodeo stuff everywhere in Jake's home. Feels good.

Sunday 17 November 1991

Up early, grabbed my war bag and walked downtown to locate the church. A storeman said the LDS building was in Nogales. Bought a blackberry turnover for breakfast and stood on the road with my thumb out, a prayer in my heart for a safe ride. Within ten minutes standing in the chilly wind, a bookstore man going to Tubac to open his shop stopped and took me right to the church steps.

Used church facilities to get cleaned up. The Spanish session was going. Beautiful people. About every twentieth word sounded faintly familiar. Stayed for the English session, too, which was more meaningful to me. Met someone who knows Adeline Halvorson and Ben and Delores Brown. Small world. I sat by Charles Corday, a government veterinarian who inspects animals for border crossings. He said I should not take my animals across the border, as a ten-day quarantine is required for their return to the U.S. I planned to spend several days riding in Mexico, but there went my extended over-the-border visit.

Got a return ride to Patagonia with an electronics worker I met at church. Jake had gone to gather wood, so I didn't see him, but Abby was home. I checked in back home with Sally and with Fritz. Called Kelly in St. George to report on Sugar and coordinate her drop-off. Then I called cousin Lynn in Mesa, Arizona, to come down tomorrow to take animals and me from the Mexican border back to Phoenix.

Chapter 20

Monday 18 November 1991

I did it! Made it to Mexico today! One half of my dream complete.

This morning cousin Lynn Waddell and Art Freeman's son, Lewis, brought Art's trailer and met me at the border. They watched as I rode down a dirt road toward a flimsy barbed-wire gate held closed by only a bale string. A sign was tacked to the gate which read, "Please close the gate." I nudged Teancum up to it, lifted the bale string, and the gate collapsed under its own weight. I led Sam and Teton through into Mexico. It was that easy. So much for national security!

Surely the quarantine doesn't apply for a quick photo shoot.

As I sat on Teancum, looking into Mexico, a warm feeling started in my toes and slowly traveled upward, reaching the top of my head. I took off my hat, ran my fingers through my hair, and gingerly waved my hat above my head while the other arm supported my rib. The warmth in my head seemed to turn and travel back down my neck and concentrate in my heart. I heard Brittany's words again, "I knew you could do it, Grandpa." These words fueled me much of the way when discouragement threatened to overtake me. Dreams are impossible only if one believes them to be. Oh, how I hope to always have a dream to look forward too.

A man on the Mexico side told of drug runners armed with machine guns who pass through the gate a couple times a week; sometimes up to thirty cars cross at that point in a single night. Everyone here turns a blind eye to the traffic and is extremely careful not to ask questions or be in the wrong place at the wrong time. Can you imagine only a flimsy barbed-wire fence tied with twine to keep folks in or out, when most other spots have checkpoints?

Lynn snapped some pictures as I watched the grass gently sway in the breeze and looked out over the Mexican landscape. My emotions were a jumble. First, relief–no more water or forage worries, and I'll get to rest my rib. Second, triumph! I knew I could do it. Third, sadness. It was over. Still, I was left with a sense of excitement to share my experiences with family and friends. Then, next summer–to Canada!

Lynn and Lewis helped me load up the ponies. We drove back to Abby and Jake's home to thank them, but both were gone. Left a note. Then Lynn and Lewis hauled me to Phoenix to leave the ponies and gear with Art.

Presently I'm with Lynn and Janet in Mesa. Spent a restful evening and enjoyed Lynn's beautiful singing voice. We even sang a duet or two around the piano while Janet played.

I called around to arrange a ride home. Earlier, I'd lined up Lamar Garrett and Leland, but Lamar is on an extended trip to Dallas and Leland is out doing some search-and-rescue work. Don England couldn't come until Friday, so I tried Blake Chapman, a friend from Jackson, but he was gone flying his plane to Seattle. Blake's wife Sandy pointed the finger at Bill Scott, a Jackson Holer, holed up right here in Tempe. It turns out he'd brought horses from Jackson to winter down here and was going back with an empty trailer. After all my phone calls, however, now it's too late to call him. I'll check with him in the morning.

Tuesday 19 November 1991

A whirlwind day! At 7 a.m. I phoned Bill Scott, who said he had room for me, my gear, and my horses. He was leaving at 2 p.m. Picked up my ponies from Art Freeman, then Lynn and I ran around to secure horse health certificates to cross state lines. Bought "take-home fruit," then hauled the horses and gear over to the stables, where we met Bill. L.J. Dewitt from Mesa met us at the stables with Sugar, who's made a full recovery.

Departed Tempe at 5:30 p.m. Bill and his assistant drove steady and fast. We stopped for soup in Flagstaff, where I called Kelly so he could meet us in Kanab to pick up Sugar. Bill lay in the sleeper cab while his assistant drove, and I huddled by the drafty passenger door. Beautiful, clear moonlit night. We had to slow down for fifteen elk who were crossing the road north of Panguitch, Utah. Also saw lots of deer, and nearly hit several.

Next morning, stopped in Cokeville for breakfast. Arrived in Alpine, Wyoming, by Palisade Dam at noon. Fritz Kaufman met us there and hauled me and mine the last hour–a wonderful, lickety-split trip home! Cold and snowy here in Alta, Wyoming, but my heart was aflame as I showed Hunter the sweet kiss I'd carried in my pocket. A symbol of love, yes. But it also stood for the faith and trust so many had shown, both in me and in the Lord, that I'd be successful in my journey. Thanks be to them; thank you, Lord!

How I relished Brittany and Simone's butterfly hugs again, and wrapped my arms tightly around Sally. Couldn't let go.

DECEMBER 1991

Home sweet home! Wrote Thank-you's to Utah District Rangers for their trail construction. Also wrote notes and status letters to each person who'd helped or befriended me on my journey south.

Then on December 21st, I got a phone call from Scottsdale, Arizona. Seems a fellow had watched *Arizona Cowboy* on TV and wanted to join me on my ride north. Will keep him posted. L.J. Dewitt also phoned to report he'd seen me on *Arizona Cowboy*.

Sally had gathered and saved all the newspaper articles written about my ride south. Enjoyed very much reading them and reliving my trip.

My ride south has left me thirsting for more. Instead of feeling like I've completed a milestone, I feel half baked–neither done nor beginning.

JANUARY 1992

Back to teaching and grateful that I can. I'm feeling a bit stronger and no longer have to lie down to teach, but my white count is still low and cancer is still present, as evidenced by ribs that frequently pop loose or crack. But I'm excited to start gathering maps for the ride north. This anticipation keeps a bounce in my step.

SUMMER 1992

Rats! Can't ride to Canada yet, 'cuz I'm still trying to piece together a route. I've spent my after school hours, up until now, pondering over maps, in meetings, making phone calls, writing letters to Montana/Idaho Parks and Recreation Rangers, USFS officials, and Idaho/Montana Back Country Horsemen Clubs, all in hopes of ascertaining and confirming northern trails/routes. Much harder to get information on trails going north.

I've beaten the eighteen month prognosis. I'm in my second year. And though I'm grateful for each day, I worry my health can quickly turn for the worse. I'm frustrated it is taking so much precious time to find a route north. Each day that passes gets me closer to that three year prognosis but no closer to Canada.

It's interesting that I seem to have more supporters now that I've made it to Mexico. Many of those who were on the fence before Mexico are now squarely in the, "You can make

Canada," camp. It's nice to have the support, but those who believed before I even started, are more deeply treasured.

My time home with Sally has been sweet. She's anxious about my north trip and wonders why I feel like I need to ride to Canada, too, but is supportive as always and we try to make every minute count.

December 1992

Just recently I stood on the Alta Cemetery knoll and watched as dirt fell over the casket of my friend Ty McCowin, who passed away December 4th. The icy wind whipped at the bottom of my coat. My gloved hands, tucked deep in my coat pockets, periodically came out to wipe at my dripping nose and eyes. My black Stetson, the one I wear to funerals, was pulled down low in an attempt to protect my face. But despite the wind, it was a beautiful day, a day Ty would have liked. Blue sky framed the Tetons, white snow sparkled like piled-up jewels, and loved ones murmured condolences. I thought of our ride south and the trail mishaps he'd endured without any complaint or regret. He'd lived his life the same way—without complaint.

After the graveside service, I went to my horsetrailer that stood on the outskirts of the cemetery, unloaded Bow and Arrow, and led Ty's blacks over to the fresh dirt mound. Bow sniffed the ground, Arrow stood as if at attention. Sally came and stood beside me, as we each took turns reminiscing and sharing our favorite stories of Ty.

Our bodies tired, our tears spent, we loaded up the blacks and drove away from the cemetery with a piece of me missing, left back on the hill.

CANADA-BOUND

Chapter 21

Thursday 1 July 1993

"Leaving" is such a hullabaloo! Noise, worry, forgetting things... Like most beginnings, I headed off amid a jumble of chaos and order, pandemonium and peace, lost and found.

Quite a caravan of outfits had turned out this morning as we left Alta. Eleven men will be riding with me on this first leg: nine from Utah; plus Fritz, my life-time friend, who practices what he preaches and shares with me the distinction of wearing pantyhose; and Rudy, a young, friendly college professor, a man who tells a great story and laughs easily. Rudy and the Utahns will ride with me for three days, until we get to Interstate 15, while Fritz will ride a little longer.

Son Leland, daughter Janelle, and Jube and Laurel came to ferry our vehicles. They'll leave the trucks and trailers near I-15 for Rudy and the Utah guys' trip home.

Got a good early start, close to six-thirty, headed for Bechler Meadows in Yellowstone Park. I'd planned on riding through Yellowstone, but found the park was closed to horse travel until mid-July because of late high water on the trails. So we hauled the animals forty miles west over to Sheridan Creek and got up close to the Continental Divide Trail at Island Park by the Centennial Range.

Rudy backed his mule, Jeep, out of the trailer. Jeep's companion mule, Wildflower, followed after like a nursing kitten. My heart warmed when I saw Wildflower. Her name reminds me of dear friends and the Tetons.

A couple of years before my eighteen-month to three-year life-expectancy prognosis, I'd decided I wanted to raise mules. My jack, named Flapjack, produced four foals; Teancum was one of them. But after being diagnosed with cancer, I started giving things away, including three of those four young mules. One I gave to Leigh Ann, Rudy's wife; I knew she'd give her a loving home. Now, several years later, this same Wildflower is serving as my pack mule on our ride north.

Fritz, who wears his hat comfortably pulled down just right, finished snugging the ropes over his packhorse's back. Fritz owns only horses, and we spend more than a few minutes each day in friendly banter over which is better, mules or horses. A pair of folding lawn chairs laced tightly on the top of the pack appeared like woven wings, inspiring the image of a giant horsefly.

"Are we going to the beach?" I smiled as I tightened Buster's cinch.

"You'll thank me later," he replied, patting the chairs.

I'm leading two mules: Buster, who is mine, and Leigh Ann's Wildflower. I ride my mule Teancum, who hasn't quit on me yet. Teton just recently gained back all the weight he'd lost on the ride south. It took one and a half years, but now he's returned to his gassy self; I'm so glad to hear it. He earned a rest. Instead of Sam, I'm packing Buster to give him the experience.

Had my monthly chemo right before I left, and am feeling good. I've also been taking Fosamax to slow my bone loss. Seems to be helping. I'm physically stronger now than when I rode to Mexico, so I don't need the ten-pound cloth bags, but I still pack small and light.

Got lost right off the bat; went too far north. Turns out I was using the wrong side of the map! Hell, was I mortified when I had to admit an hour and a half of circling was my own fault. If a camera in the sky had recorded our "excursion," the twelve of us would've looked like a snake looping slowly back and forth, trying to find its way through a ground-squirrel maze. Finally got found. The route actually was good, but it needs more signs in the meadows and by each road. Swarms of mosquitos pester both human and animal. We'll try to stay hugging the Continental Divide mountain ridges as much as possible.

No wrecks today. With so many riders, that's something to be grateful for. So peaceful and relaxing to be back on the trail. I'm inspired by the fresh wilderness and new country. Snow banks remind us how high we are. What Lewis and Clark must have thought!

"How do you like the beach?" Fritz asked after dinner, grinning over at me as I lounged in his extra lawn chair.

I nodded and caressed the chair arm. "Heaven; I've learned to never doubt you."

"Then you'll trade in your mules for horses?"

"You just lost your credibility," I chuckled, shaking my head. I'm out-numbered for mule support. Most of these men ride horses. Rudy and I alone hold the line in defense of long ears and Roman noses.

"Would you like some fudge?" asked Fritz as he carefully removed the waxed paper wrapper from the brown ball he cradled in his lap.

"Ohhh, would I!" Hand outstretched, I bounded from the lawn chair, my eyes the size of a full moon. Rudy, tying horses and seemingly out of earshot, must have the gift of echolocation. He too nodded and scampered to gather round, as did the others as Fritz neatly sliced the fudge ball into twelve pieces. Each man savored his portion; some moaned, others licked fingers to get every speck.

The creamy confection in my mouth reminded me of a similar fudge treat from years ago. Visiting the Idaho Teton County Fair, I walked past a candy booth and a plump lady in a red apron called out, "Would you like to try a sample of our B fudge?" Skidding to a halt and beelining in her direction, the thought crossed my mind, "Isn't this the County Fair where everything is judged? Why not A fudge? Surely B fudge is inferior to A fudge…"

Stepping up to the counter, what the woman held up looked like every other fudge I'd ever seen. Expecting substandard taste, nonetheless I plopped a brown square into my mouth. Instantly my taste buds sang like angels. "Why call it B fudge?" I'd asked, wrinkling my forehead and licking my fingers.

"Oh honey, it's beef fudge, not B fudge." She chuckled, her jiggling belly reminding me of Santa.

"Beef-f-f-f fudge?" I repeated, looking at the full sample plate.

She slid it towards me with a nod. "We're the Cow Belles. Our husbands raise cattle and we all do our part to promote beef. We cook a beef roast, run it through the grinder, add some sugar, milk, butter… and there you go, beef fudge," she explained.

"Mmmm, meat from home. Thanks, Fritz," I said, nibbling off a corner to make it last.

Rudy, already done, licked his lips and squinted. "Meat like beef?" Then his eyebrows raised in a wrinkle. "No need to ask, 'Where's the beef'?"

Rudy's Journal Entry, July 1, 1993

"Rudy, you and Leigh Ann come ride with me," Chuck had said on the other end of the phone. It was early June, 1990. We hadn't seen Chuck for several cold months, but warm weather often brought an invitation for us to ride with him. Leigh Ann and I had each picked up different phones at the same time and we agreed to come

the next day. Knowing he'd been sick, we inquired after his health.

"I can ride, provided you help me get on my mule," he said with conviction.

So the next day Leigh Ann and I brought our horses from Rexburg, Idaho, to Alta, Wyoming. Inside Chuck's earth-shelter home we found him in the living room, lying on a high plywood bed. My heart sank. He looked much different than when we'd last seen him. He struggled to sit up, his back pain making him grimace. At this point he didn't know it was cancer, but was trying several different doctors in an attempt to find the source of the pain. We all decided he better not attempt a ride. Leigh Ann and I left his home with heavy hearts, saddened and worried about the shape he was in. In Chuck's mind he thought once he was in the saddle he could ride well enough; he thought the only problem would be getting on the mule. I worried it was much more than that.

Leigh Ann and I rode up Teton Canyon. On our way, she glanced right and left as if taking mental notes. On the ride back down, she climbed out of the saddle at certain spots to gather wildflowers for Chuck. She hand-picked only certain flowers, ignoring others close by.

After loading our horses and driving out of the canyon, we stopped again at Chuck's place. Leigh Ann handed him her bouquet as he lay flat on the plywood bed. Holding the flowers up in front of his face, smiling, he said, "Mules Ears." He gently caressed each green leaf that resembled a mule's ear, their stalks topped with yellow and white blossoms.

"And Steers Head," Leigh Ann chirped, pointing to the blossom that looked like a cow's face with horns. Her face beamed. "I picked each flower specially for you."

"The Wyoming State Flower." His fingertip stroked the wispy, red-orange Indian Paintbrush.

"And Mountain Lover," Leigh Ann said softly, referring to the predominant bouquet filler of vibrant green leaves with small, red blossoms.

Upon hearing the name of this flower, Chuck swallowed hard. "Thank you. I wish I could have gone with you," he whispered, closing his eyes.

Leigh Ann, too, nodded, her eyes watering, the tears threatening to break free and flow down her cheeks.

The bouquet rested atop Chuck's chest, its colors vibrant, its scents intoxicating. He inhaled deeply and appeared to be transported to the mountains for a few moments. "So thoughtful. Thank you," he murmured.

Chuck had spent several previous summers clearing trails for the local Forest Service, and with volunteer help, had built a horse-transfer camp in Teton Canyon. Creating the transfer camp also included cutting a trail to connect to the existing mountain trail, clearing trees, building ramps, and constructing a corral and hitch racks with feed stations. He was to be honored at the transfer camp dedication in September 1990, shortly after his cancer diagnosis. He called Leigh Ann and me and invited us to attend. Several Forest Service personnel, family members, and friends were also in attendance. One of the four young mules he'd raised from his jack, Flapjack, was tied to the hitching rack. A plaque, expressing gratitude for Chuck's service in the mountains, was attached to a large boulder at the head of the camp.

Following the presentation, Chuck called Leigh Ann up to the front. She hesitantly complied. Then he began: "The backwoods have always been therapeutic for me. This spring, at a time when hope was waning, Leigh Ann gave me a simple gift of mountain flowers. They lifted my spirits, partly because the flowers were from the Tetons and partly because the thoughtfulness of the gift was overwhelming. But what she gave me was so much more than flowers; she brought me hope. Thank you." Then, with tears flowing down his cheeks, he untied his mule and handed its halter rope to Leigh Ann. "She's yours. I want you to have her," he said. "As payment for a bouquet of wildflowers."

Surprised at the gift, Leigh Ann inhaled sharply, covering her open mouth with her palms. "Ohhh," escaped her cupped hands. Chuck explained that the mule was sweet and gentle and needed a good home. He said that Leigh Ann's heart was such that she could provide that kind of care.

"I'll call her Wildflower," Leigh Ann said, recovering her voice.

FRIDAY 2 JULY 1993

Second day, and we started off with nice riding on a clearly-marked trail. How comforting to see signs periodically and know we're where we're supposed to be.

Lost the trail again. Yup, sailing along secure on a good trail, and then all of a sudden there were the Tetons in front of us. *Not* where they were supposed to be! We'd ridden 180 degrees on a Table Top Trail. Heckle, heckle from the peanut gallery. Retraced and got straightened out, but then the trail got jungly. Rudy's mule, Jeep, true to his name, could've motored anywhere. Rudy just hung on. From there we rode to Little Table Top. Fritz got us camped by a mountain lake with grass and timber. Looks like it's getting ready to rain or snow.

Very tired. So good to settle in for the night. Again, forgot to bring a bunch of stuff on this departure. I feel ok, 'cuz Fritz did, too. Remembered my overshoes, though!

I offered Rudy a spot in the tent with Fritz and me, but he wanted to bed down outside under a tarp.

RUDY'S JOURNAL ENTRY, JULY 2, 1993

"How can you ride so long without getting saddlesores?" I asked Chuck while riding today. My tender backside prompted the question.

"Calloused behind. Just let yours toughen up. You'll get used to it," Chuck replied. *He glanced over at Fritz. Was that a wink they exchanged? Something was up.*

"Just wait and see," Fritz said, muffling a snicker with his hand.

Tonight I took Chuck up on his offer, crawling into the tent, whining about my backside. While relaxing on top of my sleeping bag, I noticed Fritz and Chuck give each other a slight nod and then begin to undress. My eyes widened when I saw "ladies-legs."

"I can't sleep in a tent with men who wear pantyhose!" I yelled, snatching up my bag and backing out of there fast! Laughter followed me out of the tent. I laid out my sleeping bag not far away and staked a tarp over it. Then I nestled in. I noticed that one of the jokers had hung the "lady-legs" at the tent opening for my viewing. I chuckled, trying to think of a way to get back at them. Sky looks ominous. I hope I don't have to swallow my pride and crawl back in with them.

SATURDAY 3 JULY 1993

We awoke to rain and six inches of wet, heavy snow. We'd covered our supplies, but slushy puddles were everywhere. Stayed in bed late, waiting out the weather. The clouds lifted a little, but we decided to linger in camp and dry out. Lotsa fun visiting, sharing stories, eating, and lounging around in those lawn chairs. Had to eat more crow, of course, since I used Fritz's chairs again today.

Came time to ride and it was still too cloudy and foggy. Couldn't make out which direction to go. Lots of concerned "scouts" reconnoitered individually to determine where the trail was. Then twelve different norths were picked out. The sun appeared and settled it. Whew!

Toward evening we threw up camp in Mule Meadows

by a dark, glass-like volcanic rock. Fritz stepped over to the obsidian. "Top quality," he said. He'd tried his hand at making arrowheads with this type of rock. He polished a smooth side and we used it as a mirror.

We built a fire and propped up some logs on which we could drape damp saddle blankets. The sun had shone all day, but last night's rain and snow left us still damp. It didn't take long for the radiating heat to warm bodies and hearts, the fire burning down to a pile of perfectly glowing, ashen coals. "I'll throw some steaks on the fire for you," I volunteered. The Utah cook nodded, handing me the meat.

At that, we each went about helping to prepare the meal. Some cut potatoes and onions; others prepared cobblers; we even had corn on the cob. I've never eaten so well while camping. The Utahns seemed to have brought along an entire grocery store. I threw two steaks on the embers, then reached for the third.

Rudy cleared his throat. "Um, Chuck, that looks like a good piece of meat, so shouldn't we use a pan?" he asked. The camp had turned quiet, all eyes focused on the steaks sitting directly on the hot coals. Only Fritz knew what I was doing. He sat back in his lawn chair, corn husks dangling from his hands, amused at the distraught looks on the other faces.

"This is the way it's done; you'll see," I reassured them, glancing around to each man and silently encouraging him to continue his chore. Some returned to food preparation right away, others not so fast, as they watched me until twelve prime steaks, covered in gray ash, lay in the coals. About this time I said a silent prayer. I didn't want this to be the first bad meal since we'd started.

Rudy crouched nearby, stirring the onions and spuds. "When did you start cooking meat like that?" he asked, pointing with the spatula.

"When I forgot to pack my pans," I answered. I tonged a

steak from the fire and blew the ash from the meat. "When nothing sticks, its done." With the browned meat on Rudy's plate, once again activity ceased around the fire. Rudy made a great show of untucking his shirt-tail, tucking it up into his collar, then extending his pinkies as he drew the knife blade back and forth. The steak's pink middle secreted clear juice as knife and fork pierced the browned exterior. The bite-size portion on his fork was brought under his nose; steam disappeared up his nostrils as he slowly inhaled. At last he plopped the meat past his lips, chewed, then swallowed. "Steak-master!" was all he said as he waved the empty fork in the air. Steaks plated, we all ate. Success–thank goodness!

After dinner we sat around swapping tales–which grew into tall tales as the evening went on. I continually wiped tears as we hee-hawed; we even ended up buying into some of the stories.

One man babbled on as if he were an auctioneer, using strings of offbeat words as filler in his fast-talking story. He jumped so quickly from word to word, I was left wondering whether they were made up or genuine unknowns. He ended each sentence as if it were the 11th commandment. When his story was done, we could have heard chipmunks from Canada. Then we erupted as if on cue, roaring so hard one Utahn fell right off his log bench.

Towards the end, I shared some poetry, then dragged my spent body to my tent. My flashlight hangs from the tent ceiling. I write this entry facing the open tent door. Some of the men sit still surrounding the crackling fire, some slouched in lawn chairs, others on logs as they rock back and forth like a team of horses in a pulling contest, each out-doing the last one. Others bend forward, straining to hear, then lean back, jiggle-jawed. As my mind fades into slumber, I smile to bits and pieces told about a chicken derby...

Rudy's Journal Entry, July 3, 1993

I should have braved the "ladies-legs." This morning I woke when Chuck nudged me with a boot toe in my back. I'd pulled the drawstring of my mummy bag so tight that it left only a little circle for air round my mouth and nose.

"Are you hibernating?" Chuck asked. I mumbled, trying to shift into a more comfortable position. I felt as if I were trapped in a dentist's chair, pinned under a hundred-pound lead apron.

Chuck must not have noticed my attempts to move, for before I could try again, he was kneeling and frantically brushing snow from my tarp. "Rudy, Rudy?" His raised voice was laced with concern.

I poked my head out to show him I wasn't a frozen corpse. "I'm fine. I'm stuck in my burrow, though." Still, he kept brushing away the snow. Only after he'd uncovered my tarp was I able to turn, look him in the eye, and say, "Squeak."

I used to feel guilty about my nice tent and foam pads whenever I saw Chuck pull off his saddle, line up the saddle pads, lay his sleeping bag on the pads and cover up with his duster. He claimed the saddle made an excellent pillow. Now, I was the one roughing it and realized it wasn't that bad—other than the packed-down-by-snow part.

Chuck cooked up steaks last night that could've won him a purple ribbon at the county fair. His chili, Dutch oven dinners, and cobblers are mouthwatering. So I wasn't concerned a few years ago when he called and invited me to join him and Fritz for a ride—lunch furnished. He said to come right then. I had no time to pack, but took Chuck at his word. I remember riding and riding, the lunch hour long past. I was hungry. I eased Jeep up alongside Teancum and inquired when we might stop for a bite, whereupon Chuck pulled a cold wiener and apple from his saddlebag and said, straightfaced, "There you go."

Now, I don't eat wieners when they're cooked, let alone raw; "lunch"? No... Regardless, I thanked him and fell back in line behind Fritz, who was chewing on some jerky. Fritz smiled as big as the sun and handed me some jerky as we rode along. I gobbled the apple and made the jerky last all afternoon, but forgot to take the hotdog out of my saddlebag when I got home. I remembered several days later, when a rancid odor wafted out of my tack room.

Since that time, I've ridden with Chuck when dinner consisted of macaroni noodles and an onion in water, all cooked in a tin pot about four inches across the top and two inches deep. And that was for both of us! No wonder he's so thin! I've realized when Chuck fixes food it's either feast or famine. Now, I pack jerky and trail mix in my pocket, just in case.

Today when we came to a ravine, Teancum balked, then fussed and wouldn't go further. We all pulled to a stop as Chuck cranked him in a tight circle. Soon they came charging by all of us and Chuck yelled, "I'll be right back; I'm going to mule school." We waited, then they came charging past again. School was still in session. After persistent kicking, flipping of flanks with the lead rope, and verbal "encouragement," Teancum finally made the leap. Chuck jumped the mule back and forth over that ravine probably ten times. Boy! Can Chuck sit a saddle. I want to be an excellent rider like him when I grow up.

Chuck also taught me about using a choker. He once had a bay mare who bucked for the first few minutes before every ride, then settled down. His kids were afraid to get on her, so he'd ride her until the bucks were gone, then the kids could climb on. Tired of this routine, Chuck checked out a book from the library and found one way to stop the bucking. He'd tie a rope to the saddlehorn, loop it low around the horse's neck, then retie it to the saddlehorn, essentially cutting off the horse's air supply when she'd put her head down and causing her to bring it up. No more bucking! Chuck's a problem-solver.

Sunday 4 July 1993

Nice night, cloudy but not stormy. It took us until 1 p.m. to get packed up. Surely there's peace when one chooses not to let the world hurry him. Now I hope we can find the Utahns' pickups and trailers in the canyon where we think they ought to be.

We cut off too soon from Little Table Top, found a promising trail, then lulled ourselves into false security. After riding three miles too far, we found a sign and had to backtrack. Lost again! Made it great the second time around. A little more embarrassing when you get lost with a large following versus getting lost by your lonesome. The Camas Creek country is beautiful and open. Seems like it goes on forever—a sweet feeling.

We found the trucks and trailers! When we arrived at the freeway, there sat Dave Green, a friend from home. He'd come the day before to join us and had camped by the trailers, waiting for us to exit the mountains. We got Rudy and Jeep loaded along with the Utahns, then sent them on their way. I'll miss the large campfire gatherings and great food. What fun they've been.

Dave, Fritz and I rode across Modoc Creek, traversed it one and a half miles downstream, and camped not far from I-15. Stayed close to the road so Rudy could find us when he returns tomorrow with our replenished and forgotten supplies.

Rudy's Journal Entry, July 4, 1993

I slept in the tent last night. Cozy. It doesn't matter a bit what folks wear when your eyes are closed in sleep. Enjoyed a restful night and woke at 5 a.m. to a "rooster" singing "Amazing Grace." Peeking out of the tent, there in the trees stood Chuck in his underwear, singing to the world. I wish my friend luck on his journey. I wish I could ride longer.

Chapter 22

Monday 5 July 1993

Woke dry, no sweats! Cause for celebration! It is certainly the exception.

Enjoyed a peaceful night. The hobbled mules stayed close to camp. Rudy and Leigh Ann arrived at nine with all the things we needed. They'll shuttle Dave's outfit to Bannock Pass #2, and when we get there in a few days they'll join Fritz and me. From there, Dave will head for home. We discovered #1 Bannock Pass by accident. Should have figured there was a #1 if there was a #2, but didn't.

Dave and Fritz are comfortable company, like my favorite jeans. Even their horses meld with my mules. Glad they're here. We got on our way shortly after noon and decided to ride the Continental Divide Trail fenceline, since the new country fools many of us. Traveling on the top of creation. Surely beautiful. Lotsa steep ups and downs, much winding around, so in four hours we traveled about seventeen miles of trail, but made only six miles as the crow flies. The Continental Divide Trail signs surely are comforting.

Saw much wild game today: three pairs of cow and calf moose in one draw, many deer, about fifty elk in three bunches, and two wolves–one of which was squatting on her den mound just fifty yards from us. Our ponies eyed most wildlife with mild interest; however, the wolves peaked their interest a little more. Teancum used his special lizard eyes to track their movement as well as focus on the trail. I'm so proud of him I still could burst a button.

Nearly all this country is open hills, and one can see for a long distance. Spied an approaching hailstorm, so we pulled down off the watershed onto a Montana by-loop and camped in a stately fir glade by Scheiberger Creek. Not wishing to experience a "hail of a trail," we had picket lines tied and camp set up before the storm hit. Only lasted a short while. Then we came out from hiding and cooked dinner.

Ah, so good to be in the hills.

Fritz's Journal Entry, July 5, 1993

Chuck is fussy when it comes to the Forest Service's leave-no-trace-behind policy. He's clearly read the camping/horse regulations and follows them explicitly. When we leave a campsite, the garbage is packed on a horse, manure is broken up, and pawed holes are filled in. Even the trees are left unblemished due to special two-inch nylon tree-saver straps he uses when he strings the picket line. I know no one who loves the backcountry more than Chuck.

My ulcers are bothering me. The painkillers I brought aren't doing the trick. I might have to leave when Dave does. I was hoping to continue riding when Rudy and Leigh Ann join Chuck, but I don't know. I so enjoy the mountains. I completely understand why Chuck is on this ride. If I were in his shoes, I might be doing the same. The mountains do for me what I think they do for him.

I'm glad to be able to share in this ride with my "horse brother."

Tuesday 6 July 1993

Traveled twenty-five miles today, Fritz leading the way. His bay thoroughbred, Bullet, stepped out and hurried. His packhorse, Sonny, kept pace. Teancum is learning to really stretch out, too. He now oversteps by fourteen inches to keep up with Bullet. Buster, pulling Wildflower, just gave up and jogged most of the time with Wildflower also trotting. Dave, on his feisty black mustang, Midnight, had no trouble keeping up, even pulling his pack-horse, Ribs. Not sure if Ribs was named for his protruding ribs or if Dave was just hungry at the time.

Got lost only twice today. That doesn't sound like much of a badge of honor, but put into perspective, I'll wear it proudly. Saw lots of elk and a few deer as we rode up Sawmill Canyon, some of the most majestic and beautiful high country I've *ever* traveled! Maybe next summer I'll bring Leland and anyone else who'd like to join us up through Sawmill and across Bannock Pass to Nicholia-Tendou Creek Junction on the Montana side. This is country truly deserving of the title "Continental Divide."

Today we met up with a bunch of *real* cowboys, riding the high range and mending fence. One had an unwaxed handlebar mustache that hung ten to twelve inches long on each side. Friendly and interested in our ride, they greatly admired our outfits and mules. When they joked about Fritz's high-riding lawn chairs, Fritz only smiled, knowing they, like I, would in fact vie for a chair around the campfire.

Bannock is a huge, open, sagebrush-meadow pass, a fitting finale to a memorable day. We camped under high transformer lines east of Gilmore. Cooked up chili and spuds for supper, then the rain started.

So grateful for the tent this go-around. In these conditions, the fly I used going south wouldn't have worked.

WEDNESDAY 7 JULY 1993
Could tell it was freezing outside before I opened my eyes. The fingers on my left hand were crushed by a post-pounder when I was a young buck, and they stiffen up in cold weather. The doctor said they wouldn't heal well, that I'd gradually lose the flexibility and usefulness of those fingers. They healed fine, only a bit flat, like smashed sausages.

I stepped from the tent and saw frozen rain coating everything. The ponies looked frosty, the day gray and gloomy. As the morning progressed, sheets of thin ice slid off the tarp that protected the saddles. My spirits rose as the gray lifted. Skies were sunny by the time we left camp and for the rest of the day. My, aren't we children of the sun!

This morning I tethered Buster and Teancum with hind hobbles. There was absolutely *no* place to tie them while packing up, and we couldn't afford the hassle of traipsing after them. Buster stood pretty still once hobbled, but Teancum was dancing and winning the battle when Fritz suggested that we blindfold him. Wow, the magic pill; he stood like a milk cow. Fritz's knowledge is amazing. If I were to ever get lost for longer than a day or two, I'd like it to be with Fritz. He knows which roots, flowers, and mushrooms are edible, and his calm personality relaxes all who are around him. I've surely enjoyed having Fritz and Dave for company.

Cattle were lowing all morning. Got away mid-morning. I led Wildflower and turned Buster loose. It was fun to watch him eagerly move to the front, then wait his turn and fall back in line. Back and forth, back and forth.

Late this morning, near a spring, Fritz jumped a four- or five-year-old bull moose in velvet. Evidently it was the only water for some distance, because in a few minutes a five-point bull elk, also in velvet, waited his turn to drink. Despite his left horn being broken off above the brow line, he was magnificent.

Today I spied some pitch to the side of the trail, so I climbed off and collected it. When you spend so many days at a time in the mountains, you appreciate anything that helps start a fire. Even when water-soaked, pitch will still light. I couldn't pass it by.

Today we rode about twenty-four miles. More grandeur. Got lost only once; my badge is getting bigger. We passed a group of ten backpackers who'd taken three days to cover what we did today. Am I glad to be riding.

In the late evening we camped at the head of Rock Creek, above Nicholia. Watched eight elk above camp for our evening entertainment. Then we bathed in a bowl. Mmm, felt good. Teancum thought about leaving and actually started to, so I had to tie him up.

THURSDAY 8 JULY 1993

Made only about fourteen miles today. I was reminded several times how frail I am, in spite of the bone-strengthening meds. Between Simpson Creek and Morrison Lake, we dismounted to rest. When it was time to leave, I gathered up Teancum's reins, stepped into the stirrup, and threw my weight up into the saddle. Unfortunately, it was loose and started to turn, my upward motion pounding my rib cage into the saddlehorn. The impact knocked the air out of me. Pain shot through my chest. Blackout. When I came to, I was flat on the ground, grunting and gasping for breath. It was as if a steamroller had run over my chest. My lips moved, but muscles cramping in my chest kept my lungs from expanding. Fritz and Dave hovered over me.

"Take it easy, Chuck," Fritz said calmly, his hand resting on my forearm. Focusing on my friend, at last I began to get some air into my lungs. I lay there until my breathing was even and I no longer felt lightheaded. I ran my fingertips along the sore rib and felt the broken ends, which luckily hadn't punctured the skin. Dang! Not just cracked but snapped. Don't know if it had broken on the saddlehorn while climbing on, or sliding off, or when I landed on the ground. Fritz gave me a couple of his pain pills, which seemed to help.

After about twenty minutes, Dave and Fritz lifted me onto Teancum. Both were long-faced, their complexions pasty, like mine, I suppose. Grunting and groaning and wiping away tears, I made it a couple more miles before we had to stop, deciding to camp above Indian Creek, west of Whitworth Ranch. They gently eased me from Teancum's back. My face was dripping and my shirt was soaked with sweat. Dave unpacked my ponies and wrapped my sleeping bag around me, while Fritz set up tents and started dinner. We thought about trying to remove my wet shirt, but realized we couldn't pull my arm through the sleeve.

I didn't eat much, but lying flat here in the tent feels good.

FRIDAY 9 JULY 1993

Slept pretty well, considering; rolled only once during the night, and it jolted me awake. I quickly returned to the stone-like prone position and fell back asleep.

Rode about eighteen miles hunched over to protect my rib and took shallow breaths to minimize chest movement. The pain pills keep me going, but I can't lift a thing. Dave had to do all my packing; I couldn't even get my arm high enough to bridle Teancum. Dave tied Wildflower behind Ribs, and Fritz tied Buster to Sonny.

Along the trail we jumped six ragged, gray mountain sheep ewes on a snowbank, then spooked up twenty or so elk. Came to a place that looked like the Continental Divide Trail making a big "U" loop in the canyon, so Fritz decided to shortcut it. I objected, but went along, grumbling under my breath. Every steep spot, every rocky place, every jostling tangle I registered my complaints, but all within myself. It's interesting how negative, unhappy, and critical I become when I'm hurting. I could learn a lesson from those who suffer chronic pain and still remain upbeat.

Flies buzzed thick in the hot timber. When at last we left the trees, we rode out through a herd of cattle mixed in with one hundred-plus elk. Wow, what a sight! Fritz said, "Glad we took the shortcut, or we'd never have seen that big bunch." But I was in too much of a sulk nursing my wound to agree. Turned out we were two canyons too far south from the Continental Divide Trail, which had veered north behind the "apparent" "U" loop, so we had to bushwhack down through sagebrush to Wildcat and Frank Hall Creeks.

Along the way we rode up behind a gal and guy leading three pretty llamas. They'd quit the Continental Divide Trail for the same reason we had–trail confusion. However, they carried an Idaho road map that they shared with us. With our bearings set, we turned right at the next fork and rode two to three miles, camping along the roadside by a stream below Bannock Pass #2.

I lounged around camp while Dave and Fritz went down to Leadore, Idaho, to pick up groceries and call Rudy, as we need to coordinate Rudy and Leigh Ann's arrival tomorrow. But when Dave and Fritz returned, they were long-faced and Dave issued an ultimatum: "We're going home, and you need to come with us." It seems Fritz isn't feeling good, his ulcers giving him grief.

Fritz met my eyes and spoke quietly but firmly, tipping his hat brim back above his forehead. "You need to come home with us for a week or two and recuperate, Chuck."

I struggled to my feet from my lawn chair. "QUIT? No! I'll lie around a few days and make it on my own," I argued. "You just brought plenty of food. I only need horse grain, and can do without that for a while." I felt backed into a corner, pressured to give up. I was also annoyed with myself for letting a tiny carelessness threaten a two-year dream. Dave stood behind Fritz, head down, the toe of his boot boring a hole in the dirt. Fritz smiled sadly and let out a sigh. Both men knew to press the point was useless.

I melted as I looked Fritz in the eye. He was hurting, too. "I'm sorry you don't feel well," I said softly. "Is there anything I can do?"

"No, I'll rest when I get home. Why don't you come, too?"

"I'll be alright," I said, knowing I couldn't bridle, saddle or pack my animals. But I'd convinced myself to believe if I rested for a day or two, I could make it.

We suppered on spaghetti and I went to bed very sore, disgruntled but resolute.

"Dream, or desperation?"

FRITZ'S JOURNAL ENTRY, JULY 9, 1993

It's too painful to keep riding; I'm going home. While in Leadore I called my son, Roger, to come get me. Then called Rudy and Leigh Ann and told them of Chuck's injury and that I'd try to convince him to go home. Dave phoned his daughter and asked her to notify Sally, Leland, and Janelle that Chuck is hurt, but doesn't want to leave the mountains. He's injured too badly to continue. Please don't be stubborn, Chuck.

SATURDAY 10 JULY 1993

In the middle of the night I awoke from a dream where Leland and Janelle were calling for me to come home. I lay on my back, looking up into the tent darkness, wondering if I needed to quit. After a time, I dozed off to a fitful sleep.

After breakfast, Fritz's son Roger showed up to haul Fritz home. Leland and Janelle followed him into camp, driving my truck and pulling my trailer behind. I gritted my teeth, prepared for the confrontation ahead. Leland stepped from the driver's side and Janelle hurried over to check on me. They'd left Alta right after Anita had given birth to Jed, Leland's second son. Hearing the news, my resolve wilted as I dabbed at the tears.

Leland showed me a snapshot of Anita hoisting a blanketed bundle with tufts of red hair sticking out the top. "He needs to know his grandpa."

I needed no more convincing. I *was* glad they'd come, and decided to give in. I was kinda relieved. It turned out that another son, Eddy, had called Leland last night, worried that I was hurt in the mountains.

They loaded Dave's horses into his trailer. Roger tried to get his dad to rest in the truck cab while he loaded Bullet and Sonny, but Fritz wouldn't rest until his horses were taken care of. My three mules were anxious to load, as if they knew we were going home.

Curled up in the truck cab with my arms cradling my ribs, I realized how much softer truck upholstery is than saddle leather. I wondered why I'd been so stubborn, so irrational. Is reaching a goal more important than family?

Monday 12 July 1993

Early this morning, at home in Alta, Wyoming, Sally drove me to the local clinic. I have a broken rib, broken collarbone, and sprained shoulder muscles. The doctor gave me lotsa pills, a bigger brace, and a severe scolding.

Total miles ridden so far: about 1,400. I'm about 700 to 800 miles short of the Canadian border. How's that for stinky!

Chapter 23

Friday 16 July 1993

After nearly a week convalescing, I've decided to make another run at it. I know one thing for sure–if I don't start moving, I'll never get there. I'm afraid, with time ticking, I might be too sick to try again. I guess stubborn wins out in the end. I'm bandaged and wrapped up, so Leland and Jube will haul me up to Bannock Pass and ride along to help saddle ponies and lift everything.

Saturday 17 July 1993

Fun abounds! We got lost for three hours in a snowstorm amid a lodgepole jungle, atop a mountain. Then, circled here and there and finally got out on a point just when the sky lifted a little, so we could identify Eight Mile Creek Basin. We followed the Continental Divide Trail fence and got snowed on a second time. So wet and cold!

Dry camp. Takes quite a bit of tossing and turning to adjust my achy shoulder, rib and arm.

Monday 19 July 1993

We traveled an endless lodgepole jungle. Then went down a steep, steep shale rock trail. I'm sure Teancum wondered what was the matter with me!

Even so, traveled twenty-five miles. We're camped in a wet meadow with thousands of mosquitoes. A long night ahead.

These last few days have been much harder on me emotionally than I'd anticipated. I was ready for the pain associated with broken bones and sprained muscles, but wasn't ready for the blow to my emotional well-being as a result of being so dependent on Leland and Jube. My personal motto has always been: "Do for yourself." I feel like a child waiting for a parent to come do or fix. That weight is harder for me to bear than the pain of broken bones.

Tuesday 20 July 1993

Good journeying, bad country. We did lotsa zig-zagging on steep, up-and-down climbs. Some of the trail is still under snow, which causes us to do a lot of jumping and scrambling. The jolting is painful, but not to the degree that I felt in my heart this morning while I watched Leland saddle Teancum.

Tonight I'm twenty-five miles tired!

Wednesday 21 July 1993

It snowed and drizzled till noon, so we huddled under a folded tarp, wrapped in saddle blankets. The sky cleared and we packed up. The blazing orange trail markers painted on rocks to the side of the trail gave us assurance. Then the blazes ended abruptly and we did much circling–no trail. Rained again. Bushwhacked with much floundering. We traveled eighteen miles today, but only five easy ones.

Wet and cold. Broken rib and collarbone are too sore. We're going home again. After coming to that conclusion, the knot in my gut hardened as I thought of the doubters. Then, sanity took over. What was I thinking? I can't push through at all costs. Sometimes I can only achieve by knowing when to stop so I can continue another day, a day when I can do for myself. Irrational as it sounds, I feel like I've not really completed this portion of the trail–because I needed help. However, I'm grateful for Leland and Jube's support, for encouraging me to try, and for allowing me to fail instead of coddling me.

AUGUST 1993

It's been a little over a month since my return. Rib and collarbone mended; back teaching school… Eager students make my profession rewarding and I love being around my family, but I yearn for the trail. The mountains are calling.

DECEMBER 1993

A few days ago, I stood with my black Stetson pulled low over my ears and my coat pulled tight, waiting to file past the casket for a final farewell. A cloud-covered sky released puffy snowflakes that softly settled on the fresh mound of dirt. All was peaceful and quiet, except for the sniffles and crunching snow as people made their way past the burial plot.

My turn came. I stood by the casket with a hole in my heart. I'd been on this knoll just one year ago for Ty's burial. Didn't like it then, nor now. My dear friend, who wore his hat just right, was gone. Fritz passed away December 14, 1993. His "ulcers" turned out to be colon cancer. He was diagnosed on Labor Day weekend, about one and a half months after we came home from our ride last July.

As falling snow coated the flower arrangement on the casket, our last conversation came back to me. I'd gripped his hand that lay on his bed cover. His hands had once been massively strong, but now were frail. We laughed, cried, and remembered. As the hour passed, the palm of my free hand continually wiping the stream of tears from my face, he told me he'd been unable to keep food down for several days, but that he'd wanted one last drink of water from Cold Springs, a stream close to his boyhood home. Ken, Fritz's second son, had gladly obliged, carrying his father to the truck and driving to Cold Springs. Fritz waited in the truck while Ken snowshoed a half mile to fill a glass with water. The water stayed down when all else wouldn't. After that, Fritz was unable to go to Cold Springs himself, but Ken went daily to bring back water for his father. As Fritz described the sweet experience, I recognized his feelings. Truly a mountain brother.

"I'll be looking for you," he'd said, smiling his classic smile. He was lifting me when it should have been the other way around.

"I'm not far behind," I said, giving his hand one final squeeze. Then I stood, bent over his bed, and lightly kissed him on the forehead. He was a cowboy to the core, but there was no embarrassment, only a slow blink of his eyes and a widening grin. Farewells are hard.

Now I stepped away from the casket, allowing others to say their goodbyes. I knew no one finer; the honor had been mine. I pulled my coat tighter, but the warmth in my chest deemed it almost unnecessary as I made my way over to say "Hullo" to Ty.

As Sally and I drove away from the Alta cemetery, I felt I'd left another part of me behind. No more would I hear Fritz say, "God looks out for little children, fools, and Chuck."

MY FINAL RIDE NORTH

Chapter 24

Friday 17 June 1994

Well, well… we'll try this again. I've got the same donks with me: Teancum, Buster and Wildflower. Had a chemo treatment last week. Feeling good. Outlived doctor's estimate of eighteen months to three years–every day a gift.

Jube and his trademark grin accompanied me for a few days from Leadore, Idaho, to Salmon. Having him along felt like wearing a comfy wool sweater. His horse, Lady, still has no love for mules, but his packhorse, Sandy, is as sweet as ever.

We had a major change in elevation the last day Jube was with me, dropping to within 2000 feet above sea level. Started out with six inches of snow on the ground. The sardines in my sandwich froze, reminding me of bean sandwiches when I was young. Back then, after doing chores, I'd go to the house to get my lunch that Mary, our house-helper, had made for me; then I'd hook up the sleigh and trot up to Spring Creek where our neighbors Oscar and Wayne were logging. We'd find the trees that the forest service had marked, then dig the snow from around them so we could saw them down. One day Mary had made me a navy-bean sandwich, and by the time I bit into it, the beans had frozen solid. From then on, I called them my "bullet" sandwiches. Oscar and Wayne often kidded me about my poor man's sandwich. Today's frozen little sardines were much like those frozen beans of yesteryear.

After the high country snow came a pelting rain and

wind, afterwhich we bottomed out to flowers and peach trees. One minute I'm eating a "bullet sandwich," the next I'm sniffing at flowers and peach blossoms.

We ended our steep decline into Salmon by watching men fish in the Salmon River. Laurel met Jube to ferry him home. He left with a holler, "Live and laugh!" I returned with cupped hands around my lips, "You too!"

WEDNESDAY 29 JUNE 1994

Made the ride from Salmon to Lost Trail Pass just fine. Somehow I lost my pencil, which is why I haven't written for a few days. Two friends from Kaysville, Utah, ElDean Holliday and Elwood Clark, joined me at Lost Trail Pass. Luckily, Elwood had brought several pencils with him.

ElDean claims that the horses Elwood and he brought had named themselves, with one exception: his packhorse, a beautiful big blond Clydesdale that his daughter named Juice, as she loves grape juice. ElDean rides a tall gray called Jumping Jack. Elwood rides a strutting strawberry roan named Rooster; he leads two packhorses, a white Morgan named Snow and a bay, Romeo.

Longtime friends, Elwood and ElDean are like brothers. By the law of association, many of their mannerisms are similar. Often when listening, their heads are angled in the same direction, nodding together when appropriate and ending with a combined "mmhum." Even their hats are similar– Elwood's is black, ElDean's is brown, and both are worn just above the eyes, comfortably tipped back revealing two pairs of hazel eyes. Not to mention, how many people do you know whose name starts with El? We rode today with ElDean starting a story and Elwood finishing it. Fun company.

SATURDAY 2 JULY 1994

Before sunup I heard Elwood holler, "Mule in camp!"

Buster was sneaking in for some grain. After four tries to drive him out, I finally succeeded. It feels like snow is coming. I hope not.

Last night deer kept scurrying past our camp. Fun to see their inquisitiveness.

Sunday 3 July 1994

Rained hard last night, steady and heavy. Don't know what I was thinking, sleeping under a fly that was strung over a rope while my tent was packed nicely away. Awoke around 2 a.m. with the fly hanging low, heavy with rain. I trenched along my bag, bare-handed, trying to irrigate around my bed, then hunkered in as best I could, waiting for morning light. This morning there was an inch of water in my cup that I'd left out over night. Elwood and ElDean were cold in their tent, but at least were dry. I'll be using my tent from now on. Rode chilled all day long.

Monday 4 July 1994

Snowed double what it did last year at this time. We woke to a foot of new powder. This high up July often feels like December. ElDean, Elwood, and I stayed in camp all day, close to the fire. Since ElDean is an excellent cook, he spent much of the day hard at it. Such a variety. The task of eating fell to Elwood and me. Oh, to get snowed in more often!

The cooking, however, started off a little rough this morning. It turns out that ElDean's packhorse, Juice, loves pancakes, so when he fixes them we find Juice crowding camp, only content to leave and continue grazing after she's had one or two fresh flapjacks. But this morning's menu consisted of meat and potatoes. We weren't paying attention and only noticed Juice when her backside was sticking out of ElDean's tent. She must've smelled the pancake flour, and by the time we got to the tent, it looked like we'd been chasing bears in there. The white powder scattered inside didn't look much different from the snow outside.

It was a good thing we'd planned to stay in camp to wait out the storm, as it took most of the day to clean up.

Tuesday 5 July 1994

We left camp knee-deep in snow, but it didn't take us long to come to clear spots on the trail. Glad we all had coats, though; kept 'em buttoned.

ElDean injured his left knee today doing a good deed. We met some riders coming down the trail, chatted for a moment, and continued on. Not far up the trail we came upon the last rider of the party, a heavy-set girl who was attempting to climb onto her horse, which kept dancing and circling away from her. "Can you help me get on?" she sniffled, close to tears. We pulled our ponies to a stop.

She explained that she'd stopped for a bathroom break without telling the rest of her group. Eagle Scout ElDean climbed off Jack and strode past me before my boots hit the dirt. "You bet. What would you like me to do?"

I stepped to the horse's right side to box it in and took ahold of its bridle. Then the girl placed one foot in the left stirrup. Hopping on the other, she called out to ElDean, "Now, grab my bottom and push."

At this, I looked over at ElDean. I smiled at his stunned, sunburnt face, and glanced over at Elwood, who was holding all our ponies, smiling.

ElDean shook his head. "Never at anytime have I..." he began, then squatted and bent forward. "Here, sit on my shoulder and I'll lift you up." When the girl placed her full weight on his shoulder, his face turned even more "sunburned," and the vessels bulged in his neck. He took hold of her ankle with both hands. After several tries, he straightened his legs and lifted, getting the job done.

By the time we set up camp, ElDean's knee was bothering him something fierce. We filled his camel-back water pouch with cold water to use as a cold pack to bring down the swelling.

Saturday 9 July 1994

ElDean's knee is swollen so badly his jeans can't fit around it; had to slit his pant leg up the side. He thinks it's a torn meniscus. We'll get him to Elk City, Idaho, so he can see a doctor.

Sunday 10 July 1994

ElDean's daughter and husband met him in Elk City and took him home. He left Jack, Juice, and his gear for Scott, a son of a friend of mine, who'll ride with Elwood and me.

At the designated rendezvous outside Elk City, Scott, age twenty-three, joined us wearing a straw hat, drugstore style with a tight rolled brim and stampede strings. It looks to have been edge-burned and factory-holed to lend the appearance of rough riding and experience. After the first few hours of wearing it tipped back on his crown, Scott straightened the hat so it rested just above his eyebrows, the way Elwood wears his. Then it became apparent why he'd kept it high on his head: because it was a tad too big. Now he has to tip his head back in order to see out from under the brim. He's anxious to learn, and he grins continuously. Even after our bare-bone dinners, which appeared immediately after ElDean left, Scott still smiles. He's like our personal sun.

Tuesday 12 July 1994

While riding through a meadow today, we met some locals who told us that the elk around these parts are so salt hungry they'll steal your saddles. So now we're sleeping on ours. Imagine... attacked by elk! Sure enough, before dark a cow trudged into camp. Well I'll be danged!

Teancum stepped on my heel coming down the trail–surprised us both. Despite that, he's doing very well.

WEDNESDAY 13 JULY 1994

Early this evening, we were following a Forest Service trail that was more like a wild game path. I was in the lead and kept losing it. We doubled back three times, then gave up. I peeled off from Elwood and Scott to search for a way down the steep canyon to Meadow Creek. It wasn't too high, but the canyons here are like deep holes. Scott and Elwood stayed together, scouting for the trail in a different direction.

"I think I've found it," I heard Scott holler not long after we'd separated.

I wasn't convinced and wanted to continue scouting. "Go ahead and try it. I'm going to keep looking," I called back in the direction of Scott's voice. Before long, I also came across a trail, but the rim seemed to drop off into the canyon. I crawled off Teancum and stood on the edge, following it with my eyes. As far as I could tell it went completely to the bottom, so I led the ponies slowly down the narrow trail, which proved to be sound.

It was getting dark by the time I got to the bottom of the canyon. Leading the ponies over to where I thought Elwood and Scott would be coming down, I called up into the shadows, "I've found a trail to the bottom!" My stomach sank as I heard Elwood's strained reply...

ELWOOD'S JOURNAL ENTRY, JULY 13, 1994

Chuck had gone off scouting a trail. Scott thought he'd found one and was encouraged by Chuck to try it. I peered down the trail where Scott pointed. It looked better than what we'd seen so far, but still seemed to be very precarious. We got off our horses and prepared to lead them down the steep trail to Meadow Creek, but not before Scott slid the bead on his hat's stampede strings tight up under his throat. I led Rooster and Snow, leaving Romeo to follow on his own. Scott led Jack and Juice. Periodically, Scott glanced back at Jack, whose hooves were crowding the heels of his boots. Juice's outside hind foot either caught on a small root or her back hoof missed the trail altogether; suddenly Scott felt Juice's lead rope go tight. Behind me I heard Juice scrambling to get some sort of footing. I dropped Rooster's rope and squeezed past him, Snow and Romeo, and saw Scott hold on as long as he dared, then let go of Juice's rope. Her eyes filled with terror, and with red nostrils flaring, she disappeared from view. I looked on in horror as the end of her rope whipped from the trail and vanished over the edge.

"No!" I yelled helplessly. Scott's eyes were like saucers, his mouth wide open but silent. Juice's screams mingled with the clanging of metal items from her pack, bouncing off rocks and brush, some of them sliding down the steep bed of shale faster than she was. Tumbling, rolling, and sliding for a couple hundred feet, she would have continued rolling down the steep mountainside to the bottom of the canyon had it not been for a massive log. She appeared dead, lying with her shoulder wedged tightly against the cracked log and her head resting on it.

Visibly shaken, Scott stayed with the four horses on the trail while I half slid, half crawled down to Juice, grabbing hold of shrubs and roots to keep myself from falling. Arriving at her side, I found Juice wheezing, her windpipe nearly shut off from the extreme pressure on her throat. I worried that her neck might be broken. A deep gash about four inches wide and two inches deep bloodied her left shoulder. I pulled the pack off her and set it down, only to hear it roll off down the hill. We'd retrieve it in the morning.

At that point, I heard Chuck calling up from the bottom of the canyon; he'd found a trail. I called down to him and told him about Juice. He said he'd come up to help. It was dark as I made my way back up to Scott. By the time Chuck and his mules had climbed up to help us with the animals, we decided it was too dark and dangerous for any of us to move. We'd have to leave Juice and check on her again in the morning.

We tied our animals to ragged bushes and camped right there, halfway down the steep hill, lying on the trail. We half sat, curled around bushes, wrapped in our jackets, waiting for daylight–a fitful night spent worrying about rolling stones and listening to Juice groan.

At daybreak Chuck, Scott, and I, using ropes, scrambled down to where Juice lay. She was still groaning, but when she lifted her head the wheezing stopped. Luckily, she'd come to rest on a wide flat spot so we could work without fear of us slipping farther down the mountain. Her neck seemed okay, though it was still pressed tightly against the log. With a rope tied around her throat, we pulled and managed to give her enough wiggle room so she could shuffle forward into a standing position. She looked alright, with the exception of the shoulder wound. Gazing upward, we could see the trail wind down around near to where we were. So Scott stayed with Juice as Chuck and I climbed back up to our animals. Then he and I started leading them slowly down the trail until we were close to where Scott and Juice were.

Before we'd reached the flat area, though, Buster suddenly baulked, slipped sideways, and plunged off the trail similar to what Juice had done. Again we looked on helplessly as mule and pack contents banged and bounced down the mountain–this time without the screams. After a few seconds the rolling ended with a solid, sickening thud near the bottom of the canyon. Chuck stood white-faced and in shock as he gazed down on Buster's lifeless form. Rousing himself by cupping his hands over his face and rubbing vigorously, he balled them into fists and dropped them to his sides. Then with clenched jaw he went about doing what needed to be done.

He squinted out over the vertical mountainside, now littered with pack items from Juice and Buster. Realizing it would be hard to find what he needed, he sidled over next to me and asked, "Do you have a gun or knife in one of your packs?" Scott swallowed hard as reality registered on his face. I pulled out my six-inch pocket knife and handed it to Chuck. Apparently he'd lost his sometime last night. He pocketed my knife, gathered up Teancum and Wildflower, and we began our careful descent, Scott leading Juice, me leading Rooster and Snow. Jack and Romeo followed on their own.

About halfway down, we came to a hairpin corner and my lead foot slid out from under me on a patch of loose gravel. Reaching out to catch my fall, I felt a bone snap in my right hand. That was all we needed—a major injury!

When we finally got down the mountain, there was Buster, standing and eating as if nothing had happened! At the unexpected sight, Chuck shook with relief, a sob escaping his lips. He handed back my knife and asked for a prayer. We knelt, with him first thanking the Lord that we'd made it out of the terrible mess, and then ended with a tearful thanks for sparing Buster and Juice. Afterward, his voice was solemn but hopeful. "There was a divine signature stamped on today."

Chuck splinted my hand with a couple of whittled twigs and wrapped it with tape from his first aid kit. We spent the rest of the day gathering pack paraphernalia off the mountain. We think we found most everything. Some of the cooking kettles were dented—one doubled almost in half—but Chuck hammered them out with a rock. Juice's pack was easy to spot, having landed upright on a bush as if the bush were a saddle tree.

I'm upset that I can't help Chuck more. He's doing most of the work. Sometimes while riding, he slumps over, wraps his arm around his ribs, and clenches his jaw. Without a word of complaint he continues to ride, then sets up camp, fixes dinner, and recites poetry. He seems to do all of it on guts alone.

Chapter 25

THURSDAY 14 JULY 1994

We discovered more injuries this morning. Rooster has a punctured right coronet (the band around the top of the hoof from which the hoof grows) and Buster suffered a bad split and puncture hole in his penis sheath by the cedar knot. It's terribly swollen. I applied peroxide and blue wound powder to Rooster, Buster, and Juice. Snow and Romeo have scrapes and cuts on their legs. We've got too many sore, achy animals to travel, even though Teancum, Wildflower and Jack seem to be okay.

FRIDAY 15 JULY 1994

Juice's shoulder wound appears infected–bubbling froth. It's open, the edges curling back, creating a hole the size of my fist. She's so stiff. We doctored with more peroxide and wound powder. Gave her some penicillin, but I'm worried I don't have enough.

Rooster lost a shoe coming down the hill Wednesday, and is tender-footed. But worse, his punctured coronet is filled with puss, causing him to limp and tiptoe along. Elwood stood by apologetically, cradling his injured hand, as I nailed a new shoe on Rooster. I reassured him all was well, but I can tell he feels bad about his limited ability to help. Scott helped me pack up camp, Elwood doing what he could, then we followed the canyon bottom to the trailhead. Passed several Louis and Clark Expedition route markers, but we were too worried about Juice's shoulder wound, Buster's sheath, Rooster's coronet, and Elwood's hand to stop and reflect on that historic adventure.

Wednesday 20 July 1994

Juice gave out today and dropped in her tracks–just a few feet before a fatal ledge. Eventually got her up and moving.

Thursday 21 July 1994

This morning we came upon a bear track on the trail only a fourth of a mile from camp. Will keep our eyes open.

I gave Juice the last of the penicillin several days ago. It wasn't enough. The cut is terribly red and oozing pus. The 1,400-pound horse has lost about 400 of those pounds the last few days and is very sick due to infection. She needs a vet, but the closest town is days away. As horse grain and groceries have been consumed, we've packed less and less on Juice. She's stripped to only her packsaddle now.

My heart felt hollow. As we rested along the trail, I was resigned to the inevitable. "Elwood, we need to put her down." Juice lay panting, in shock, sweating heavily, her pretty blond hair now more like a dark, dirty rag.

Elwood crouched by her head, stroking her velvet nose. His face hidden under his hat, he uttered a soft but resolute, "No."

I knelt next to him and ran my hand over Juice's body. She felt on fire. "She's suffering," I coaxed, pointing out the obvious.

"I can't. She's a family pet. It'll break ElDean's daughter's heart if I come home without her. I'd feel awful."

"If she were mine, I'd have done it a day or two ago."

"No." That was that. We let Juice rest for a while; then we pulled and prodded until she shakily found her legs, the sweat coursing down her neck. ElDean's pet horse may die before we can get her out, but we'll do all we can to save her. At every stop she swayed as if she were going down. We coaxed her as she continued to stumble and stagger up each incline, each step seemingly her last.

Elwood's hand is swollen and painful. I loosened the tape around the splint, but kept the sticks where they were. Each day Scott helps Elwood take down and set up camp, then comes to help me pack or unpack horses; but the lion's share falls to me to pack and saddle all eight horses. I'm exhausted. My back is hurting more each day. The rib belt does little to ease the pain.

Traversing the base of a mountain, we held our breath as we watched Juice shakily place each hoof ahead of the other. If she dropped here, the discussion about putting her down would be moot. The trail wasn't overly steep, just constant enough that if she rolled, we wouldn't be able to stop her; her momentum would take her to the bottom. She kept trying to quit, but we were pulling her downhill. Three quarters of the way down, Buster's pack rolled off center then under his belly. Scott had helped me pack him today, but it could have easily been my fault. I'm tired. The fact is, packs sometimes roll, even on a good day. Buster ran kicking, trying to lose the "lion" gripping his underbelly. Once more, pack gear was spread across the mountainside.

Three strikes! We're out. Enough! Time to go home. I'm ready; we're all ready. Disgusted and discouraged, I would've walked away and returned home with only the half that Wildflower carried, but the sight of so much scattered debris spurred us to climb the hill and gather it all up.

I shared some poetry this evening in an attempt to raise our spirits. It didn't work.

Saturday 23 July 1994

We came to a forest road at Kelly Creek, which is actually a river famous for trout fishing. We followed it to a campground, where Elwood called ElDean to request a ride home and told him about Juice. Then I called Leland and asked him to come retrieve Scott and me.

Late evening, ElDean stepped from his truck, walking stiffly. Turns out he was right: the doctor had confirmed and treated the torn meniscus in his knee. He was carrying a long penicillin needle. Scott, feeling responsible, met ElDean not far from the cab, and offered apology after apology.

ElDean calmed him by placing a hand on his shoulder. "Are you glad you went?" he asked.

Despite the mishaps, Scott let in the sunshine, showing every tooth he had. ElDean nodded and patted Scott's shoulder. "Glad to loan you my horse," he said, walking past Scott to doctor Juice. We loaded her first, penning her off from ElDean and Elwood's other horses. She's in bad shape. She stood in the front of the trailer, thin and shaky, with pus oozing from the cut. I hope she makes it.

About an hour later Leland arrived and loaded Scott and me up. Trip over.

AUGUST 1994

At home, making up school lesson plans, I paused to call ElDean to check on Juice. The vet had loaded her up with lots more penicillin, and she's made a full recovery. I'm so glad Elwood had been unwilling to put her down.

Rooster and Buster have recovered as well. ElDean's knee is loosening up and he's getting around better. Elwood had a doctor check his hand, and it seems you can now call me "Doc," as my temporary crude splint had done the trick.

CANADA-BOUND ONCE MORE

Finally Finishing What I Started

Chapter 26

Friday 7 July 1995

Yup, I'm a stubborn one. Gonna give it yet another go.

I feel like I can just write "Ditto" here: Had my chemo and wonder if this will be the summer I finally complete my ride to Canada!

I first called the Forest Service to make sure the snow had melted from the high country. They reported that the usual melt-out was two to three weeks behind schedule and that I'd need to start after July 4th.

Jonah is with me–the boy I remember of yesteryear–genuine smile, short hair, looks me in the eye. He's a mechanic and loves it. Sharon and Betty, members of an Idaho chapter of the Back Country Horsemen of America, are also riding with me. We met the ladies at Sage Junction on Interstate 15 and caravanned up to Superior, Montana. Left our rigs in Superior and rode west up the canyon to Hoodoo Meadows to spend the night. Sitting around the fire, we calculated 325 miles of remaining trail to the Canadian border.

Again I brought along my four trusty steeds: Teancum,

Buster, Wildflower, and Sam (for Jonah to ride). What a reunion that was. I wondered if Jonah mistook Sam for Sugar.

Sally had gotten ahold of Sharon just before she left and sent a message with her. It seems shortly after I'd left Alta, Sally was in Victor, Idaho, about twelve miles from Alta, Wyoming, when a friend told her some French folks had come to town asking about Chuck Christensen. The friend had given them directions to our home. Having finished her errands in Victor, Sally had started to drive home when she saw four horsemen and thought they might be the ones who'd inquired about me. "Are you looking for Chuck Christensen?" she asked, pulling off the road. One spoke English, the others only French, but they all recognized my name.

At this point Sharon paused in her story and waited for me to quit chuckling. Why would they want to meet me? I wondered. I didn't know any Frenchmen that I could remember.

Sharon resumed Sally's story. "I'm Sally Christensen, Chuck's wife." The English speaker translated, at which all four became excited, smiling and nodding. Apparently, they'd heard about my ride and had started out from El Paso, Texas, stopping on their way north to visit me. "He's actually on his way to Canada right now," Sally explained. "He left just a few days ago."

Disappointed, wishing they'd set up a rendevous, they huddled, considering what to do next. Sally suggested stabling their horses in Driggs, then invited them home for breakfast. She said it was a little strained due to the limits in communication, but they all smiled a lot and enjoyed the pancakes. Then she took them back to Driggs and their horses.

Sharon finished Sally's story with, "Cool, huh? You're known internationally!"

I nodded, then rolled my eyes. "Yeah, yeah," I chuckled. I hope to meet them on the trail sometime.

Saturday 8 July 1995

I woke thinking how good it felt to be back in the mountains. A cow elk, not 100 feet from camp, called as I flipped back the tarp covering my bag. The ladies sleep in a tent, but Jonah and I prefer open air and stars when the weather's good. Several other elk joined the one doing all the bellowing. We've seen scads of whitetail deer, too. There must be an old salt lick close by to draw them here.

After breakfast we saddled ponies. We're especially mule-strong on this trip. Betty rides a mule named Astor, adding one more to my four, and packs a pinto named Ace. Sharon rides Oneida, a fancy Appaloosa.

Got away by mid-morning headed for Hoodoo Pass to get on the proposed GWT. After two hours of riding, we approached a cow elk who stood eyeing us. When we got thirty feet away from her, she circled and stood trembling, but was rooted. Teancum tightened, as did I, in case she charged and we had to retreat. But we tiptoed quietly past, her only movement was her darting eyes. She must have had a calf in the grass and was ready to defend it.

The tall bear grass was gently blowing at Hoodoo Pass, a remote area with lots of wildflowers, elk, deer, and evidence of bear. I did bring Leland's gun this time around; thought it might be good to use as a noise-making warning. It was cold up on top of the world under the clear blue sky. The trail sometimes had us staring steeply down into Montana.

Rounded a bend and came upon a massive snowdrift covering the trail. I kicked Teancum into the snow, pulling Buster and Wildflower behind; Jonah and Sam followed. Teancum floundered, sank to his belly, and went down. To avoid being washed under him, I half stepped, half fell, then bailed off into the drift. Sam lunged through the soft snow, and went down, sending Jonah sliding downhill. He only managed to stop by doing a spread eagle, digging in his fingers and toes.

Gathering ourselves up, Jonah and I, along with my four mules made it to a small clearing on the trail. Betty and Sharon tried to veer above the drift, but couldn't, instead forging a different trail through the snow and joining us in the clearing. Betty had to repack Ace, as his saddlebags had slid considerably with all the hopping and jumping.

I went ahead on foot to check the advance trail. "Snow gets deeper. We need to go down the snow slide to the canyon floor and find a different way," I said to three long faces.

"It's so steep," Jonah said, brushing snow out of the fold of his coat collar.

I tied the reins around Teancum's saddlehorn and asked Sharon to hold him. "You give me a head start of about ten minutes, then let Teancun find his own way down to me. Then, one at a time, let your horses go and follow them down. I'll catch the ponies as they come down the slide." Sharon nodded. "Go slowly through the snow. We don't know what's under it," I cautioned.

The snow was so deep my bottom scraped it with each step, but I made it down without a problem. Looking on from the canyon floor, I could see Teancum confidently, meticulously working his way back and forth down the steep, drift-covered mountainside. Buster and Wildflower followed; then Sam appeared, working his way down carefully. A little behind Sam came Jonah, scooting and sliding on his bottom. I caught and hobbled Buster and Wildflower, then tied a cowbell on Sam. Before I had a chance to grab hold of Teancum, wandering nearby, Astor, Ace, and Oneida came leaping into view, wide-eyed, nostrils flaring as they came down. A photo of their churning descent could have graced the pages of Western Horseman magazine.

Then potential tragedy. The horses, floundering and leaping, were about to trample the slower-moving Jonah, sliding along right in their path. "Jonah, get out of the way!" I hollered. The horses were almost upon him before he rolled sideways to avoid their crushing hooves.

After arriving at the bottom of the canyon, the motley herd took off in a frenzy at a dead run, with hobbled Buster and Wildflower bringing up the rear. I checked on Jonah, then we scurried after our mounts, who by then had disappeared into the trees. Sharon and Betty were nowhere to be seen.

After about four hours, Jonah and I managed to round up the animals and gather up the scattered gear. Ace had managed to lose Sharon's sleeping bag, but we think we found everything else. I was repacking Ace when Sharon, limping, her arm draped over Betty's shoulder, found us. "Sorry it took us so long to get down," she explained, hobbling over to where I stood. "I whacked my knee on a rock, and I can't feel my toes." The women told me they didn't need to follow the cowbell Sam wore, because they could easily hear the verbal abuse I was heaping on the ponies. Ahem... will do better in the future.

We spotted a place where we could climb back up to the trail past the snowbank, but it was steep and the timber was thick. As we started up, Ace balked, pulled free from Betty, and returned to the bottom. Buster, too, had had enough, and planted his feet. I yanked, threatened, prodded... but he lay down and was done. I got off Teancum. "Buster, I'm in no mood for this." He didn't move. So I found a short stick and busted it over his head, whereupon he sprung to all fours faster than you could say, "ouch."

Finally convincing all animals to make the climb, we once again reached the trail–only to find more snowdrifts. Crossed several, a good deal easier than the first, and came to Illinois Peak, and still more snow. Made it about halfway through the drift onto a shale rock clearing. Our choices were snow, shale, or a dropoff–and the last option wasn't really an option. I gave Teancum his head and led Buster and Wildflower across the rest of the snowbank. Jonah and Sam followed, making it alright. Sharon, on Oneida, started, but the shale rock caused Oneida to slide backwards down the mountain and he began flailing like a cutting horse keeping a steer in a corner. Sharon leaped from his back and was pulled by his reins as she tried to halt his slide. Her arms awkwardly flailing, her feet scrambling, one hand managed to grip a tree branch, the other still clinging to Oneida's reins. Oneida continued to scramble, perilously close to the cliff's edge.

"Let go, Sharon!" screamed Jonah in a panic, clearly afraid she'd go over along with her horse. Determined to save her mount, Sharon held tightly to the reins, pulling the bit from Oneida's mouth. But being no match for the horse's superior weight, she was forced to let go. He rolled once, rose up on his haunches, then slid over the edge. We listened for the expected thud, but heard only what sounded like a saddle being shaken.

Sharon lunged toward where Oneida had gone over. "You stay there! I'll check on your horse," I called to her. I knew she'd have a hard time making it back up to us with her hurt leg.

I peered over the edge and saw Oneida standing on a ledge only about twelve feet down. I had Jonah throw a lariat to Sharon, who in turn flipped the end to me. She lashed her end to the nearby tree, while I began tying my end around my waist. I stopped tying, realizing that if I did what I was thinking of doing, I'd end up with several broken ribs. To stay clear of my ribs and back, I slid the loop down to just below my bottom. Then like a rappelling beginner, I slowly backed over the edge. Oneida seemed fine, with the exception of minor scrapes on his legs from the shale. His bridle still hung from his neck and the saddle was intact. Surprisingly, the ledge we stood on gradually angled up with crude stone-like steps that helped us, step by precarious step, make our way back to where Sharon and Jonah were.

We then turned our attention to Betty, who stood with Astor's reins in hand, stranded on a shale point close to the canyon edge. Ace had them boxed in and wouldn't move an inch—and there was no way he was going to go back to wallowing in the snow. I shuffled over to Ace and got him turned around. First, with me sweet talkin' and then with me growling, we slowly crept through the snow to join Jonah and Sharon. Betty followed.

However, the circus, it seems, had only reached a brief intermission. For no sooner had we all joined Teancum, Buster, and Wildflower, than Buster's pack rolled, causing him to buck, then fall to his side and slide toward the cliff's edge, stopping just short of a dropoff. Then, peering out over the edge, it was almost comical to watch as he came to his senses. One roll and bye bye Buster. Calming himself, he let out a guttural groan and held absolutely still until I came over to help him. All in all, it was a traumatic two miles of deep snow, treacherous shale and steep slope.

We led our animals until we were past the narrow, side-hill trail. Hopefully, no more snowdrifts.

Camped for the night in a saddle by two hikers who'd been fishing in the lakes we passed earlier. They offered us a couple of speckled brook trout for supper. Fabulous, but the looks on the ladies' faces showed little appreciation for the free meal. They were a little glum as they reflected on how our first day had gone. I encouraged them with, "It only gets better from here; the first day is usually the toughest." I hope it's so.

I gave my sleeping bag to Sharon, who joined Betty in the tent. I slept out under the stars with all our coats piled on me, covered by my tarp, with Jonah beside me. I figure we traveled about eight and a half miles today, since mules travel about 3 miles per hour. Not bad, considering the pitfalls and hardscrabble terrain.

Sunday 9 July 1995

Of course it rained last night! The pitter-patter on the tarp woke me, so I crawled under a tree and kept dry enough. Maybe I should use my tent. Jonah, burrowed in his bag, slept peacefully.

The fishermen came over while we were fixing breakfast and offered us some beer. We declined, but asked if they had any water. Ours was gone and ponies were dry. They drained the ice water from their cooler and gave it to us; they also told us of a campground about three or four miles down the trail where there might be water. There was.

Rode by Eagle Cliff, a shear rocky face with blue mountains off in the distance. Reflected again on Louis L'Amour's *The Far Blue Mountains*.

Rode a good twenty miles today and camped at a place where trails crossed by the side of a logging road. Grass. Tied a rope picket line for the animals. I'd thought it would take us three days to reach this point, but we did it in two.

After setting up camp, Jonah and I thought we'd hitchhike into Superior, ferry our truck and trailers farther up the road, replenish the grain for the animals, and buy a new sleeping bag for Sharon.

Got a ride from a logger right to our horsetrailers. Worried about Sharon and Betty 'cuz it started to rain, but it was late and we were tired, so we got a motel room in Superior and spent the night.

Monday 10 July 1995

As we drove my truck and trailer back up the logging road to our camp, the fog became thicker and dropped lower. Even with lights on, it was hard to see. Pulled into camp about 10 a.m. Sharon and Betty had everything under control. Sharon's knee is doing well—the feeling in her toes returned yesterday. It'd rained all night, but they'd kept dry in the tent.

I dropped off the grain, Sharon's sleeping bag, and the few supplies we'd needed, then thought it better to ferry the truck and trailer to Mullen, Idaho. Sharon and Betty stayed in camp while Jonah and I drove to Mullen, where I talked to the Forest Service about trail conditions and snow melt-off. They didn't want us riding through the Selkirk Mountain Range—thought it would upset the elk study they were doing. We'll try Troy, Montana, across the Kootenia River, up Deer Creek Road, Idaho, to Canuck Pass in the Purcell Mountains; from there we'll go on to Copper Lake and across the Canadian border.

Misty, foggy, and gloomy most of the day. Hitchhiked back to camp, arriving late afternoon. Betty and Sharon had the horses packed, ready to ride. The fog had lifted, so we decided to go. Skirted Ward Peak, which rose snow-covered and intimidating. There is contrast here with high, cold mountains towering above low-lying valleys trimmed with blooming flowers. Beautiful! We rode into a patch of bear grass in bloom, which only happens for one week each year. Lucky to see it.

Camped high, looking down on Clear Lake. Plenty of grass, but no water for ponies. Oneida's legs are better—scabbed and sealed. Rode seven miles today.

Jonah enjoyed sleeping outside, throwing his bag under a spruce tree.

TUESDAY 11 JULY 1995

Rainy and foggy this morning, with low clouds hugging the hillsides. Everything is wet: blankets, saddles, even toilet paper. Jonah is soaked to the skin. He warmed himself by the fire, but is feeling a little sick.

I made a lean-to so the ladies could fix breakfast and stay

dry. Then I hung ropes so Jonah's bag and mine could dry. The tarp I used to cover my bag had protected it on the outside, but sweats soaked it inside.

Before ten the weather seemed to clear, so we packed up and left camp an hour later. Overcast and cold. Passed Crittenden Peak, Dominion Peak, and Bald Mountain, following State Line Trail signs. The trail turned into #391, then funneled us onto the Idaho Centennial Trail.

After riding twenty-plus miles, we camped by some grass at Roland Summit. The trail up to the summit is wide and clear. Nice! The map showed water farther down the trail, so Jonah and I went to get some while Betty and Sharon cooked chicken noodle soup and raisin-rice pudding.

Jonah has been coughing all day; his lungs gurgle every time he inhales.

WEDNESDAY 12 JULY 1995

We headed out close to noon. More rain and clouds. My map was wrong; it said to go straight, but I walked up the trail and it progressively got narrower and finally petered out. A logging truck came along; flagged it down and asked for directions. The driver was a big help. He said to go left (west), and it proved right!

We followed an old railroad bed where wild raspberries were in bloom. Rows of wildflowers framed the railroad bed: daisies, blue bells, Indian paintbrush, yellow mustard, and some unknown white flowers. Reminded me of the bouquet and how sweet Wildflower had gotten her name.

Midafternoon, after riding some twelve miles, we came to Lookout Mountain Ski Resort. I'd parked the trailer nearby. We crossed the St. Regis River, then rode along Interstate 90 for about a half mile. Both ladies tied up their horses and appreciated the resort's modern restroom facilities. By now the weather had turned hot and dry, and they wanted to splash water on their faces.

Meanwhile, Jonah and I decided to take my donks into Mullen to find a place to board them, then check with the ranger station to see if the trail will be open tomorrow. One of the rangers told me a crew was out clearing the trail, and the Shoshone Mounted Posse had added switch-backs to make the steep areas safer for travel. But he also said no one had ridden all the way through, and he thought we'd never make it. Hmmmph! Felt my gut knot up again.

We returned to the ladies and horses a little after five and told them that the Hale Trout Farm would board our animals. We dropped the horses at the farm and turned 'em loose in the field, but then decided to stake Oneida and Buster on a picket line as run-away insurance. As night fell, we drove into Mullen and got a motel room; each of us took a bath and washed our clothes. Bought groceries, cough medicine for Jonah, and roast chicken at the only cafe in town. Then Jonah and I drove back to the trout farm to be with the horses while Sharon and Betty stayed in the motel.

Thursday 13 July 1995

Jonah woke with a fever; he feels lousy. We picked up Betty and Sharon at dawn on our way to Wallace, seven miles down the road. Needed to buy salt, rope, grain and additional cold medicine for Jonah, but the supply store wasn't open until 7 a.m., so we ate breakfast. Decided to leave Jonah in Wallace—needs to recuperate. Called Jonah's dad and asked him to come get him. Sorry to leave him behind, but Jonah assured me he'd be fine.

Drove back to the trout farm and the animals. Oneida had worn a rope burn around his ankle from the staked rope. He obviously didn't think the thirty-foot picket was long enough. Got the ponies packed and left after ten.

Climbed a steep, twenty-five percent up-hill grade for

seven miles. Had to rest animals often. On top, the trail seemed level, but we were still climbing. After passing Burke Summit and Glidden Pass, I took out my binoculars to locate another trail far across the valley floor. Pointing, I told the ladies, "That's where we need to be." They just looked on in silence.

By and by, we followed a steep side-path and came to a shale rock cliff. From there I had a better view of the trail we needed to be on. But I could see that part of it was covered by a rockslide. So, securing Teancum to the only tree in sight, I went ahead on foot to see if the trail opened back up. It was windy; my hat sat tight, though. Such rough shale, only mountain goats could travel here. Must turn around; map wrong again!

Our alternate route was Pear Lake, Blossom Lake and Thompson Pass. Passed lots of trees with splintered trunks and their tops sheered off about fifteen feet above the ground. I wondered if an avalanche had sheared the tops off. Must have been tall trees. Looked like Big Foot could use the splinters to clean his teeth. We could tell the Forest Service had been clearing the area; only a few trees still lay strewn on the trail.

Came to an old road with lots of grass along it, so we threw up camp. A creek ran along the road, but the water was yellow. I got some water for cooking, but warned the ladies of giardia, advising them to boil it for at least five minutes. Betty scowled at the water in the bucket and compared it to the yellow kerchief around her neck. I believe she boiled it much longer than five minutes, but the color never changed.

I shared some stories about Chief Joseph and we sang some hymns as we sat around the fire. Got to bed late and tired. The eighteen miles we rode felt even longer due to the steep climb.

Chapter 27

Friday 14 July 1995

Last night was the first night it didn't rain on us. Clear blue skies, no fog or clouds.

Oneida is limping, his rope burn infected. Had Sharon ride Sam. I led Oneida, tied Buster's halter rope around his neck, and let him tag along behind on his own.

Struck camp at a half past nine and rode past Dixey Pass and Black Peak. When we got to Bloom Peak we noticed someone had hung tiny, handcrafted wooden birdhouses, about twenty of them, in the surrounding trees. Not only lodging for birds, but also enjoyment for us.

Four times today the map has turned out to be wrong! Much of the time I had to guesstimate the trail. I knew we were smack-dab on the Continental Divide, because the Idaho valleys run west and the Montana valleys run east.

Rode through snow, across fields of shale and around downed trees all day long. Ran out of drinking water, but found a small runoff stream. So grateful. We filled our canteens, then let the horses drink. They were thirsty; none of them had touched the yellow water yesterday.

Rode past Lost Peak and camped at 87 Mile Peak; plenty of grass but still no water. Tired. The right side of my back is hurting. Is my kidney going?

Sharon boiled her canteen water, added salt, and tried to clean Oneida's ankle. He kept jerking away. The wound is pus-filled and swollen. I suggested that we put salt on a wet first-aid elastic bandage, then wrap it directly on the wound. Oneida didn't like it, but we got it done. Sharon taped the bandage top and bottom. Hope it stays.

Rode twenty-four miles.

Saturday 15 July 1995

Dry camp, so we packed up early. I continued to lead Oneida, who's limping even worse than yesterday. We were relieved to see the bandage had made it through the night. Sharon rode Sam again today.

We've happened upon several old silver mines over the past few days. Rode mostly on unmarked trails–thick brush, lots of downed trees. I chose the right turns over and over. Whew, finally got to a dirt road with signs. One sign said "Idaho Panhandle Forest," another, "Kootenai National Forest." But neither sign told us where we were. I guessed: Porcupine Pass. What's the use of a sign if it doesn't give you all the information? Disgusted!

We roamed Gem Peak for hours, trying to find a safe route down. Followed old prospector trails that haven't been traveled for many, many years. Some went straight down the mountain; others zig-zagged across the slope. Came across some aged telephone poles with old glass resistors and wires still attached.

Near noon, we rode through another wildflower field: sego lilies, blue bells, white and yellow blooms. Gorgeous! Found a mud hole; animals sucked at it for moisture.

Also came upon a grizzly bear track in the mud, clear as day. Some think bears won't charge unless threatened. But it doesn't matter what people think; only what the bear thinks. Worried the mules would smell bear and stampede, we all sat at the ready, but the ponies must have been distracted strain-ing mud through their teeth. I've been packing Leland's gun in my saddlebags for easy access, if I need it. No need, it turns out.

We finally found good water this afternoon. Later, camped by an old road with grass. No water, but thick with overly affectionate mosquitoes and flies. Tried smoking them away with fire, but they were a hearty bunch and didn't give up. Sharon removed Oneida's bandage to check his ankle. It's worse.

Rode sixteen miles today.

Sunday 16 July 1995

Horses are thirsty. Rode out early looking for water, munching breakfast in the saddle. Clear, blue skies.

Passed Divide Peak, Buckskin Saddle, Delyle Forks, and Dry Creek. Rode along an old road and got a little worried when we heard the sound of gunshots too close for comfort. Hoped my orange Ralide boxes would catch any hunter's eye before he pulled the trigger.

Decided to shortcut through the timber to a road I'd spotted while up on the Continental Divide. The shortcut was extremely steep, thick with timber, and when our excited animals started lunging we had to bail off. Ponies slid down the steep part and landed on the road; then the whole herd bolted. Impossible to contain them. Only the sound of thundering hooves and whinnying could be heard as they disappeared down the slope, out onto the flat, and around a bend.

Finishing the slide down on our behinds, we went looking for the renegades. Two legs are not as fast as four. We needed a ride. As we stood along the hot, dusty road with our thumbs out, I had time to meditate on the "gatorbait." What I'd thought were my million-dollar mules had crashed on the "stock" market, worth nothing, free for the taking. The third truck that came by stopped and offered us a ride, cold water, and cans of pop. The driver was releasing Peregrine falcons into the wild. I kept an eye out for our motley bunch as he told us about the birds.

About two miles down I began spotting tell-tale signs: shredded reins and bits and pieces of gear along the road. Felt a little like Hansel and Gretel following the bread crumbs. At last we found the ponies near a trailer home surrounded by no trespassing signs. Buster and Wildflower had rolled in the dust and their packsaddles hung under their bellies. Ace's pack hung off to the side, threatening at any time to shift and roll under as well. Pack items lay littered everywhere. Bridles, reins, and canteens that had been tied to the saddles were busted. Didn't have time to stew. We jerry-rigged the bridles, repacked quickly, and rode out before the homeowners appeared. Didn't want another "private property" conversation.

I led Buster and Wildflower at a fast clip. Betty followed close behind with Astor and Ace, while Sharon rode Sam, pulling Oneida, who was still limping badly. His bandage had come off in the free-for-all and the wound looked bad. How come he wasn't limping when they all bolted? Didn't slow him down then.

Got to Clark Fork, Idaho, just before supper time, a day ahead of schedule. A couple of boys told us we could stay at the railroad park, so we rode over to it. But before setting up camp I thought I'd better first check it out with the town constable. While Teancum and I were gone, Buster and Wildflower started calling for Teancum, bringing a man named Cody, along with his wife, wondering what all the ruckus was about. They turned out to be mule people, who offered us water, pop, pasture, and to drive us wherever we needed to go.

Sharon phoned a vet. He wanted a hundred and fifty bucks to come out at night, so she said she'd buy her own penicillin; but there was nowhere to get any. Cody had some ampicillin, which he kindly offered. She used that, hoping it would help Oneida through the night.

We showered and did laundry at Cody's home. He and his wife didn't have much, but were the welcoming kind—very generous with what they had. The man told of two grizzly bears nearby who wore transmitters so rangers could track them. I wondered if the track I'd seen at the mud hole belonged to one of them.

We nestled in at the railroad park. The trains didn't scare the horses; they were too tired from running the race track. I stayed behind while the ladies went to dinner at a restaurant, and brought back food for me and rock salt for the horses.

Traveled twenty-four miles; so tired, I can barely write.

MONDAY 17 JULY 1995

Cody offered to take Sharon and Oneida to the vet in Sandpoint, Idaho. We helped load Oneida in his trailer, a rickety contraption with wobbly sideboards and cracks between the floorboards where you could see road. We prodded the horse inside and secured him with bale twine tied behind his rear end. Despite the worn trailer, we were grateful!

Betty and I were packing animals when Sharon and Oneida returned from the vet. Turns out he wasn't going to release Oneida if Sharon was going to continue the ride. Good thing she'd already decided to bail out.

She helped Betty finish packing Ace. I know Sharon wanted to ride all the way; I could see the disappointment on her face and in her body language. She and Betty each grabbed an end of the top pack to toss it on, but it sailed over Ace and landed on the ground, sending up a small puff of dust.

"Look what happens when they come to town," I chirped, cinching the last knot on Wildflower's pack. Sharon cracked a smile, her mood lifted. She handed me her one good rein, which I tied opposite the halter rope I'd been using. Now I'll have two reins again after mine had been shredded. Up to this point I'd made due with a halter rope tied to one side of the bit. As a result, after his mad dash down the road, Teancum and I had made a lot of circles.

Cody gave us directions to Lightning Creek Road, Rattle Creek, Keffer Creek, and on to Troy. He explained that the last forty miles to Troy would be all dirt road. I invited him to the Tetons so I could reciprocate. Hope to see him.

A friend of Sharon's will meet her in Sandpoint to pick up her and Oneida. They'll ferry my truck to Copper Creek Campground, Idaho, one mile from the Canadian border. So I'll have to at least make it that far–if I want a ride home, that is.

As Betty and I rode out of Clark Fork, I looked back at Sharon and waved. She returned my wave halfheartedly, looking melancholy. I'd seen the same expression on Jube last time we said goodbye.

WEDNESDAY 19 JULY 1995

Today Betty and I made it to Troy, Montana. It was like riding atop a piece of sizzling bacon, fried over-easy. Betty's husband was waiting in Troy to haul her home. I left my tent, stove, and most of the food with them. Want to travel fast and light from here on. Called Leland to see if he wanted to ride these last few days with me, but he was uncertain about taking time off work.

I'll make a run for the border tomorrow, stripped down to my dancing shorts.

THURSDAY 20 JULY 1995

Skeeters continually chewing on me–traveling fast–but can't outdistance 'em. Just my ponies and me, no mishaps. Anxious. Getting close!

FINISHED

Chapter 28

Friday 21 July 1995

The man who couldn't and the mule who wouldn't, made it! Cheated death!

This afternoon my ponies and I stepped into Canada. The border itself looks like Paul Bunyon ran his lawnmower through a dense pine forest, cutting a swath about 50 feet wide. The minute I crossed into Canada something sweetly changed inside me–profound peace replaced fear, doubt, and hopelessness. The hard knot in my gut disappeared. I just sat there on Teancum and, with leaky eyes, thanked the Lord for allowing me to finish what I'd started. I knew I wasn't alone in my struggle. With a silent "hallelujah" in my heart and an imaginary jig in my boots, I inhaled the mountain breeze, felt its cleansing power, and took in the greenery all around, renewed.

It was humbling to sit and think of all the statesmen and laborers who'd planned and cleared the swath. After belting out "O Canada" and "America the Beautiful" as best I could, I got off my trusty mount and walked up a crest to where stood an obelisk of brass, painted white. About five feet high, it read: *Treaty of 1846, United States, Canada, surveyed and marked 1903-1907.* It was sign post # 220. I assume there's a sign post on each summit along the border, beginning at the west coast and going east.

I climbed back in the saddle, just thinking, feeling. A part of me that has been dead, is now alive. The cancer is still silently working within me, hollowing me out; but I am at peace with myself, the cancer, and my God. My ride has gradually taught me that cancer is actually a kind of friend, a friend who gives me perspective and time, like a grace day when a library book is past due–so I can still get it right, without penalty.

Now my fear is gone. I feel like a frozen man thawed. I'm no longer angry or discouraged. Cancer doesn't mean an end of hope. I'm not just a host to a deadly disease. My disease isn't me. Multiple myeloma can only steal what I let it steal. A loving God has given me a second chance to prioritize, a chance to harmonize my life on earth with my reason for being here. A warm feeling spreads through me when I acknowledge that I cannot change the fact that I have cancer, but I can change my attitude. Cancer is no longer an enemy, bringing dread and fear, but an uninvited visitor who is making me a better, wiser, kinder, more patient man. I can now see the beauty in the complete experience of life, the good and the bad, the hard and the easy. The chronic nature of cancer? Good... it means I'm still here on earth for it to affect.

An important lesson I've learned from the "schoolmaster" is that no matter how bad you feel, or how terrible the outlook, you must get over the crying and self-pity, then pick yourself up and wring every morsel of sweetness out of life. There are still wonderful and rich things to do. I must look for what sunlight there is. It's so easy to grab hold of and focus on the bad things, but as soon as you do that, you might as well give in. That is one of the most important things I've learned.

When I think that someday one of my kids or grandkids might also be diagnosed with cancer, I want him or her to remember to focus on the good, to know he or she is Heavenly Father's child, and that it's still possible to see bright light off in the distance. I'm grateful for the experience; it has schooled me. The lessons I've learned from this illness will not be wasted.

Teancum shifted under me, disturbing my reverie. I'm sure he wondered why we were just standing still in an open area. I reached down and patted his neck, realizing I have nothing to prove to anyone, except myself. I'm ready to go home. Though I wanted to linger in the quiet solitude, I turned Teancum and rode straighter, with my head up, back into life.

I entered Copper Creek Campground and trailered the ponies, then climbed in my truck and pointed my face south. While driving, I found myself thinking of and anticipating the simple pleasures of home: the smell of Sally's lilac bush, a gentle hug, the picturesque view of the Tetons from my livingroom window, a hot shower, Sally and our children, our grandchildren's loud chatter, a good porterhouse steak smothered in onions, and some No Bake cookies. A deep sense of peace and contentment settled over me.

Eager to get home, but I couldn't help but think, *"Accomplishment is just a springboard to the next dream."* What next?

Epilogue

Chuck always believed that he was the first horseman to ride the Great Western Trail from border to border. True or not, he hoped he had been of service to the GWT with his first-hand knowledge of the trails and of areas where there was limited water and insufficient feed for animals.

After completing the ride to Mexico and then up to Canada, Chuck accepted the invitation to be the Idaho representative for the GWT, and traveled throughout Arizona, Utah, and Idaho, recruiting trail enthusiasts and informing others of the GWT. He often showed slides of his trip in hopes that others would in turn help with the trail. In some areas, the GWT idea has met resistance. A few folks feel that the GWT is unnecessary because of the already-existing Continental Divide Trail that stretches from Mexico to Canada. Some people living along the GWT didn't want existing trails to be part of the trail system or to be renamed. Chuck's idea was to have locals and area Forest Service offices create and maintain their own sections of the GWT.

Chuck returned to Utah in the summer of 1996 with three of his middle-school students to help clear parts of the GWT. He took along faithful Teancum, who never did give up.

Teton has since passed on, but Teancum, Sam, and Buster, Chuck's beloved mules, are alive and well-cared-for by his family.

In June 1996 Chuck retired from teaching, and underwent his last chemotherapy treatment in December of the same year. In all, he completed six and a half years of chemotherapy, but stopped because the urine test to monitor the disease by checking protein levels was changed to a less convenient blood test. He spoke with Merrill Wilson, an oncological surgeon who'd helped with diagnosing his multiple myeloma, and learned about carrot juice. Merrill's wife had cancer and they strongly believed in the health benefits of carrot juice. The idea came from a German doctor who thought cancer was caused by a virus and could be fought with diet. Chuck began a daily regimen of carrot juice, which gave his skin an orange hue but seemed to keep the protein levels down.

There were several times when Chuck's health turned for the worse, and his family worried that the Lord had finally come calling. In February of 1997, while in Pittsfield, Illinois, serving an LDS church mission, he contracted pneumonia. Previously, doctors had said that pneumonia could be fatal due to his fragile immune system. After ten days in the hospital he was discharged, but not before a protein test was performed. He hadn't had carrot juice for ten days and his protein was up. Amazingly, once Chuck started drinking carrot juice again, the protein count went down. Whether or not the carrot juice was what made the difference, Chuck believed it did, and he drank it the remaining eight and a half years of his life.

Congestive heart failure plagued him from then on. This, along with the high altitude of the Tetons, contributed to his breathing problems. He couldn't walk to the barn without pausing every few feet just to breathe. Sally, peering out the house window, often would see him lying in the grass and would send someone running to see if Grandpa was alright. He'd always cheerfully reply, "I'm just resting, enjoying the sky." Over the years he received four blood transfusions to battle his bouts of constant fatigue. Each helped boost his energy level for a time.

In February 2000, Chuck, then on another church mission, collapsed in the Family History Library in Salt Lake City. This is his written description of the incident:

Monday morning went to the library; an hour into microfilms

I got dizzy, vomity, and weak. Made it to the restroom, but when I decided to go up to the third floor and lie down in a lounge, I couldn't make it, so I lay down right on the bathroom stall floor. My! If you want to be the center of attention, lie down in a restroom and look like you're dying. Lots of security men, a priesthood blessing, a gurney, a wheelchair, an ambulance, then two hours in the ER before I felt like I was really going to stick around.

Blood pressure in the ER was 60/35. Interesting. I was surprised to find the ambulance ride and ER visit exactly like they show on TV. In the hospital, the doctors admitted they didn't know what caused my collapse. After a three-doctor conference, they decide the culprit was high potassium. Normal is 3-5; I was 7. The higher the potassium, the slower the heart rate, thus explaining the twenty-six beats per minute when security picked me up off the restroom floor.

Then came the price: multitudes of IV's, catheter, stomach pump, and a #28 needle in the jugular. I was in the hospital for three days, rested for four more, then went back to work on Monday. Still, there are some good things about being sick: folks make a fuss over you and bring you delicious meals; you're the center of attention for a time; you get to rest until you get tired of resting and actually WANT to go back to work; and probably best of all, the blessings of health and life are brought clearly to your mind. In addition to the gift of continuing here in mortality for a little longer, all the friends and family who came to see me, and the professionalism and efficiency of the security and medical people, two blessings from the Lord stand out in my mind. First, during an early-morning walk alone up to the Utah Capitol building, the Lord didn't let me collapse then. Had I done so, Sally wouldn't have known where to look for me. Secondly, He let me be too sick to get to the third floor lounge. That place is often used for naps, and nobody would've thought twice about me sleeping on the floor.

These may seem like small things, but they were the difference between me living and not living. I'm grateful He's giving me another chance to learn and obey.

The first Sunday in August, 2000, Chuck again collapsed at church in Driggs, Idaho (closest town to Alta, Wyoming). Eddy started unbuttoning his dad's shirt to administer CPR. A nurse attending the service pushed Eddy aside and ripped the shirt open, and they both applied CPR. Four minutes later Eddy and the nurse had raised a pulse. Chuck needed to be life-flighted to Idaho Falls, Idaho, but the helicopter wasn't available, so he was driven the one and a half hours by ambulance. The cardiologist in Idaho Falls did an angioplasty (balloon in veins to open them up) and also put two stints in heart valves to keep them open. Chuck was then taken by ambulance, a three and a half hour ride, to Salt Lake City. After four days and a combination pacemaker/defibrillator had been installed, the cardiologist said, "So far as your heart is concerned, you'll live forever unless you fall off a mule."

"Howzat for a wonderful blessing!" was Chuck's reply.

Chuck later participated in an experimental medical study, where his pacemaker/defibrillator were to be checked every three months. After receiving the pacemaker, Chuck could again walk to the barn without stopping to rest.

But yet another malady soon appeared to slow him down. His vertebrae started collapsing like a stepped-on cardboard box, and he needed to start IV's again in order to put a special type of calcitonin in his system to harden them.

In the summer of 2004, less than a year before he passed away, Chuck went with Leland and a family group into Yellowstone Park on an annual four-day ride. Chuck's body hurt so badly while in the saddle that he had to get off and walk much of the way coming out of the Park. With saddened heart, he pronounced that it would be his last Yellowstone trip. He got to the point where he couldn't ride without pain and was so weak he couldn't drive his mules. He hadn't the strength to stop a potential runaway. Content to just ride along as a passenger or sit as a spectator as his mules competed in pulling contests, he received great enjoyment from watching loved ones participate in events that they loved doing. Despite his discomfort, he continued doing and learning: braiding halters, lead ropes and lariats, checking out library books, learning new knots, and using them in the keychains he braided for gifts.

November 9, 2004, five months before passing, Chuck saw the doctor for deep sternal pain, a constant pain similar to when he was diagnosed with multiple myeloma. Worried that the cancer had become more aggressive, he began to plan funeral arrangements. Yet in visiting with the mortician, in Chuck's mind he could see the man smoothing his hands in anticipation; he felt like the fly being welcomed by the spider. No, Chuck was going to have his own style of funeral: no mortician, no embalming, no viewing, and the family would wash and dress his body.

In the spring of 2005 Chuck decided he wanted to learn all about converting cooking oil into a fuel that would run diesel motors. Problem was, he knew little about engines and cars. He checked out books and talked to his brother Jim, Jube's dad, who'd successfully converted cooking oil into a gasoline substitute. For several years Jim had been driving a diesel truck and had the equipment for purifying vegetable oil–dirty and chunky with bits of leftover food–into clean, pure fuel. Jim would gather used cooking oil from fast food establishments, the local college cafeteria, and small mom-and-pop shops, all who were eager to rid themselves of their used oil. Chuck read his books and often drove to Rexburg, Idaho, to watch Jim work at his "still."

On Saturday, April 9, 2005 in Rexburg, Chuck was learning and watching Jim out at "Cow Patch," the affectionate name given to the place where the still was set up. Chuck had just purchased a used diesel Volkswagon Rabbit, and he couldn't wait to see if the oil would work in his "new" car.

Anxious to get this project up and running, he'd excitedly called his sister Morrissa in Salt Lake at 6 a.m. before going out to Cow Patch, asking her to keep an eye out for rabbits and used cooking oil. He frequently called Morrissa to bounce ideas and schemes off her, and now she was ready to go hunting. Only after several minutes of politely agreeing to gather cooking oil and to look for rabbits, Morrissa finally realized Chuck was not planning a big dinner with fried rabbits as the main entree.

Chuck arrived at Cow Patch at 7 a.m., driving his diesel Rabbit. Jube, along with multiple extended family members, gathered to watch the launch of Chuck's "new" car. Before the trial run, the entire group picnicked on pizza and soda. But shortly after lunch, Jube, Jim, and Chuck jumped into a pickup and headed to Rexburg to get a part for the VW. Rexburg was only a few short minutes from Cow Patch, but along the way Chuck said he wasn't feeling well, attributing it to his unhealthy lunch. Pale, feverish, bloated, and having a hard time breathing, he let out a groan, at which Jube pulled to the side of the road. He tried to take Chuck's pulse, but there wasn't one to find.

I, LeAnn Bednar, lived in Virginia at the time Jube brought Dad to the emergency room. I received a phone call late Saturday afternoon, informing me of the situation. Dad had pulled through so many other times, I remained hopeful. In my eyes he was Superman, the sort of person who could catch bullets in his teeth and jump tall buildings; despite being unconscious and plugged into a myriad of machines in a faraway hospital room, he could beat this.

Still I worried. I was told the next twelve to fourteen hours were critical and would determine the outcome. After several calls to update his condition, I received the news that I dreaded: his bodily organs were shutting down and Mom was keeping him on life support just long enough so all six of his children could say their goodbyes. Leland was there in person, but the rest of us were spread over several states.

Mom held the phone to Dad's ear and, between sobs, I said goodbye and sent my love to my dear father. His death certificate stated the cause to be "massive organ failure." He loved life, always had a project going, and continued learning to the very end.

On Sunday morning, April 10, 2005, Charles Morris Christensen passed away peacefully, surrounded by loved ones. His special magic, that only he could summon, was gone. He would now be clearing trail in Heaven to make it easier for those who came after.

Within three hours of his death, I was on a plane flying from Virginia to Wyoming. The extended family was gathering and preparing for Dad's special brand of funeral, the outline of which he'd written down and reviewed with Mom.

To gather information, plan, and prepare for the inevitable, my parents had visited several funeral homes. Dad had declared each one to be too impersonal and too expensive. Wanting only those who loved him to take care of his remains, he went on line and made phone calls to research how to do a proper and personal family burial.

Morrissa has a woodshop in her backyard and does beautiful woodwork. Dad had asked her to make his casket, together researching state laws, requirements, appropriate woods, etc. Both Ed and Morrissa built the casket. Morrissa had called Dad just the week before his passing with the news they'd finished the task. It was beautiful, crafted with love, and finished with three horseshoes on each side panel to be used as handles.

In a final farewell, family members penned messages of

love on the underside of the casket lid. I wrote this:

Daddy,

You are my HERO! You lived life to its fullest and life loved you. Your fire for life was contagious and we loved you for it. You never gave up and always had a dream that spread to those around you. I will think of you when I see a mule, a beautiful flower, feel a breeze from the Tetons, read a good book, when I'm camping, or learning something new. I see you all around me because you loved all that was around you. I love you, Dad. Until we meet again, your loving daughter, LeAnn

Earlier, at the hospital, when the emergency room staff learned that the dying man was Jube's uncle, every accommodation was made. Jube was a paramedic volunteer, and was well known and liked by the hospital workers. The ER doctor, however, was concerned about releasing the body to the family, having never had one request it. The family assured him he could release Chuck's body to them, because Dad had done his research. A mortuary was not necessary if certain conditions were met, such as burial within three days. The doctor, not knowing dad's love of research, made a few phone calls, then signed the release. Jube secured a body bag from his paramedic group. A cousin and her husband, Marlene and Arlin, just happened to be visiting at the time and had driven their Chevrolet Suburban. It was used as a hearse to bring Dad's body home to Alta.

When I arrived at the family home, Dad's body was in the cool storage room of the vacant earth-sheltered, solar-heated house next door, awaiting burial. This unusual house had been one of his dreams.

Monday, the day after Dad's death, was very busy. The family had only 72 hours to get the word out to friends, plan a funeral, write the eulogy, write up an obituary for the local newspaper, and perform the funeral and burial. Our local paper printed the obituary, but the Rexburg and Idaho Falls papers declined; since the family hadn't used a mortuary, they couldn't verify his death, and they'd experienced too many pranks in the past.

Family and friends streamed in from out of state all through the day. We were ever so grateful for the food and flowers delivered by so many. It eased our minds that there was plenty to eat, leaving us free to do the task at hand—that of burying Dad.

Tuesday, April 12, at noon, we held the funeral for my father. We were surprised that on such short notice the chapel was completely full. Many people loved my father for his welcoming, inviting spirit, his contagious enthusiasm, and his tender kindness. He had come full circle; no longer a bully, he was now loved by many.

Dad's life was atypical, as were his funeral plans and his ride to the cemetery. The church leader conducting the funeral opened with, "Many of you have asked, 'Where is Chuck?' He's home, right where he wants to be. As you can see, this funeral is a bit different from others, but we're doing it Chuck's way."

Janelle offered the eulogy and told of her skydiving with Dad, Leland related hunting whales with him, I shared climbing the Grand Teton together, and Eddy told of a lesson learned while fixing a neighbor's fence in the rain. Daughter Catherine led the music; son Mat offered a prayer; grandson Hunter sang Tim McGraw's " Live Like You Were Dying." Those wishing to drive to the cemetery were asked to break tradition and go ahead of the casket and family en route. There, they would greet the funeral procession.

Lying in a casket made by his loving sister and brother-in-law, Dad made his final ride, carried along in the beautiful pioneer-style covered wagon he and his brother Barrie had made. The canvas had been removed to display the casket, and the United States and Wyoming State flags flew from poles attached to the side of the wagon. Two of Dad's mules, Blue and Thinker, were at the head, pulling. And a beloved, saddled, yet riderless Teancum, led by grandson Hunter, clopped behind. Sally followed in a horse-drawn buggy, and a long line of family and friends walked along behind.

Father was buried, not far from Fritz and Ty, on the knoll at the Alta Cemetery, with the song "How Great Thou Art" on his lips, the smell of wildflowers in his nose, the beloved Teton Mountains before his eyes, and mule hoof-prints on his heart.

Later, we found atop Dad's grave a rusty horseshoe with an attached Veteran's Day poppy tucked between the flowers–a sweet tribute. Dad surely loved horses, and he loved his country.

Two weeks before Dad passed away, grinning, and with a book tucked under his arm, he left the local library. The book was entitled "Mongolia." The Lord knew it was time to bring him home.

Author's Note

Writing this book and reflecting back on how my father lived his life, I've come to realize his ride through the mountains was the perfect setting for him to achieve what he'd come to earth to accomplish. My concerns and worries have been put to rest. After his ride, he was a better father, husband, brother, and was closer to the Lord. I've come to understand it was I who had been selfish, not him.

That day when dad had paused and considered not going on his ride, I was sure that I was in the right. But I've learned we can each reach our destination traveling on different paths. Mine is not always the right way. I, too, have been schooled.

Our eyes see only a short distance, but our hearts see into eternity. Until then, Dad, until then.

LeAnn

"I may have been given a bad break, but I've got an awful lot to live for." - Lou Gehrig, 1939

"Never give in. Never give in. Never, never, never, never..." - Winston Churchill

"If you can dream it, you can do it." - Walt Disney

The Great Western Trail

"Something somewhere for everyone."

The western United States hosts National Forests and other Public Lands in which a corridor runs from Canada to Mexico through the states of Montana, Idaho, Wyoming, Utah, and Arizona. The Great Western Trail (GWT) is more than just a trail. It is a corridor of paralleling routes that accommodates all kinds of trail users and allows them all to access and enjoy our public lands. The diversity of terrain and natural wonders cannot be found along any other trail system. The GWT traverses lush alpine meadows and dry dusty deserts; rocky mountain ridge tops and carved sandstone canyons; and densely forested mountains and cactus covered deserts. With minimal new construction, the GWT links together exiting trails and roads to create a network of trails and passageways for horsemen, hikers, mountain bikers, skiers, snowmobilers and other motorized trail enthusiasts.

The GWT is designed to link together communities and bring economic opportunities to rural areas by allowing the trail user to easily access those communities and their resources. The GWT will connect the user to *Points of Discovery* that highlight the unique culture, history, and traditions of the Old West.

The Great Western Trail Association is a non-profit corporation that represents the trail users. They coordinate efforts to develop, maintain, promote, and designate the GWT through partnerships between federal, state, and local land management agencies, as well as private businesses, property owners, individuals, and user groups.

For more information, visit the website at gwt.org.

Mike Browning, Executive Director, Great Western Trail Association